THE DEATH OF THE SOUL

STUDIA PHILOSOPHICA

Jordančo Sekulovski, *General Editor*

The Death of the Soul

Critical Essays on the University

THOMAS S. MARTIN

CHISOKUDŌ

Cover design: Claudio Bado

ISBN: 978-1546779421

Nagoya, Japan
http://ChisokudoPublications.com

for Linda Martin

Contents

"Tradition means giving votes to the most obscure of all classes, our ancestors. It is the democracy of the dead. Tradition refuses to submit to the small and arrogant oligarchy of those who merely happen to be walking about. All democrats object to men being disqualified by the accident of birth; tradition objects to their being disqualified by the accident of death. Democracy tells us not to neglect a good man's opinion, even if he is our groom; tradition asks us not to neglect a good man's opinion, even if he is our father. I, at any rate, cannot separate the two ideas of democracy and tradition; it seems evident to me that they are the same idea. We will have the dead at our councils. The ancient Greeks voted by stones; these shall vote by tombstones. It is all quite regular and official, for most tombstones, like most ballot papers, are marked with a cross."

— G. K. Chesterton

Introduction

The following is a selection of essays from a dissenting campus newsletter entitled *The Examined Life*, which I have been publishing for over twenty-six years at the University of Nebraska at Kearney, a state university in the heartland of America. Beginning in 1988, I set about examining my university, which was then a state college, by scrutinizing our mission statement, course offerings, Faculty Senate, affirmative-action hiring criteria guideline, push for diversity, Chancellor's correspondence, campus architecture, athletics, political correctness, entrance requirements, as well as any one of the plethora of campus missives and announcements clogging my email daily. This journal was sent to the faculty, administrators, regents, governor and several hundred additional off-campus readers. Working from Socrates' injunction that the unexamined life is not worth living, I found that the unexamined university is also worthless.

These pages are my attempt to be mindful about the place in which I have been placed as a philosopher. While this may be similar to Socrates' being attached to Athens to keep the statesmen, poets, philosophers and citizens from falling asleep in the care of their souls' need for the truth, I am no Socrates. I do not, however, think it an accident that I landed here in 1986. After applying to 125 colleges and universities for an entry-level professorship of philosophy for a year and a half, I was hired to develop a philosophy program at a state college hoping to become a university. I had no experience other than the preparation that comes with completing a doctorate in philosophy at the University of Missouri while living on a forty-seven-acre farm with my wife Linda and three of our four children, Zachary, Seth and Katherine—Rachel arrived in Nebraska. While applying for a position, I had been working on a neighbor's farm feeding greyhounds, building fence, clearing brush, etc., which was a perfect fit, I thought, for qualifying me to establish a philosophy program (clearing brush with students). Coincidentally, what was then Kearney State College had previously been the state normal school where my father, aunt and uncle were the first of their family to graduate from college. A. O. Thomas Hall, where I have taught for thirty years, was originally the lab school where my father Robert taught for the Nebraska State Teachers College.

I teach philosophy as I was taught by Professor Dick Wood at Northern Arizona University, the old-fashioned way: by examining the ideas of one thinker at a time with students, who, like myself at their age, are not in the habit of thinking about much other than "Will I need a coat?" or "What is my boyfriend doing right now?" My Socratic endeavor, then, is to get students to think about ideas, for example, "Which is better, to suffer an injustice or to commit one?" and to understand that the ideas of their intellectual ancestors have consequences that affect their lives. One of the first facts about learning to think is obvious: only a person can think. Corporations, government agencies, committees, universities, etc., cannot think, not because they do not have brains but because they have no souls, no minds by which to see. What holds for the whole necessarily holds for the part. Man is *capax Dei*, a living soul made in the image of God. He is made to know.

Plato's "Allegory of the Cave" is the ancient form of what currently passes for education, for instructing the young. Imagine a cave where people are chained to a wall by their arms so that their heads can only look forward at a flat wall upon which shadows are cast by men who are standing behind those chained beings on a parapet before a fire and holding up cut-out images of objects found outside the cave.

These prisoners have been here since childhood at the mercy of those in a position of authority over what they can view. The people on the parapet are teachers, ministers, government officials, newscasters who control the visions of the cave dwellers. To pass the time of day, those chained to the wall have contests to see who can remember the order of images passing before them and award praises to those who do so.

This is the picture of the lecture format of learning in which a subject matter is distilled into a textbook administered by a person who is no more than a talking textbook. Imagine a student with a large funnel placed in hole drilled into the top of the head so that information can be poured into the funnel. Then imagine a continually dripping faucet spouting forth from the student's mouth. At the end of the week, when the faucet is opened, out pours the information, which is shortly to be forgotten—thus, the leaky faucet.

Little can or will change until the person chained to the screen starts to think for himself and to understand what it is to have a soul, a mind moved by principle. The *Republic* is founded on the principle that one ought not return a harm with a harm. Socrates is the soul of an education which releases each student from the mundane realm of his view, his opinion, by questioning what he assumes to be reality.

My introduction to philosophy, which began in wonder forty-four years ago, shows what it is to be troubled by ideas. During my sophomore year at Northern Arizona University, I took the philosophy course "Man and Reality," taught by Dr. Richard Wood. Twenty-five of us were seated in the classroom when in walked this man with his hair slicked back, wearing brown jeans, a western shirt, a bolo and cowboy boots. He stopped and stood eyeing the class. While twitching the corner of his mouth and straightening out his mustache with his forefinger and thumb; he frowned and looked about as though he were searching for something to say. He took a puff on his half-smoked cigar and began to read the roll.

After reading a few names, he suddenly stopped and asked a student sitting in the front row, "Do you have a mind?"

"Yes," the student responded.

"Well, then you will like this course and reading Descartes' *Meditations* because he also has a mind about which he is going to tell us. Do you have anything in your mind?"

"I have lots of things in my mind."

"That's nice, but could you give me an example of one thing you have in your mind?"

"Well, currently I have you, Professor Wood, in my mind."

"I am in your mind?"

"Well it is not really you that is in my mind, but an image of you which has come through my eyes to my mind."

"An image of me has come through your eyes and is in your mind?"

"Exactly!"

"So do you see me or do you see an image of me?"

"I see an image of you."

"Have you ever seen me?"

"No, I have only seen an image of you?"

"Then how do you know that it is me if you have only seen an image of me?"

"I don't."

"Then to whom are you speaking?"

No response.

I went home very confused—Who was this cowboy? This was the first time in my life I had been confused in school to the point of thinking and rethinking the discussion. How could it be that I could not see what was right before my eyes? Man has a soul, a mind, the ability to think by nature, but he does not think by nature any more than he speaks by nature, though he has the potential to speak. It depends on his formation. Just as speaking takes practice and the good fortune of a home with literate parents, quality teachers and the will to learn are necessary for thought.

His questions forced me to use my mind and, by so doing, to develop the mind needed to wrestle with Descartes' solipsistic idea of how the mind works. Eventually, I saw Descartes' confusions were brought about by the misuse of ordinary, everyday words.

This was the start of the adventure which follows after being freed from the cave of information into the light of the formation of my mind. By studying the ideas of Plato, Descartes, Berkeley, Hume, Wittgenstein, Dostoyevsky, Camus, etc., I learned to think and be responsible for my life and was grounded by "you shall know the truth, and the truth shall set you free."

The foundations of my university, which was a state college several years ago, are much older than this university herself. The word "university," for example, houses an idea that comes from the Latin *universum*, which in turn grew from the neuter of *universus*, the base from which the word "universe" evolved, meaning the whole body of things and phenomena observed or postulated. Similar in meaning is the word "cosmos," a systemic whole created and maintained by the direct intervention of divine power.

The focus of the university rests on the first sentence of Aristotle's *Metaphysics*, "All men by nature desire to know." This is obvious, Aristotle noted, because of the delight we take in our senses, especially the sense of sight, in that we are able to see the difference between things. This is sensible. Aristotle elucidates the directive principle of the university in the first sentence of *Nicomachean Ethics* when he states "Every art and every inquiry, and similarly every action and pursuit, is thought to aim at some good; and for this reason the good has rightly been declared to be that at which all things aim."[1]

The university was founded in the Middle Ages, when God still was creator and continued to maintain the universe. All the students and faculty were members of the same body on their pilgrimage through the world. A common inscription over a scriptorium or monastic library *Tota Bibliotheca unus liberest, in capite velatus, in fine*

---

1. Aristotle, *Nicomachean Ethics*, trans. Martin Ostwald (Upper Saddle River: Prentice Hall, 1999), 1094a, 1–3.

manifestus (The whole Library is one book, in the beginning veiled, in the end manifest) succinctly summarizes this.

Man has two eyes. He has an external eye, which looks out on the world of chronological events streaming right before him. This is the quantifiable eye, the scientific eye, which measures everything by size, shape, color, speed and quantity. The second eye is the internal eye, the qualitative eye, the eye of the heart looking deep down into the soul throughout time. This is the eye of memory and self-examination which is anchored by a conscience and the moral judgment necessary to distinguish between what is just and unjust, good and evil, smoke and mirrors.

The external eye can be taught to see and describe what is right before it, and its medium is the natural sciences. The internal eye looks back in time through the lens of history, literature, philosophy, art, scripture, etc., to learn the necessary art of being. This eye requires learning moral principles to guide the soul between good and evil, the just and unjust. And while science builds upon itself, every man is born internally ignorant and must start from scratch in finding his purpose in the world.

Deprive a student of either one of his eyes and you have a Cyclops with the myopic vision that makes for a narrow mind. He will be all head and no heart or all heart and no head. The former leads to heartless abstraction and the later leads to mindless compassion.

In all of this, it is important to remember that a university is not housed in its buildings. A university is housed in the minds of her faculty and students who can see only as far as they can read. It is necessary to have both eyes wide open in search of not merely the cutting edge of the present, but also those permanent ideas gained through understanding in the study of the Humanities.

The modern university is but a smattering of what she once was. Though universities were founded to sustain faith by reason and to maintain order in the soul, they have fallen to being secular rather than universal, aimlessly offering, at best, a servile education based on the technique and procedural knowledge necessary to present and/or perform a service. From kitchen and bathroom design to neuro-surgery, from accounting to industrial distribution, from music therapy to elementary math, education no longer provides students with the whole picture. Faith is not in the province of the mundane and the need for order in a man's soul has been forgotten or denied. Remember, "university" comes from the Latin *universitas* which means "the whole." However, in this age, "university" is applied loosely as they have sunk further and further into the provinciality of place and time. Along with advancing the ordered knowledge of the sciences and history, a university which fails to offer her students the literature and philosophy of her intellectual ancestors leaves her students blinded in the world.

Without any introduction to a higher sense of purpose in their lives, computer scientists, accountants, teachers, graphic artists, counselors, lawyers, physicians, and the like, are left grounded at the lowest level of existence to scratch out a life. We are a prudent, practically-minded people, interested in attaching ourselves to the means of making a living, but not in addressing the ends of living.

Post-modernism, or the Age of Dotage

I do not know when the modern world became the post-modern world nor when the pre-future age might begin. However, it is obvious that we, the living, have history all to ourselves when it comes to naming the age in which we have accidentally landed. Our historians would have us believe that Socrates was wandering about in the Ancient world; the Romans created an empire in the Neo-ancient Age and produced a variety of civic-minded philosophies which ended in debauchery followed by the sacking of the Vandals, which brought, in turn, the Dark Ages of St. Benedict's monastery from which St. Francis awoke to find himself in Middle Ages; then Descartes (who so smartly separated his mind from his body) enlightened the world to the "firm and constant knowledge in the sciences" by doubting his senses, thereby opening the door to the Modern Age, which preceded the Post-modern Age in which we are now (supposedly) living.

However, it makes as much sense to look at the Greeks and say they were not Ancient but Young. And as with all youth, they were innocent—so innocent that their imagination was filled with gods and goddesses, Harpies, Cyclops, Hydra, and nymphs. Until, that is, they were awakened to their ignorance by Socrates in the search for self-knowledge, as well as the virtues prescribed by Aristotle to achieve the "highest good." All of this was merely the precocious pursuit of youth enamored with Reason but without love, forgiveness, or a sense of evil.

It can clearly be seen that the freedom and spirit of innocent youth gave way to the Teen Age of man: a proud and passionate age of intense desire, of learning to think, of conquest and of revelation. It was a willful age marked by physical strength and the longing to find meaning in life. It was the age of philosophers, of Caesars and of God the Father. The teachers of the Teen Age were split between the Epicurean delights, Stoical resignation, Caesars of the soul ranging from Caligula to Constantine, and St. Paul's deliverance of the stone the builders had rejected to Rome.

Seneca captured the spirit of this hormonal age ("It is a gathering of beasts!") by directing his lectures to the practice of virtue as the conflict of the soul and body and so to assist in the battle between the higher man and the hedonistic desires of the flesh. Epictetus taught the universality of virtue: all men have capacity for virtue, with which he coupled, "I am a citizen of the world." Marcus Aurelius' meditations offered consolations for the pangs of the flesh and the horror of the nothingness that awaits the soul after death by prompting man to live in the moment, "Consider thyself to be dead, and to have completed thy life up to the present time; and live according to nature the remainder which is allowed thee." The Teen Age was marked by the power of man's will and his potential to be trained to action, to athletics, to performance of civic duty, to be counted as a true son, brother, and citizen. Nevertheless, philosophy remained mortal in the face of death. How natural.

To this age St. Paul delivered the good news of salvation: there is a way for a boy to get beyond being a teenager and become a man! Man is not a child of the flesh but a child of God whose soul is not fulfilled by his own will, philosophies or law. Praise God eternal, not Rome. "For when we were in the flesh, the motions of sins, which were by the law, did work in our members to bring forth fruit unto death. But now we are delivered from the law, that being dead wherein we were held; that we should serve in newness of spirit, and not in the oldness of the letter." This good news freed man from the bondage of the flesh and the state, releasing him to be a son of Our Father who art in Heaven. Thus began the sojourn of the Church on earth until the end of time.

However, as all who have been involved in the education of the teenagers know, the hormonal flow of youth is such that while the spirit is willing the flesh is weak. Thus many were prone to chaotic behavior, acting like barbarians, until the seat of reason was vandalized by the desires of the flesh, which resulted in the virtues of the new civilization of faith, hope, and charity being exiled into darkness.

Thus St. Benedict was driven from the decay of Rome into the Dark Age of the daily grind, a penitent age of deeper silence and aloneness with God where man labored by the hours. This was an age of single-minded devotion to one mistress, as a house became a home and soulful parents rose like monks to Matins in beginning the daily routine necessary for the transformation of the children to the spirit of the Word. And thereby began the labor necessary for our own lowly bodies to be transfigured into copies of His own glorious body.

In all of this, it makes good sense to see St. Francis as Middle-aged, stigmatized for turning his back on the dreams of practical men. They, like his mercantile father, were more concerned with how much their sons made in the world than what their sons made of the world. So Francis, with little more than the words "Francis, seest thou not that my house is in ruins? Go and restore it for me," tried to steer the world away from commerce to rebuild the Church by collecting the stones the builders had once more rejected.

And it still makes fine sense to see that Descartes was well past the middle of his life when he sat by the fire in his dressing gown and separated his mind from his body. It is a perfectly natural thing for a man who is approaching old age to muse that this body could not possibly belong to me! Descartes is not the Father of the Modern Age, but the father of Old Age and he started by doubting his senses. They do "occasionally deceive [him] about things which are barely perceptible and very far away." Perhaps he was too proud to admit he needed glasses to correct his blurry vision or to acknowledge that his taste buds were fading. Therefore, he rejected his senses for the "firm and constant knowledge in the sciences." Thus was his mind freed from worldly cares, leaving him to meditate in a "serene retreat in peaceful solitude." He achieved this solitude by saying, "I think, therefore I am." Descartes got it exactly backwards. He became his own god, creating his own existence via the ideas within his own mind. Senility at its best!

Descartes' world led to the Post-modern world, an age populated by multiple creators, each thinking his own reality, without any possibility of adjudication. To the Post-modernist, the world does not possess values that have reality. For him, the world has been reduced to a "text" in which each author gives a reading of his own observations of the world, which, like its author, is in flux. There are no ideals in this universe of immediacy; there are simply detached creatures seeking a quality of life free from suffering.

It makes perfect sense that we, the oligarchy of the living, should look back through the family album at our youthful and then teenage years, followed by our dark and middle age, then our more recent old age, and realize that we are currently living in our Age of Dotage for it may well be that we have shown up at the last act of a play and the curtain is about to fall. Look around!

We are in the depths of an insecure age accented by excessive fondness for life and the frailties of victims. This is an age when youth acts as though it were in old age: the automobile is a self-propelled wheelchair for people too weak to walk, let alone ride a horse or bike. Microwavable meals, fast food, and junk-food are available for those who cannot cook. Climate controlled cars, homes, and office buildings are the iron lungs for those suffering from respiratory ailments. And television is for those who lack the imagination to live.

In our Age of Dotage our senses have been dulled, and now we need salsas to awaken taste the buds and the electrically-charged stimuli of video games to shock eyes too blind for insight and ears deaf to all but bites of sound. Despair is treated with Prozac while the Viagra stock is rising on the Dow Jones.

In Dotage, love is infertile so sex is "safe." If some fetuses threaten us they are removed and disposed of like a cancer from the skin. Self-examination is replaced by "feelings" which are positive or negated. The old trials, which supposedly tempered the character of the soul, have been replaced by the longing to possess a healthy "self-image" found floating in a Postmodern Nirvana.

All ideas of an education rooted in Latin—bringing a person up on ideals by which he could live—have been replaced by the practical politics of schooling the student on the importance of financial security in the twenty-first century, a century in which Social Security will be replaced by the corporate pension plan for the worker (who will survive down-sizing only if he has accumulated enough to enjoy his "golden years").

In the Age of Dotage, people think and experience after the moment in which they live. We are like Descartes, who received from his senses an idea of reality—of which he could not be certain beyond a reason of a doubt. So now in our Alzheimerian haze, somewhere between reality and remembrance, each person is left to interpret his experiences—with no way of knowing if he ever participated in a rewarding moment.

And so it goes.

UNK: A University Education without Testosterone

The Asst. Director of Waste Management started the meeting with a brief overview of the history of the Philosophy Department at University of Nebraska at Kearney. The first philosophy teacher was hired in 1986 to establish a minor in philosophy. Dean Becker-Theye of the College of Fine Arts and Humanities introduced Tom Martin to President William Nester, whom they happened to run into as he was talking with the architect under the newly constructed Yanney-Peterson Memorial Carillon Bell Tower. It was high noon and the bells started to chime. The three seemed to exchange cordial greetings between the first and fifth chiming of the bells, with none able to hear the other. All was well and good. (The carillon was a gift of the Yanney and Peterson families who thankfully remembered their start in higher education at Kearney State College—the state college which preceded the change to a university.)

The carillon is adorned with frescos from the Parthenon, the temple of Athena, which depict the Panathenaic procession from the Dipylon Gate in the Kerameikos to the Acropolis. The original castings are from the British Museum, replicas of which line the walls of the Art Department. Athena, the Greek goddess of wisdom, war, the arts, industry, justice and skill was the favorite child of Zeus.

---

* The following are the minutes of the staff and faculty fall, 2013, meeting of *The Examined Life*, now in its twenty-seventh year of publication at UNK.

14

After having admired the replicas in the Art Department used to cast the friezes for the carillon, the Asst. to the Asst. of Waste Management noticed the men and horses on the Carillon were emasculated.

The Director of Anti-Intelligence reported, upon further investigation, that Ray Schultz, professor of art, was commissioned to cast the friezes from those hanging on the walls of the Art Department for the carillon. President Nester approved the project and it remains a mystery whether President Nester ordered the emasculation of the horses and men or Schultz took artistic liberties. There were whisperings that Nester feared the students would be offended by such nudity. To date, no one has claimed responsibility.

The first and only philosopher to serve as a faculty senator made a motion to the faculty senate that no administrator ever be permitted to oversee any artistic work on the campus. The motion failed by a vote of 39–1. So much for faculty senators being concerned about emasculation chiming from the Carillon.

The Asst. Understudy of Student Publications reminded the staff that Mark Bates, the student editor of the 1988 Blue and Gold yearbook, dedicated the last page to the new Carillon with a full size photograph entitled Neutered at Night… under which hung the caption: The carillon bell as it appears at night, complete with "adaptations" of the friezes that appear on the Parthenon in Greece.

The Asst. to the Administrative Director of Mascots and Mottos had recommended the administration change the mascot of UNK from the Antelopes to the Fighting UNicKs so that Louie the Loper would be replaced by Charlie the Castrati and that the motto of the college would be "Try as we Might."

The Asst. Associate of Carillon Studies noted the similarity between UNK's carillon and that at Tarkington College—immortalized by Kurt Vonnegut in the novel *Hocus Pocus*, where all the students were learning-disabled. The bells at Tarkington College also no longer swung, but had been welded to rigid shafts. The clappers had been removed and hung in order of size on the wall in the foyer in the library. However, here stops the similarity, as the UNK bells have always been clapperless, having no dings or dongs but a carillonneur with an electronic keyboard.

The Asst. to the Asst. of Ideas and Images observed that while the bell tower is a symbol of liberty and the friezes from the Parthenon a symbol of Democracy from those ancient Greeks who believed that they alone were civilized among barbarians, the emasculation of the horses and men before Athena has turned the temple of wisdom into pigeon perch from which their droppings are plopped on the students below.

The emasculated men and horses of the bell tower now serve as a fitting symbol for the new General Studies Program at UNK, which lacks the necessary testosterone to enrich the growth and development of civilization. Every student at UNK can satisfy his Humanities requirement without taking a course in literature, history or philosophy. This requirement can now be satisfied by taking a 200 level Spanish, French or German class—mumbling ability—and a cross-cultural speech class.

UNK's general studies curriculum caters to students who disable themselves by avoiding the reading of history, literature or philosophy in college. This is especially attractive to campus administrators in the recruitment of foreign students wanting a university degree though remaining functionally illiterate in English.

The Senior Executive Assistant for On-and-Off Campus Billboards, Buffets and Feed-lot Studies noted the lack of testosterone in the General Studies Program results in the cutting of students from Humanities, which is essential to the enrollment game being played by the UNK administrators for budgetary purposes. UNK's 7,000 plus student body includes everyone who takes more than 0.5 credit hours. Why not 0.2 or 0.1 or 0.0? The foreign students enrolled in the English language immersion program are signed up for 1.0 credit hour, though not yet college students. This also includes all the students taking on-line courses—numbering several thousand—which explains the empty classrooms.

At UNK, students can graduate without any humanity and cut off from their tradition. Without a historical perspective or a grasp of the intellectual ideas of their ancestors, both necessary to examine their souls, how can they survive in the struggle to realize who they are and how they ought to live in this world? Our functionally illiterate grads can read and write with the best of them, but do so at a childish level. They can flip through magazines, read short newspaper items with enticing pictures, short stories with sex and violence, the menu at McDonalds and even text while driving.

The old saying that those who cannot remember the past are condemned to repeat it has given way to those who don't know their past are in a vacuum, ready to believe whatever is given without question.

This institution prides itself on offering up a servile education for slaves and clerks, trained to follow instruction in the form of questionable policies and procedures handed down from on high.

In closing, the Asst. to the Asst. Senior Director of Strategic Planning on Mondays, Wednesdays and Fridays foresaw UNK going the way of Tarkington College, which had modernized its campus with luxurious dormitories, a theater, a spacious dining hall, a new administration building and athletic facilities (that were the envy of the institutions with which it competed, including Hobart, Cornell, Amherst and Bucknell), all of which provided an excellent campus in the transition of Tarkington College to Tarkington State Reformatory, a part of the New York prison system.

Go UNicKs!

The Death of the Soul

There is only one way, then, in which a man can be free from all
anxiety about the fate of his soul—if in life he has abandoned
bodily pleasures and adornments, as foreign to his purpose and
likely to do more harm than good, and has devoted himself to
the pleasures of acquiring knowledge, and so by decking his soul
not with a borrowed beauty but with its own—with self-control,
and goodness, and courage, and liberality, and truth—has fitted
himself to await his journey to the next world.[1]

Imagine reading those words with students today.
Socrates' admonition would strike the majority of students as contrary to the purpose they have set for themselves in an
educational system that is increasingly becoming more vocational than
liberal. The reason Socrates' advice falls on deaf ears reflects the way
we think of ourselves. It is common to think of one's self as a material creature with desires that need to be satisfied in order to be fulfilled; it is uncommon to think of one's self as a spiritual creature in
need of self-control, courage, liberality and truth in order to become
a human being. Why has this come about? Perhaps it is because man
has come to think of himself as existing in a world where a vocation,
a vocation alone, is sufficient for self-fulfillment, and the idea that we,
like Socrates, are embodied creatures has been denied, dismissed, forgotten, or, perhaps, never heard.

1. Edith Hamilton and Huntingron Cairs, eds., *Collected Dialogues of Plato* (Princeton: Princeton University Press, 1961), Republic, 114e.

The concept of embodiment is understood as the giving of a body to a spirit and also as the spirit being restricted by the body. Embodiment thus consists of two parts: firstly, the immediate, which is the mortal, physical side of man as experienced by the senses; secondly, the spiritual side of man, which is the immortal side as apprehended through the inwardness of reason. In this light, every individual is embodied: possessing a soul bound by a body. Socrates further realized that the embodied soul must rule over the body; otherwise, a person's desires would enslave him. Before grasping the idea of self-control as necessary for becoming human, let us look at some familiar examples of being bound. A person may be bound by his spouse, family, friends, and prison.

A man unites with a woman in the bond of marriage, committing himself with the promise "… in sickness and in health unto death do us part." The vows of matrimony restrict a man from all but his wife: in choosing one woman all others are denied. The vows of matrimony present each couple with the task of fidelity as their relationship is tested by sickness, financial crises, and the possible momentary attractiveness of infidelity. Though a promise binds a husband and a wife, one's word may be broken; there are legal and illegal means of separation. The courts have avenues by which a promise may be renounced; they can also decide whether or not there will be alimony and, if there are children, custody, visitation and/or child support. One may also escape a relationship by fleeing to another land.

Regardless of the outcome of the bond of matrimony, a man has the ties and expectations of his birth. Being born into a family places him in a situation he did not choose. Brothers, sisters, mothers, fathers, aunts, uncles, etc., are not chosen in as much as they are accidental relationships. Though there is unity in a family, there is also diversity as members' personalities often conflict. This diversity creates friction within the family, requiring acceptance and forgiveness if unity is to be maintained. In other words, a struggle is involved in relationships. If, however, the members of a family are too overbearing, a member may denounce the striving necessary for participation and move out.

Friendships are another form of embodiment as one is bound by obligation. The foremost characteristic of a friendship is the enjoyment of another's company, be he man or beast. But, unless one is only a fair-weather friend, it also means sharing another's life. Sacrifice is evident in friendship as the giving of one's self places a person in the position of a servant. When a person is in need, a friend will heed his call, whether it be to pull a car out of the mud in the middle of the night, listen to troubles, give money, offer a defense, etc. Having friends means that a person's time is not his own; that is why self-centered people have more acquaintances than friends.

Finally, a prison is a form of restraint for those unfit to participate in society. A prison tries a person's character as boredom, hostility, and perhaps torture are to be endured by him who longs to walk freely. Like the aforementioned forms of restraint, expectations are placed upon the prisoner. Though not as easily left, escape from prison is possible, especially if Crito is waiting in the wings.

These examples of vows, relationships, and walls are forms of restraint where a person is bound to struggle in order to persevere, as is readily understood by anyone who participates in social and civic relationships. Though these relationships are confining, they can be cast aside.

We know Socrates was bound by marriage, family, friendship, and prison. We also know that he could have, but did not, escape any of these forms of restraint. Why did he not escape? The embodiment confining Socrates was not one from which he could have been legally or illegally separated, moved, or dragged. Socrates was bound by an insight, a revelation which separated him from his fellowman, that led him to believe he was eternally bound by being foremost spiritual in nature. Unlike a person in the Christian world, Socrates was ignorant of the eternal goodness; however, his ignorance did not dampen his spirits. O. K. Bouwsma captures Socrates' dilemma:

Perhaps we can understand Socrates as a man who thinks of himself as a subject, as a servant, but he does not know what or whom he serves nor how. This is his ignorance. We might say that he knows he should be virtuous but he does not know what virtue is. Now I am for once clear about Socrates' ignorance. This would, of course, not have bothered him except that he still has the burden of his being a servant, a servant from the beginning. It is as though he knew there must be a Moses or other prophet who would know what he does not know. Was Socrates distressed about this, worried? He did not show it. Socrates is a little like those who expect a Messiah—who does not come. He, the Messiah, will come later. He will. There is a risk.[2]

Can we understand Socrates' predicament? In order to do so, one must imagine himself bound as a servant is bound to his master. Perhaps the analogy is misleading. A servant may reject his master by refusing to obey; likewise, a person may turn his back on God. In the first case a servant can be free of his master. In the second case man, though he refuses, does not break the bond; it is not a relationship which can be refused.

By admitting to the condition of embodiment a person comes to understand that he has a nature. I am a spirit, and this self that I refer to is crude if I do not polish it. There are, in the realm of polishing, proportions ranging from the dullness of sandstone to the luster of a cut diamond. Each person is what appears to be a dull stone. Some men, "who are favored by heaven," have found that they might be polished to sparkling brilliance. The fascinating thing about this polishing is that one can only do it for oneself. Another cannot be hired to come in with a sandblaster and knock the moss and rough edges away. A finishing school can only deal with the superficial, providing a smooth surface that does not change the dullness. No one, for example, can give you musical ability in the sense that enough money might procure a teacher who dispenses abilities devoid of struggle. A teacher can-

2. Richard Bell and Ronald Hustwit, eds., *O. K. Bouwsma, Notes, Essays on Kierkegaard and Wittgenstein* (Wooster: The College of Wooster, 1978), 39.

not force a student to practice or study; that is the individual's task in awakening.

Implicit in the notion of the individual's awakening is the idea that the truth comes from within; it is revealed. This is not to be understood as man being the measure of all things. Socrates was concerned with an eternal truth that, by its very nature, transcends sophistical relativism. It is a truth revealed from within, in that the eternal was cradled within man before he existed. The eternal truth comes to surface in time; this is a paradox precisely because that which is eternal must be timeless. So man had the truth before him but forgot it by coming into existence. "And if it is true that we acquired our knowledge before our birth, and lost it at the moment of birth..."[3] then the subject, Socrates, is removed from the eternal in that he cannot go backward out of time. It seems that the task now becomes one of laying hold of the eternal truth through existence in time. It is impossible to contemplate speculatively the eternal continually, for this would be taking oneself out of existence through thought. The individual must lay hold of the truth in existence or lose it forever. In understanding the truth within himself, a person cannot approach himself objectively in that existence cannot be understood as an object of thought. To understand existence one must study one's self through existence. If, while examining one's self, a person is confronted by someone who lies, cheats, hates, or envies, then he must cast that part of his self aside and put on a "new man." Existence, thus understood, is an ethical task. And that is what Socrates viewed as his task.

The spirit, until it has mastered the body, is continually struggling, as it were, against itself. The nature of embodiment is that within every man exists Michelangelo's David, a sculpture displaying man's fullest heights, and also the fury and rage of Macbeth. To put it in the Platonic idiom:

3. Phaedo, 75e.

He that is on the more honorable side is upright and clean-limbed, carrying his neck high, with something of a hooked nose; in color he is white with black eyes; a lover of glory, but with temperance and modesty; one that consorts with genuine renown, and needs no whip, being driven by the word of command alone. The other is crooked of frame, a massive jumble of a creature, with thick short neck, snub nose, black skin, and gray eyes; hot-blooded, consorting with wantonness and vainglory; shaggy of ear, deaf, and hard to control with whip and goad[4].

In a sense, at birth we are given equally tuned pianos. It is important to note that when Socrates speaks of the soul he thinks there is an agreement, a tuning, amongst souls. If we were all strictly individuals, unique, each different from the other, with only our opinions, we would be differently tuned. Any attempt at harmonizing two instruments would result in noise. Each of us would complain that the other was interfering with his music. Each would demand that the others drop their individual tuning and follow his. Everything would be a matter of opinion, devoid of standard.

I would like to introduce an allegory, an addendum of sorts, to the further understanding of the Socratic task. Once, when at the symphony, I remained in my seat during the intermission. In front of me sat a shabbily dressed man with a snub nose whom I overheard saying to a young man seated beside him, "A symphony is a representation of man and his various types. The complete orchestra is analogous to a nation. If a few of the musicians excel, but the rest linger, one has a nation with a few excellent statesmen and a multitude of mediocrity. In turn, if they are all quite proficient, from diligent study, then we have a harmonious society which produces splendid music."

He further added, "There is only one conductor instead of many, for only one can be responsible for making sure that they are in tune and lead them through the pieces. If each person were to play in the

4. Phaedrus, 253e.

way he saw fit some would be slow and gentle, others loud and rapid, producing no more than disharmony."

I reflected upon the overheard conversation upon leaving the concert hall. We all sit in the audience viewing an orchestra composed of three sections: winds, strings and percussion, which are analogous to wisdom, courage and temperance, or, in the Christian world, faith, hope and charity. All the players are facing us. Only one, the conductor, who is the leader, is not. In order to see him one must endure many hours of practice to become part of the orchestra which he leads; otherwise, we get only a glimpse of him as he turns to take a bow.

As the audience leaves the hall, some are left with a sense of incompleteness at having to be separated from the music. We do, however, have memories, if we were attentive, of the edifying music. In our desire to participate, we purchase a symphonic instrument and set out to learn to play. We soon realize our ignorance—I am all thumbs!—and need of instruction, so we seek a teacher capable of instructing us so that we might become part of the orchestra. Without instruction we may regress into a state that only leads us toward illusions of fame and fortune.

We must seek after the Socratic dream to "practice and cultivate the arts" if we are to be liberated from our inabilities. If we don't recognize our ignorance, then we are in a disharmonious state, susceptible to any sophist who might pick us up and tune us to his fancy: communism, hedonism, or materialism. In ignorance we follow false gods, the gods of the underworld who are not even allowed on the stage, grasping hold of their doctrines of salvation: "Let us build paradise on earth," "Let pain and pleasure be your guide," "Man is a product of his environment."

The implication of Socrates' admonition is that it involves an endless struggle. A musician, if he is worth anything, does not one day put his instrument on the shelf and say, "There, I have finally finished. There is no longer any room for improvement or need to practice." There is a lifetime of struggle in mastering an instrument; likewise, there is a lifetime of struggle in mastering one's self. There is no end to the polishing necessary as we hopefully yearn to be acceptable in the world to come.

Plato had the fantastic insight, through Socrates I surmise, that the different characters we possess dropped from a sky of sorts. If a man were just human, a species of animals, a biological classification, he would qualify as a man simply by having been born into the family of man. Therefore, he would be an unbound human, and there would not be a sense in which he might polish his self by being virtuous. True, he may be viewed as a good worker, verifiable by output, or as a model citizen by upholding laws, but this leaves him nothing to polish in the sense that he is conditioned only by that which is about him, just as an animal. Men would be like cattle kept in a pasture by an electric fence. If they end up where they do not belong, it is the result of bad fences. Cattle are not held responsible, fences are. If one has a cow that does not conform, it is not a reflection of its self, for it has none, but its owner or its physical surroundings—in short, that which places force upon its body.

Given that we are bound, a process of becoming is visible. We must struggle to be something more than the result of creative evolution or a product of "educational experiences" from a renowned university. We must continually wrestle with the material in pursuit of the spiritual. What Socrates put forth, which later became the foundation of a liberal arts education, is that man, in order to know himself, needs the truth, and that truth resides only in a disciplined life. That is why Socrates says, once again:

> There is only one way, then, in which a man can be free from all anxiety about the fate of his soul—if in life he has abandoned bodily pleasures and adornments, as foreign to his purpose and likely to do more harm than good, and has devoted himself to the pleasures of acquiring knowledge, and so by decking his soul not with borrowed beauty but with its

own—with self-control, and goodness, and courage, and liberality, and truth—has fitted himself to await his journey to the next world.[5]

Is it not a bit extreme that a person must give up his wardrobe and estate? It is not so much that we must give up the physical as it is to break the grasp it has on us. Socrates speaks of the trappings of materialism as "borrowed beauty" of no use to the soul in "his journey to the next world." Beauty is borrowed because it must be given back. The fine clothes will rest in the closet, the house will go up for sale and even the coffin will decompose. The armor that meets the eye is brittle to the eternal. Socrates beckons man to clad himself "... with self-control, goodness, liberality, and truth." The wise avoid the trappings and excuses of materialism and concern themselves with being virtuous. If we concern ourselves with the trappings of false gods, we waste the ever precious time needed to prepare for death. Time is not given in guaranteed allotments. We do not know when death will knock.

It is in the realm of immortality that the virtuous claddings for the "journey to the next world" are to be understood. Virtue is a spiritual quality that transcends this world. Only those who are embodied are capable of virtue for it is in the realm of the spiritual that instinctual urges may be overcome.

In conclusion, I have tried to rekindle the ancient idea that being ethical is necessary for becoming human. We are creatures that must free ourselves from the illusions of the material world if we are to participate in social and civic relations. Furthermore, the task confronting man is as rigorous and demanding as a musician's study: there is no putting the instrument down. Only death can take the instrument from our hands.

5. Phaedo, 114e.

The Diverse University

The Victory of the Adjective over the Noun?

The University of Nebraska at Kearney is committed to the academic value of a diverse university
community. A quality university experience must provide students
with opportunities to have contact with the broadest possible range
of people and cultures. Additionally, we believe that recruitment and
retention of a diverse work force will enhance both the recruitment
and retention of a diverse student body.

> To this end, the University of Nebraska at Kearney, utilizing the
> Recruitment and Hiring guidelines, will make specific good faith efforts
> to recruit, hire, and retain a diverse work force.

I came upon this statement of purpose for the University of
Nebraska at Kearney while surfing the web and immediately ques-
tioned the meaning of the phrase using the two adjectives *diverse* and
university before the noun *community*. This question immediately
appeared before my mind: how do the adjectives *diverse* and *university*
modify *community*?

Our language, the twentieth century philosopher Wittgenstein
noted, "can be seen as an ancient city: a maze of little streets and
squares, of old and new houses, and of houses with additions from
various periods...."[1]

The word "university," for example, houses an idea that comes
from the Latin *universum*, which in turn grew from the neuter of *uni-*

1. Ludwig Wittgenstein, *Philosophical Investigations*, (New York: MacMillan) para 18.

versus, the base from which the word "universe" evolved, meaning the whole body of things and phenomena observed or postulated. Similar in meaning is the word "cosmos," a systemic whole created and maintained by the direct intervention of divine power.

The university was founded in the Middle Ages when God created and maintained the universe. All the students and faculty were members of the same body on their pilgrimage through the world. A common inscription over a scriptorium or monastic library *Tota bibliotheca unus liberest, in capite velatus, in fine* manifestus (The whole Library is one book, in the beginning veiled, in the end manifest) succinctly summarizes this.

Also excavated from the houses in the old city, the word "academic" is from the Latin *Academus*, referring to the Greek *Akadēmos*, the groves of Academus where Plato taught and founded his academy. In this academy, wisdom was defined as good judgment in the pursuit of learning the truth about oneself and the world. Thus, it is that an academic is a member of the academy.

This being our beginning, let us examine the claim that The University of Nebraska at Kearney is committed to the academic value of a diverse university community.

The word "community" is from the Latin *communis*, which means a unified body of individuals, from which we also get the word "communion," an act of sharing, which, when capitalized, is the Christian sacrament of man's spiritual union in the body of Christ. Thus, we can shorten this statement of purpose by starting at the end and eliminating the word "community." Given that the heart and soul of a university is a unified body of scholars, teachers and students committed to the development of the intellect (known in the middle Ages as *Studium*; we call it "the pursuit of learning), it is redundant that the word "university" be used as an adjective to modify community.

Thus, we the faculty of the University, are housed by respective colleges like books in a library. We are not spread about the world but are on one campus and are devoted to a particular branch of study. The trunk of the tree, the liberal arts, is fundamental in the development of an ordered intellect. The university is open to students who desire to study the academic subjects to which we subject ourselves as masters and doctors.

The word "doctor" is from the Latin *docēre*, meaning to teach, as in the teacher of a doctrine, a dogma, a definite authoritative tenet. The highest degree in a university is a PhD, a doctor of philosophy, a lover of knowledge who seeks universal truth in a specific doctrine, such as Chemistry, Biology, English, Psychology, Philosophy, Mathematics, Music, and the like.

So, how does the adjective diverse modify university?

The word "diverse" comes from the Latin *diversus*, as in different in character or quality; not of the same kind; not alike in nature or qualities. So, how ought the faculty be committed to teaching at a "different" university?

I continued tracking our diverse university through the university website and found the "Diversity Guide:"

Diversity *may be defined* as "otherness" or those human qualities that are different from our own and outside the groups to which we belong, yet are present in other individuals and groups. Dimensions of diversity may include, but are not limited to, age, ethnicity, gender, physical abilities/qualities, race, color, sexual orientation, educational background, geographic locations, income, marital status, military experience, parental status, religious beliefs, and work experience.

May be defined? The word "diversity" is the condition of being diverse which means different from one another, as in unlike. In origin, it was identical with *divers*, more immediately associated with Latin *diversus* as in adverse, inverse, obverse, perverse, reverse. Since circa 1700, however, diverse is no longer used in the merely vague numerical sense of *divers*, but always distinctly associated with diversity.

Thus, we are told to believe that our diverse university is committed to being a community of unlike people, in which students will have contact with the broadest possible range of people and cultures who are unlike themselves. This, in turn, exemplifies "otherness" which somehow is a sign of a quality university experience for our students. Reverse U!

Should this be valued? Each student and faculty member attending the Diversity of Nebraska at Kearney already knows that he is different from everyone else. This is the principle of self-identity: I am I. Each person is an individual who can and does discriminate when opening his eyes upon the world from the seat of self-awareness in which the faculty of reason is housed. From within that house, each person differentiates and sees everyone and everything as other than himself. Thus, in the jargon of the administrators who are committed to creating a diverse university and to hiring as many adverse, inverse, obverse, perverse, and reverse people as possible, anyone can recognize I am in a state of "Iness," you are in a state of "youness," and everyone else is a state of "otherness."

What is further puzzling about the fuzzy-headed definition of "otherness" is that it starts by acknowledging human qualities that are different from our own and then promptly classifies each person as belonging to a group (ga thunk), which has

> dimensions of diversity [which] may include, but are not limited to, age, ethnicity, gender, physical abilities/qualities, race, color, sexual orientation, educational background, geographic locations, income, marital status, military experience, parental status, religious beliefs, and work experience.

The dimensions of "otherness" are then like the Hydra, the many-headed monster in Greek mythology whose head, when cut off, instantly became two heads, dividing ad infinitum.

The descent of the mind into "otherness" is the state of a soul lacking the ability to make qualitative judgments. Here we are reminded of Plato's allegory of the cave where Socrates is showing Glaucon, Adeimantus, Polemarchus, and any student who will pay attention, the effects on a mind encouraged to gaze at the diversity in front of it:

> Next, I said, compare the effect of education and of the lack of it on our nature to an experience like this: Imagine human beings living in an underground, cave like dwelling, with an entrance a long way up, which is open to the light and as wide as the cave itself. They've been there, since childhood, fixed in the same place, with their necks and legs fettered, able to see only in front of them, because their bonds prevent them from turning their heads around. Light is provided by a fire burning far above and behind them. Also, behind them, but on higher ground, there is a path stretching between them and the fire. Imagine that along this path a low wall has been built, like the screens in front of puppeteers above which they show their puppets.... Then also imagine that there are people along the wall, carrying all kinds of artifacts that project above it—statues of people and other animals, made out of stone, wood, and every material.... Do you suppose, first of all, that these prisoners see anything of themselves and one another besides the shadows that the fire cast on the wall in front of them?[2]

Here is an education (or the lack thereof) for a student who is not required to discriminate between the changing patterns passing before him. All he knows is the shadows flitting before his eyes; he lacks the ability to classify and therefore to judge. The diverse mind cannot discriminate between what is higher or lower, good or bad, just or unjust on that fluctuating wall of his mind. He treats everything as equally different. He has no ability for the classification necessary for science, a systematic study of minerals, plants, and animals, nor the ability to grasp a moral principle necessary for a virtuous life and relationships with neighbors who could never agree to see beyond their differences. His mind is a splatter which can move neither from nor towards a point.

Fortunately, one of the prisoners in the allegory of the cave is mysteriously released from the shadow-land of the senses, rising to the

2. Plato, *Republic*, trans. G. M. A. Grube, (Indianapolis: Hackett, 1992), 514a–515c.

realm of an intellect which is capable of qualitative judgment. The first subject he learns on his way out of ignorance is to calculate with numbers. Here Socrates notes,

> You know what those who are clever in these matters are like: If, in the course of the argument, someone tries to divide the one itself, they laugh and won't permit it. If you divide it, they multiply it, taking care that one thing never be found to be many parts rather than one.[3]

In other words, the students began their elementary education by learning numbers, starting with one, as in *uni-*, from which the word "universe" is derived. If a person cannot grasp one point, everything remains in flux before his eyes, in a state of "otherness," constantly dividing people into parts, by age, ethnicity, gender, physical abilities/qualities, race, color, sexual orientation, educational background, geographic locations, income, marital status, military experience, parental status, religious beliefs, and work experience, ad infinitum.

Now the prisoners, "who are like us," have transcended the realm of sensory perception and have begun to develop a mind, and with it a love of learning in pursuit of the truths in a variety of different subjects which are universal. (Imagine trying to study animals without biology or minerals without chemistry.)

In conclusion, it is troubling, as you have seen, when the administrators of the University of Nebraska at Kearney are committed to emphasizing the darkness, the unenlightened ordinary physical qualities of people, as a diversity to be celebrated rather than emphasizing the intellectual qualities in the diverse academic subject matters, which unite us. It is equally disturbing when diversity—otherness!—takes priority over ability as a criterion for employment in the academy: as though the accidental qualities of birth are superior to what a faculty member knows and is able to teach about the subject matter at hand.

And so it goes.

---

3. Republic, 525e.

People of Height
at Predominately Short Institutions

I received a brochure announcing the national conference of the People of Color at Predominately White Institutions will be offered at the University of Nebraska this November. The conference brochure suggested an assortment of topics as relevant to people of color in predominantly white institutions and invited proposals for papers addressing the following:

— Feelings and experiences of alienation at PWIs
— Mentoring students and faculty of color
— Race, gender and authority in the classroom
— Future of ethnic studies programs
— People of color and the law in higher education

From the title of the conference, I assume the intent of such a conference is to attract "People of Color" who work or attend white institutions (which, obviously, are predominately attended by whites). The people sponsoring such a conference must think there are two categories of people employed at the University of Nebraska: people of color and white people. However, since white is not a color a white institution ought be referred to as a "colorless" institution and, for the sake of precision, the conference ought to be entitled, "People of Color at Predominately Colorless Institutions."

I wondered what exactly qualifies a person to be included in the category of humans entitled "People of Color?" Freckles must count for something as people of freckle have yellow or brownish spots on their bodies which are often darker than any Latino's skin. Does a person with a ruddy complexion, a person of ruddiness, qualify as a person of color since a beet red face is more colorful than a variety of shades of brown or freckle?

I would like to know whether there is any difference between "people of color" and "colored people"? A person who claims to be a "person of color" is like a person who claims to be a "person of height." Undoubtedly a person of height, when asked about his height, is specific, responding six foot nine, six foot eleven, or, tired of being asked, "Howz the weather up there?" or "How tall are you?" responds five foot nineteen to force the greeter into a simple math problem. So, people of color must be prepared when asked what color they are to state precisely their color just as people of height are expected to state their measurements from their toes on up.

Therefore a colored person, when asked what color he or she is, ought, for the sake of specificity, to answer: brown, brown ochre, burnt sienna, deep ochre, peru, chocolate, mars orange, mars yellow, yellow ochre, aureoline yellow, cadmium yellow, melon, bioque..., etc. So now when asked, a specifically-minded colored person wanting to be independent of the group, will respond, I am a burnt sienna man, or a mars orange woman, or a deep ochre man, or a bioque woman, and so on.

This conference for the sake of precision ought to be entitled, "Shady People at Predominately Colorless Institutions."

Undoubtedly this opens up a host of possibilities for other such conferences to be held at universities in Nebraska. Several come readily to mind:

—People of Height at Predominately Short Institutions
—People of Wit at Predominately Witless Institutions
—People of Fat at Predominately Slim Institutions
—People of Courage at Predominately Cowardly Institutions, etc.

A conference addressing the problems facing people of height, "the vertically challenged," on university campuses deserves attention and ought to draw nationally. Just think of some the problems encountered by people of height.

Banging one's head on door jambs is an everyday occurrence, as well as only having available furniture lacking the necessary support for the torso. Then there are the low altitude light fixtures which short people have attached to ceilings like land mines to bruise and lacerate the skulls of people of height. And let us not forget the ever ominous ceiling fans which threaten to decapitate the vertically challenged. A person of height employed at a university is forced to ride in state vehicles, which requires him to assume unnatural positions. When traveling by air, a person of height's spine is compressed as he is wedged into a seat such that his knees may well be level with his ears. A person of height's salary does not compensate for the additional cost of clothing, the necessary larger vehicles, or the medical expenses incurred from running into those door jambs.

Furthermore, there are also the psychological problems facing people of height. A conscientious person of height is forced to sit in the back of a classroom so others may see, but thereby fostering the perception that he is a sluggard lacking interest in the class, given that most attentive students—studies have shown—sit in the center of the first two rows. A person of height, in order to be socially acceptable, is expected to make eye contact with whomever he is speaking, forcing him to look down upon the majority of people which is harmful to the neck and the spine. A person of height is naturally looked up to which encourages unwarranted anger in others who view height as a superior quality. A male person of height is forced to humiliate himself by stooping before a urinal to urinate, which studies have shown traumatizes the masculinity of a person of height.

In addition, a female person of height has a difficult time finding clothes that fit and is rarely asked to dance. In elementary school the vertically challenged are forced to stand at the end of the line when arranged by height. It is not uncommon for classmates to think people of height have been held back a grade.

In preparation for a conference on People of Height at Predominately Short Institutions, whichever campus of the University of Nebraska hosts it should, as an act of good faith, raise the door jambs to seven foot two, place a urinal and a toilet for people of height in restrooms, as well as offer several higher desks and chairs in each classroom.

It is evident that the vertically impaired have some long-overdue grievances against institutions which are practicing heightism, and such a conference would undoubtedly draw attention to this unjust treatment.

And so it goes.

Einstein on Independent Thought

The ancients knew something which we seem to have forgotten. All means prove but a blunt instrument, if they have not behind them a living spirit.[1]

Recently I found a copy of Albert Einstein's *Ideas and Opinions* in a used bookstore. I opened the table of contents to a collection of essays, speeches, statements, and letters on freedom, education, science and religion, pacifism, classical literature, scientific work and $E=mc^2$. Then I turned a page and came across the following sentence: "There are only a few enlightened people with a lucid mind and style and with good taste within a century." Who would dare to make such a statement?

Einstein.

I read on and turned to the chapter "Education for Independent Thought," published in *The New York Times*, October 5, 1952, which began with:

> It is not enough to teach a man a specialty. Through it he may become a kind of useful machine but not a harmoniously developed personality. It is essential that the student acquire an understanding of and a lively feeling for values. He must acquire a vivid sense of the beautiful and of the morally good. Otherwise, he—with his specialized knowledge—more closely resembles a well-trained dog than a harmoniously developed person. He must learn to understand the motives of human beings, their illusions, and their sufferings in order to acquire a proper

1. Albert Einstein, *Ideas and Opinions*, trans. Sonja Bargmann (New York: Three River Press,1954), 44.

relationship to individual fellow men and to the community.... These precious things are conveyed to the younger generation through personal contact with those who teach, not—or at least not in the main—through textbooks. It is this that primarily constitutes and preserves culture. This is what I have in mind when I recommend the "humanities" as important, not just dry specialized knowledge in the fields of history and philosophy.[2]

I was reminded of a public lecture some years ago at my university given by a former graduate currently employed by Dow chemical company. He spoke of the quality of his undergraduate education and of his position as the director of a team of scientists working in the area of superabsorbent polymers for diapers. At the end of his presentation, he answered several general questions before a student asked if, given the volume of disposal diapers filling landfills, the diapers were biodegradable. The speaker complimented the student on his question and responded that biodegradable material was not his area of research, but surely a problem being addressed elsewhere.

Clearly, our graduate had mastered a specialization in the area of super-absorbents for his company and, in turn, applied his research to create "new and improved" disposable diapers which helps parents clean up the mess around the house. However, while the disposable diaper saves millions of gallons in laundering the soils of daily life, it adds up to 18 billion diapers, or 82,000 tons of plastic and 1.3 million tons of wood pulp—250,000—trees a year being trucked away to landfills. Theoretically, the bacterial remains might even infest the water.

Einstein makes the distinction between the training of students for the means of life in specialized professions, such as computer scientists, business administrators, counselors, chemists, speech pathologists, graphic artists, accountants, designers of kitchens and bathrooms, nurses, physicians or undertakers, who are all prepared to perform procedures and execute techniques, as opposed to educating them for the

2. Ibid, 66.

ends of life, which offers a vivid sense of the beautiful and of the morally good.

The scientist as scientist lacks a directive principle and the prescience necessary to understand the outcomes of his research, seeing, as it were, through a glass darkly, a part of the picture but not its entirety. There is a difference between knowledge derived from past observations and forethought. Einstein, in speaking to the ends of science, states:

> For the scientific method can teach us nothing else beyond how facts are related to, and conditioned by, each other. The aspiration toward such objective knowledge belongs to the highest of which man is capable, and you will certainly not suspect me of wishing to belittle the achievements and the heroic efforts of man in this sphere. Yet it is equally clear that knowledge of what "is" does not open the door directly to "what should be."[3]

In short, you cannot derive what ought to be done from what can be done. The directive principles for establishing goals and determining value are derived from a vivid sense of the beautiful and of the morally good.

Man is more than his corporeal self.

Einstein continues:

> Intelligence makes clear to us the interrelation of means and ends. But mere thinking cannot give us a sense of the ultimate and fundamental ends... [a]nd if one asks whence derives the authority of such fundamental ends, since they cannot be stated and justified merely by reason, one can only answer: they exist in a healthy society as powerful traditions, which act upon the conduct and aspirations and judgments of the individual.... They come into being not through demonstration but through revelation, through the medium of powerful personalities.[4]

Revelation?

3. Ibid, 41–2.
4. Ibid, 42–3.

In these times of the compartmentalization of knowledge, the college graduate is too often simply trained to perform the tasks which his employer hopes he can perform. Most modern students are not well-rounded; they have little sense of tradition, having only a textbook survey of history, one course in what a teacher determines to be literature, no foreign language, several elementary composition courses, elementary math, a choice between several textbook-driven social science courses, and, at my university, an introductory economics course, though none are required to take ethics or read philosophy. While a student will have a rudimentary understanding of economic systems and the means of how the economy works or does not, he will not be able to discuss the ends of life nor have an idea of how to discriminate between courage and cowardliness, generosity and greed, self-control and self-indulgence, gentleness and apathy, motivation and sloth, all of which are necessary in the self-examination of a life that is worth living. In effect, too many universities are turning out human beings who lack humanity.

What did former head of the Federal Reserve Allen Greenspan's well-trained economic genius do for our country? When sitting before a Senate hearing, he admitted he had not foreseen that there would be greedy investment bankers who would fill their pockets while draining those of their fellow citizens: "I made a mistake in presuming that the self-interest of organizations, specifically banks and others, was such as they were best capable of protecting their own shareholders."

They are fixated on what Aristotle calls the goods of the body, or external goods, without any sense of the goods of the soul and, hence, are unaware of the moral and intellectual virtues which are manifested in the actions necessary to become mature adults.

Einstein thinks that a person who lacks a sense of moral values is like a blunt instrument who may well unquestionably follow those whom he deems to be his superiors without ever asking himself if what he is doing is beautiful and morally good.

When making the distinction between a university graduate being trained to be a kind of useful machine as opposed to being educated towards a harmoniously developed personality, Einstein reminds one of Aristotle. Aristotle thought that a person who did not develop the intellectual and moral virtues through a liberal education fitting for a free man would be a slave to be used as an instrument by his master. In Aristotle's words:

> It is also from natural causes that some beings command and others obey, that each may obtain their mutual safety; for a being who is endowed with a mind capable of reflection and forethought is by nature the superior and governor, whereas he whose excellence is merely corporeal is formed to be a slave; whence it follows that the different state of master and slave is equally advantageous to both.[5]

Neither Einstein nor Aristotle are religious, the former thinking God a creation of primitive man to answer his fear of nature and the latter viewing God as the uncaused cause who set the cosmos to order, a fact which is grasped by the faculty of reason placed in man by God. Einstein thinks the principles of morality a "cosmic religious feeling" which he finds difficult to elucidate, "to anyone who is entirely without it, especially as there is no anthropomorphic conception of God corresponding to it."[6]

What is a student to do?

> He must learn to understand the motives of human beings, their illusions, and their sufferings in order to acquire a proper relationship to individual fellow men and to the community.... These precious things are conveyed to the younger generation through personal contact with those who teach, not—or at least not in the main—through textbooks. It is this that primarily constitutes and preserves culture.[7]

5. Politics, 1251a.
6. Einstein, 38
7. Einstein, 43.

Einstein is opposed to textbook education and sees that students need personal contact with those who read the stories of humanity with students, much like parents read tales to their children to teach them values. The student must learn to understand the motives of human beings, their illusions, and their sufferings in order to acquire a proper relationship to individual fellow men and to the community.... The character of human beings is seen in Adam and Eve's disobedience, Benedict Arnold's treachery, Sam Gamgee's loyalty, Fyodor Karamazov's lust, Scrooge's selfishness, Madame DeFarge's vengeance, Alyosha's love, as well as in pondering what Charles Myriel tells his sister in *Les Miserables*, by Victor Hugo:

> Have no fear of robbers or murderers. Such dangers are without, and are but petty. Prejudices are the real robbers; vices the real murderers. The great dangers are within us. What matters it what threatens our heads or our purses? Let us think only of what threatens our souls.[8]

A machine and a dog, however well-trained, lack souls—the living spirit—and, being incapable of self-reflection, are lodged in a state beneath that of man. That man has the capacity for self-determining thought, through which he thinks about his motives and the value of his actions, is at the basis of a harmonious personality.

In "A Message to Intellectuals," August 29, 1948, Einstein notes:

> By painful experience, we have learned that rational thinking does not suffice to solve the problems of our social life. Penetrating research and keen scientific work have often had tragic implications for mankind, producing, on the one hand, inventions which liberate man from exhausting physical labor, making his life easier and richer; but on the other hand, introducing a grave restlessness into his life, making him a slave to his technological environment, and—most catastrophic of all—creating the means for his own mass destruction.[9]

8. Victor Hugo, *Les Misereables*, trans. Charles E. Wilbour (New York: Everyman's Library, 1909), 34–5.
9. Einstein, 148.

Einstein saw what some scientists did under Hitler when offered a salary, life with their families, and laboratories for their research in the areas of genetics/eugenics/race hygiene which were used in the mass sterilization and euthanasia programs. Being unable to generate wealth to equip laboratories, scientists can be at the mercy of politicians and corporate benefactors, so technology becomes especially dangerous when, "they have fallen into the hands of morally blind exponents of political power... [a] power in the hands of small minorities which have come to dominate completely the lives of the masses of people who appear more and more amorphous."[10]

The person whose excellence is merely corporeal, body without soul, is an instrument, and, if he has a good master, it is best that he be used as such, given he is incapable of reflection and forethought— his life is an afterthought. Aristotle makes the further distinction between instruments being inanimate and animate when he notes that a machine is inanimate, but a slave belongs to a class of animate objects purchased to pursue his master's directions, which are in his best interest to follow.

As in all arts which are brought to perfection, it is necessary that they should have their proper instruments if they would complete their works, so is it in the art of managing a family: now of instruments some of them are alive, others inanimate, thus with respect to the pilot of a ship, the tiller [rudder] is without life, the sailor is alive, for a servant in many arts. Thus property is as an instrument to living; an estate is a multitude of instruments; so a slave is an animated instrument, but every one that can minister of himself is more valuable than any other instrument....[11]

In effect, all men who have developed their souls are like accomplished musicians as they direct themselves in the art of preparing a

---

10. Einstein, 358.

11. Aristotle, *Nicomachean Ethics*, trans. Martin Ostwald (Upper Saddle River: Prentice Hall, 1999), 1253b.

meal, reading to children, piloting a ship, or mowing the grass. The person that can minister of himself moves by a directive principle which he wills into action.

Man, according to Aristotle, is composed of a body and a soul. The freeman uses his soul to rule over his body. If the body rules over the soul, the corruptible will be guiding the incorruptible, and this is simply not a good idea. If the body were to rule over the soul this would be an "unnatural condition, as it is clear that the rule of the soul over the body, and of the mind and the rational element over the passionate, is natural and expedient; whereas the equality of the two or the rule of the inferior is always hurtful."[12]

Slavery is the condition of the body ruling the soul, of the belly and/or the groin making decisions, as it were, instead of the soul focusing upon principles and living by conviction. A slave is a person who cannot restrain himself before the appetites of the body and the excessive desire for external possessions. This form of slavery is not a condition that can be abolished by a proclamation. Every person has the potential to fall into slavery—priests, garbage men, plumbers, corporate executives, professors, college administrators, etc. The Wall Street bankers and scientists under Hitler are slaves, doing what they are told and led by what they feel. It is an old adage, if you cannot control yourself, you will be controlled.

This reminds us of G. K. Chesterton when he said:

> Quick machinery worked by slow men will be slow machinery; efficient machinery worked by inefficient men will be inefficient machinery; exact machinery worked by inexact men will be inexact machinery; good machinery worked by bad men will be bad machinery. For there is nothing that is really cut off from man or really independent of him in the whole human world. All tools are, as it were, his extra limbs.[13]

12. 1254b 5–10.

13. *Collected Works of G. K. Chesterton,* Illustrated London News, August 4, 1906 (San Francisco: Ignatius Press, 1990), vol. XXVII, 253.

What is going to happen when in the midst of all the instruments and machinery, the soul of man becomes numb, and he is sapped of vitality as is marked by an active imagination, initiative, courage, moderation and fidelity? When he no longer uses a hoe, a spade, a pick or a computer but becomes a hoe, spade, pick or computer to be used by another person. That is what it means to be a slave.

Will we look to the politicians to bail us out?

From Anno Domini to the Common Era

Forget public schools' religious wars about intelligent design and evolution, students' religious songs and artwork, after-school Bible clubs, graduation prayers and gay sensitivity training. The latest fuss involves letters. The staff of Kentucky's education department proposed guidelines this year that would eliminate the conventional designations of years as BC ("Before Christ") or AD (Anno Domini," meaning "in the year of the Lord"). The proposed secular substitutes to shun references to the birth of Jesus Christ were BCE. ("Before the Common Era") and CE ("Common Era"). Several other states have shifted to that non-sectarian style in history curriculums, since it is preferred by Jews and increasingly observed by secular scholars.[1]

After reading this in the local newspaper, I asked a student in my Introduction to Ethics class, for the date. Surprised (at what a simple question), she responded, "September 22, 2012." "That is right," I said, "but is there any more that needs to be added to the date." A puzzled look came over her face, "No, that is the date." I wrote the date on the board, added AD, and asked the students what that meant. No one knew what the letters represented, although two students thought AD stood for "after death," to which I responded, "After the death of whom?" "Christ," they knew. (Apparently, the edict from Kentucky's education department has not permeated the history curriculum in Nebraska—it will only be a matter of time.)

1. Associated Press Published: Wednesday, June 21, 2006.

The students are partially right. AD does have to do with Christ; however, AD does not stand for "after death" but for Anno Domini, meaning "in the year of the Lord," which is marked from the year of Christ's birth. Therefore, it is September 22, 2012 AD.

In this age of cultural sensitivity and secular, state-run high school education funded by the taxpayers, it is not surprising that somewhere in Kentucky some group or board of culturally sensitive people are worried about the possibility of offending Jews. Then again, Christ, himself a Jew, had that effect on the Jews. Imagine a man claiming to be the Messiah of which the prophets spoke. Why it is blasphemy!

The very idea of Anno Domini, of this being the year of the Lord, is a replay of Jesus' trial before Caiphas in which he is charged with being a blasphemer. Here is how it went: Caiphas, after hearing witnesses who claimed that Jesus said, "I am able to destroy the temple of God, and to build it again in three days," asked, "I adjure thee by the living God, that thou tell us whether thou be the Christ, the Son of God." To which Jesus responded, "Thou hast said; nevertheless I say unto you, Hereafter shall ye see the Son of man sitting on the right hand of power, and coming in the clouds of heaven." At this point it is easy for Caiphas to judge, "He hath spoken blasphemy; what further need have we of witnesses? Behold, ye have heard his blasphemy."

Now the question for us is, either Jesus is a blasphemer (as Caiaphas charged), or he is who he claimed to be—and the apostles professed him to be. This is not a question which ought to be decided by a committee, a school board, or "secular scholars." Yet, this is exactly who is deciding what is being taught in the public schools without any sense of the implications of what changing the date from Anno Domini to the Common Era means to the freedom Americans hold to be God given.

Jesus' claim is unique. Mohammed did not suggest equality with Allah. Moses was never placed on a par with Yahweh. Nor did Buddha or Confucius ever make assertions of divinity. Not one of these religious figures professed to be the son of God, who had come to earth to redeem man, destroy death, and be present at the end of human history for the final judgment of the living and the dead.

We are living in an age in which the "secular scholar," for lack of a better term, wants everyone to adhere to his dogma of cultural relativism, which claims there are no universal absolute values but rather varieties of cultures whose beliefs and values are true for various groups. So, out of respect for people from other cultures in America the date will be changed from Anno Domini to the Common Era. All cultures are entitled to their beliefs and that entitlement ought to be tolerated and appreciated by others in America. Here is an example of the tenets of secular scholars, which come from a group calling itself the Ontario Consultants on Religious Tolerance:

> Since only one in three humans on earth is a Christian, some theologians and other authors felt that non-religious, neutral terms like CE and BCE would be less offensive to the non-Christian majority. Forcing a Hindu, for example, to use AD and BC might be seen by some as coercing them to acknowledge the supremacy of the Christian God and of Jesus Christ. Consider the analogous situation in the U. S. Pledge of Allegiance. The most recent version of this pledge includes the phrase: "Under God." Imagine what a Wiccan (who believes in a God and a Goddess), or many Buddhists and strong atheists feel when having to recite those words. Consider how a Christian would feel if the pledge read "Under Buddha" or "Under Allah."[2]

We are asked to be sensitive and imagine what a Wiccan, Buddhist, Moslem, or a strong Atheist (as opposed to a lukewarm atheist?) might feel (this being the operative word) when having to recite the Pledge of Allegiance. We are not asked to think what a Wiccan, Buddhist, Moslem, or weak or strong atheist might think when having to recite the U. S. Pledge of Allegiance because the relativist dogma of all truths being relative to the people who hold them leaves no room for a thoughtful discussion of the tenets of religious dogmas.

2. www.religioustolerance.org/ceintro.html

All truths being equal means there is but one truth: there is no truth. Therefore, why discuss the truths of other cultures which are not true.

Back to the Pledge of Allegiance and the notion of how a Christian would feel when forced to say he believes in "one nation under Buddha" or "one nation under Allah." This analogy does not work for two reasons: first, America is not a nation under Buddha; second, America is not a nation under Allah. This does not mean Buddhists and Moslems are not free to worship in America; it simply means that America is not, nor could it ever have been, a nation founded on the tenets of Buddha, Mohammed, the gods of Hinduism, or the philosophies of the weak or strong atheists.

Man is not made in the image of God for a Buddhist, Moslem, Hindi, or, obviously, a strong or even feeble atheist. A Buddhist does not believe that he has a free will: a Moslem holds all is the will of Allah: a Hindi is lodged in a caste system; and, an atheist does not have a soul, free will, or a conscience, as man is only a biological accident ultimately signifying nothing.

It is not as though changing AD to CE will change the nature of creation or alter what Christ's birth means to mankind. However, acquiescing to the secular scholar will have Christians hearing the cock crow for the third time along with Peter each day they forsake the Christian era for the Common Era for fear of not being culturally sensitive. Alexander Solzhenitsyn says somewhere, "To destroy a people, you must first sever their roots." What better way to destroy the roots of Americans than by teaching students in public schools they are living in the Common Era.

There have been other attempts to displace Anno Domini: The movers and shakers of the French Revolution did so with the French republican calendar beginning from September 22, 1792 as Vendémiaire, the first month in the new calendar. The Italian Fascists used the standard system along with Roman numerals to denote the number of years since the establishment of the Fascist government in 1922. Therefore, 1934, for example, was Year XII. (The secular scholars and staffers in Kentucky are in good company.)

There is a major difference between living in the year of the Lord and living in the Common Era. Living in the year of the Lord means that a man's life is not his own; he is living in God's creation and ultimately subject to His will. This is why Christians freely pray, "Thy will be done," as opposed to thinking freedom is permission to be led by their own wills. Furthermore, man entered creation in the image of God and entered time with his fall from grace, in an era known as BC (Before Christ), which extends to the redemptive time of Anno Domini with the birth of the Messiah, the savior of mankind. For lack of knowledge or lack of belief, the secular scholar has arbitrarily replaced AD with CE without having a point of demarcation, e. g., the French Revolution, the establishment of the Fascist government of Italy, or the birth of Christ (though His birthdate remains the beginning of CE so it is being changed in name only), with which to mark history.

Living in the Common Era is an appropriate term for a cultural relativist who denies the tenets of every religious dogma. Living in the Common Era, American students will have to "return" to the pre-American countries of their forefathers as commoners, ordinary people, without rank or distinction of any kind, lodged beneath lords, knights, and squires.

However, one could say the secular scholars have chosen well. CE is a fitting expression because, as a commoner, man is not made in the image of God, a sacred creature worthy of respect as a god—"what you do to the least of these you do unto me."

In all of this, it is important to remember the party slogan of Big Brother in George Orwell's *1984*, "Who controls the past controls the future. Who controls the present controls the past." By allowing the staffers at state departments of education and secular scholars rule the present, we forsake the inherent dignity of man who is meant for God.

So it goes.

On Research at a University

Visit the campus of almost any university in the land: you will find its classrooms packed with students, its conference rooms buzzing with the activity of faculty and administrative committees, its computer screens overflowing with electronic memoranda detailing new policies and procedures and apprising all and sundry of the latest round of internal assessment and external review of curriculum, of teaching, of research, of diversity—with goals and objectives distinguished and reduced to "bullet" or laid out on an Excel spreadsheet. You will hardly escape without subjection to at least one PowerPoint presentation. If your visit is hasty and unreflective, you may even suffer the delusion that some form of education or scholarship is taking place.... The frantic motion to and fro on most campuses, however, holds the same relation to genuine academic activity as the stampede of the Gadarene swine to the discourse of rational men. Like the luckless pigs, the university has been possessed by a legion of unclean spirits: there is feverish movement and a demonic semblance of life, but the soul has departed and all that remains is the cadaver of an educational institution.[1]

These words belong to R. V. Young, a Professor of English at North Carolina State University, and are from the introduction of "The University Possessed," in this spring's issue of *The Intercollegiate Review*. When I first read Professor Young's autopsy, I wanted to weep. A cadaver? Surely, Professor Young, there is still life in the minds of some professors on university campuses

1. R. V. Young, "The University Possessed," *The Intercollegiate Review* (Wilmington, DL), Spring 2007.

which can quicken a student's soul without the glitz of a PowerPoint presentation.

Then again, if Professor Young were to tour my campus, he would find the same "frantic motion to and fro" with the construction of new "residential" halls, the addition of "smart" classrooms, the computers lining hallways for students to surf the web between classes, the various Starbucks coffee bars, the General Studies Committee busily at work preparing for the next external review (willfully oblivious that the recommendations from the last two reviews of five and ten years ago have never been addressed), yet another new Strategic Plan, the mega-message sign announcing the employee of the month from custodial services, and the multitude of offices dedicated to assessment, diversity, research, enrollment, retention, women's issues, etc.

The modern university is an expensive resort with wads of money spent on technology, food-courts, residence halls, skyboxes and administrators' salaries, but with very little time spent on teaching students to read beyond the level of an elementary student.

This week, two educational studies in national newspapers confirmed Professor Young's postmortem. The first is the finding of a 2005 survey of 14,000 college students by the University of Connecticut that seniors had flunked the civic literacy exam with an average score of 53.2 percent; more than 53 percent could not identify the century when the first American colony was founded at Jamestown, Virginia; fewer than half, 47.9 percent, could identify the Declaration of Independence as the source for this line: "We hold these truths to be self-evident, that all men are created equal." The second confirmation, a report by The National Assessment of Educational Progress, often called the nation's report card, surveyed transcripts of 26,000 high school students, comparing them with an earlier study of student coursework in 1990. The results found that the reading skills of 12th graders tested in 2005 were significantly worse than those of students in 1992. The share of students lacking even basic high school reading skills rose to 27 percent from 20 percent in 1992. The share of those proficient in reading dropped from 40 percent in 1992 to 35 percent in 1993. Yet, get ready for this, the high school students in 2005 had averaged 360 more hours of classroom time than students in 1990. Finally, the kicker, the grade point average was a third of letter grade higher than in 1990. Let's think about this for a minute. One in four high school seniors cannot read and only one in three are proficient in reading. Soon one-half of those high school graduates go to college where under half of the surveyed seniors can identify the Declaration of Independence as the source for the line: "We hold these truths to be self-evident, that all men are created equal."

This is ludicrous. It would be like birds sending their chicks to aviaries to teach them the intricacies of high flying or dogs sending their pups to canine academies for agility training and ending up with birds that can only walk and dogs that sleep all day.

How can this be? The answers are simple: very few students have parents who read to them as children, the students are hooked on way too many electronic gizmos, and fewer and fewer teachers read formative character literature in which the student seeks to imitate the virtuous characteristics of the hero in his own life. Ergo, students do not read, like to be electronically stimulated, and do not see the point of stories that have nothing to do with them.

Not long ago I attended a dinner for honor students where a university president told his audience that the goal of modern education is to create life-long learners, that their generation has more information (thanks to computers!) than previous generations, and that those who can readily adapt to new technologies will continue to be "marketable" in the ever-changing global economy. Swell. Obviously, a university diploma should no longer certify that a student has a mind and is able to read the Declaration of Independence with understanding; in other words, not only where the line "all men are created equal and endowed by their creator with life, liberty and the pursuit of happiness" comes from, but what it means, and how it just might apply to the end of his own life when he might hope to face the creator who endowed his rights. With such leadership at the university level, is it any wonder that the world has no other goal than unbridled economic growth so that the feeding frenzy of consumerism can be fueled?

In actuality, modern education is creating students who are life-long forgetters. Most modern teaching, even at the college level, is about isolated facts (information) disconnected from a philosophy of the whole. In the words of Joseph Pearce, he is a "Techno-man, devoid of any metaphysical understanding, [who] knows how to do things without knowing why or whether they should be done." Modern man is being schooled by sociologists who compile what is, without any sense of what has been or ought to be. Our computers have memories, but no remembrances. We have mistaken access to information for wisdom. The modern university is being run by capitalists who view human beings as ciphers to be manipulated in the service of economic efficiency.

Fortunately, a university is more than her buildings, science laboratories, classrooms and dormitories. The soul of the university is the members of her student body and faculty who are doing research in the eye of the storm's "frantic motion to and fro," which has nothing to do with the quality of rational discourse on a university campus.

Professor Young understands that when a student enters a university, he has stepped on a plane with his intellectual ancestors to continue, with the assistance of the faculty—who are the faculty, the search for the truth of what it means to be a virtuous human being, a steward of the earth.

For the sake of simplification, this search takes on two forms. There is external research, that of looking out upon the world, and the internal research, that of looking within oneself for the fine art of what it means to a good and happy human being. In the origin of the word research, the prefix "re" means again, and, when placed before "search," it means to look again.

The nature of the subject being studied determines the method of research being conducted. That conducted in the natural sciences, differs from that in the humanities. Research in the natural sciences is objective; it is about an object which can be grasped by the senses, be it in biology, chemistry, or physics. Research in the natural sciences builds upon its previous discoveries and does not have to rediscover the cell, table of elements, or gravity each semester, though it does require the ability to read about and understand those discoveries.

Science advances by scientists solving problems and moving on to the next set of problems: engines fueled by hydrogen, drought-resistant seed corn, and smoother blends of whiskey. This is all fine and good in that it provides for man's mobility, appetite and entertainment. Furthermore, one does not have to be a scientist, nor understand the scientific method, to benefit from the discoveries in genetic research, of drugs which stabilize blood pressure, or in the ability to fit five trillion songs on a "smart-phone."

The humanities does not have the success rate of the natural sciences in manipulating nature because man's nature has not changed in the course of history. Research in the humanities differs from research in the sciences. In philosophy, the problem of what it means to be a human being—to know thyself—begins anew with each student. Self-knowledge is not a scientific investigation but an individual quest where being literate is the necessary proficiency.

The aim of Plato's *Republic*, for example, is to show that justice and the virtues of wisdom, courage and moderation are in everyone's best interest and are required for true happiness. This search begins anew with each student who, like all previous students, was born ignorant of the fundamental answers to the questions necessary for a thoughtful existence: Who are we? Why are we? What separates us from the animals? Is man a slave to his desires? What is a soul? What is the function of reason? Do we have a higher nature that can rise above greed and lust? Does might make right? Do we have a higher purpose than self-gratification? Should we ever return a harm with a harm? What is a moral principle? Does moral law precede civil law?

These questions are problems that are not solved; they must be lived with each decision made. So, while there are new and improved aorta valves that can be surgically implanted, there is not a new and improved program which can be downloaded on a student's hard drive which will solve the problems he will face in life. The price for answering the questions from *Republic* is being able to read because, if you cannot read the questions, you surely cannot seek the answers throughout your life in your quest for your own happiness and that of your children.

A Conversation with
Dr. Thomas Sutherland

March 10, 1992

L ast night my wife, Linda, and I went to hear Dr. Tom Sutherland speak at the "Fort Kearney Cattleman's Ladies' Night Banquet." Dr. Sutherland was one of the American hostages who was recently released in Lebanon, where he worked as the Dean of the College of Agriculture at the American University of Beirut. We went to see Dr. Sutherland for various reasons. My father-in-law and his wife are first cousins, and we wanted to welcome an American home. When one of us is held captive, so are we all.

We arrived at 6:30 for the social hour. At quarter till seven Dr. Sutherland appeared, surrounded by former teachers, students, and friends from the University of Nebraska. We went over and introduced ourselves; my father-in-law had called and told him we were coming to hear his talk. The three of us then spent the next fifteen or twenty minutes locked in conversation.

For over seventy months he was chained to a wall with a group of men. The chain was anchored to the wall and ran through their leg irons. Most of his captivity was spent with Terry Anderson, whom at first, he confessed, he resented. You see Dr. Sutherland was a college professor, and of all things, a Dean, and Anderson was a journalist. Thomas resented the fact that Anderson knew more than he did, a common problem with PhD's, that Anderson had "read everything" and could discuss ideas. "I am scientist," he told us. "For the most part I studied animals; you separate some cattle from others, run tests, do a statistical analysis and that's that. But when I was with Terry Anderson, for the first time in my life I understood what it was to be educated. He had read everything. He became my spiritual inspiration." What honesty!

I mentioned that Aleksandr Solzhenitsyn, the author of *The Gulag Archipelago*, thought his time in solitary confinement to be one of the richest moments of his life, as all the external concerns that trouble the mind were removed and he was free to think. Dr. Sutherland's eyes lit up. He had read Solzhenitsyn's *The First Circle* in captivity. (*The First Circle* is a book about scientists, mathematicians, linguists, and academics who are thrown into a special prison where they work on government projects for Stalin. If they are successful they may be allowed to return to their family, if not, they would be sent to Siberia for forced labor.) Dr. Sutherland said that he and Terry Anderson discussed the book together. They also read Arthur Koestler's *Darkness at Noon*. What a find!

We did not have time to discuss what exactly they had discussed. So as I was writing this back in my office cell, I pulled down *The First Circle* and turned to the chapter "The Fifth Year In Harness." I thumbed to an idea that Sutherland and Anderson would have come across. Keep in mind as you read this passage that these men are chained together to a wall; they may even be in "the fifth year of their harness," and they do not know if they will ever again see the light of day.

> When I was free and used to read books in which wise men pondered the meaning of life or the nature of happiness, I understood very little of those passages. I gave them their due: wise men are supposed to think. It's their profession. But the meaning of life? We live—that's the meaning. Happiness? When things are going very well, that's happiness, everyone knows that. Thank God for prison! It gave me the chance to think. In order to understand the nature of happiness we first have to analyze satiety. Remember the Lubyanka [a prison] and counterintelligence? Remember that thin, watery barley or the oatmeal porridge without a single drop of fat? Can you say that you eat it? No. You commune with it, you take it like a sacrament! Like the prana of the yogis.

You eat it slowly; you eat it from the tip of the wooden spoon; you eat it absorbed entirely in the process of eating, in thinking about eating—and it spreads through your body like nectar. You tremble at the sweetness released from those overcooked little grains and the murky liquid they float in. And then—with hardly any nourishment—you go on living six months, twelve months. Can you really compare the crude devouring of a steak with this?[1]

When Dr. Sutherland remarked about being educated, as opposed to "doing research," he was referring to this sort of passage which is packed full of ideas. Being educated means communing with the spiritual side of life, the side of man that is touched in the privacy of his own reflections on artists and authors who speak directly to his soul.

Now reread the passage from Solzhenitsyn and look at what he says. Read carefully, be patient, remember you are fixed to the wall; there is time to mull over the words and digest the ideas housed in them. Nerzhin, to whom these words belong, says that he had read men who pondered the meaning of life, but had never understood what they said, what they meant. The meaning of life? We live. What else is there? Happiness? When things are going my way, that's happiness. (This is why you only need two philosophers on a practically-minded campus.) Then Solzhenitsyn throws you a curve. Keep in mind you are chained to a wall; you probably have even thought about taking your own life—this idea will cross a man's mind, especially after months in confinement. Ready. "Thank God for prison! It gave me the chance to think." Now notice the analogy, thinking has to do with satiety, with being full, with being "thoughtful." Having the time to think is like eating soup in the Lubyanka prison, that thin watery barley without a single drop of fat. No excess. You do not eat it, you commune with it; you take it like a sacrament, savoring even the tip of the wooden spoon as you absorb the nectar of life.

1. Aleksandr Solzhenitsyn, *The First Circle*, trans. Thomas P. Whitney (New York: Harper & Row, 1968), 33.

As Sutherland read down the page he undoubtedly ran into this idea. Ready. Here it is:

Satiety depends not at all on how much we eat, but on how we eat. It's the same way with happiness, the very same. Lev, friend, happiness doesn't depend on how many external blessings we have snatched from life. It depends only on our attitude toward them. There's a saying about it in the Taoist ethic: "Whoever is capable of contentment will always be satisfied."[2]

What are the odds of the Scotsman Sutherland, and the American Anderson being chained to a wall, reading a Russian quoting the *Tao*? (International Education?) The Russian Solzhenitsyn has been where you are, too, although it was in the depths of Siberia, and he is offering encouragement. He is saying to Tom Sutherland, as Tom is reading, "Your happiness does not depend upon your external blessing; you know this, you are chained to a wall; your happiness is a matter of your attitude, it is not how much you eat, but it is how you eat." When Terry "talked" with Solzhenitsyn, I would venture that he heard much the same, and maybe Terry realized that his life had been filled with books, but he did not have time to listen. I do not know. Anyway after they read these lines, maybe Thomas and Terry read the passage aloud and then discussed it. They thought about their situation and maybe they were inspired by the words of Solzhenitsyn quoting the *Tao*, the Way, to go about living a life even while chained to a wall. I do not know if they were inspired by these ideas, and I do not pretend to understand their ordeal. These ideas are between them and Solzhenitsyn, and this is the wonder of being educated, the wonder of the "life of the mind" as a sacred form of communion where a man understands something clearly, perhaps for the first time in his life, as though it were a sacred message from his soul.

2. Ibid., 33.

What is the Way? Read on. Solzhenitsyn has Nerzhin continue to speak, "On the planet of philosophy all lands have long since been discovered. I leaf through the ancient philosophers and find my newest discoveries there.... The books of the *Sankhya* say: "For those who understand, human happiness is suffering." These words in the *Sankhya*, a Hindu work, sound almost like, "Take up your cross and follow me." Joy in suffering! Sounds like a contradiction in terms. Solzhenitsyn goes on to explain:

> Listen! The happiness of incessant victory, the happiness of fulfilled desire, the happiness of success and of total satiety—that is suffering! That is spiritual death, a sort of unending moral pain. It isn't the philosophers of the *Vedanta* or the *Sankhya*, but I personally, Gleb Nerzhin, a prisoner in harness for the fifth year, who has risen to that stage of development where the bad begins to appear the good. And I personally hold the view that people don't know what they are striving for. They waste themselves in senseless thrashing around for the sake of a handful of goods and die without realizing their spiritual wealth. When Lev Tolstoi dreamed of being imprisoned, he was reasoning like a truly perceptive person with a healthy spiritual life. (34)

An important man will not hear these words. He is too busy. In the academic community there are meetings to go to, committees to be established, reports to be given; why at this very minute we are in the process of "transitioning" to a university. On my campus some of our quasi-administrators who have fled the classroom—escaped from their cell, and with it "the life of the mind"—are currently working on how to "assess" what goes on in education as though they could objectively measure what goes on in a student, or a professor, locked in soulful reflection. (We in philosophy do this the "old fashion way" by having conversations over ideas in books with students, and by reading their papers, essay exams, and journals. There is no other way!) The man who thinks education to be public enterprise lives in a land where everything has been turned upside down. Topsy-turvy-dome. He thinks happiness comes from "how much you eat," so he ends up serving Mammon, "thrashing after goods," that will be taken from him at death. Will the people "outside of education" ever realize the privacy of the endeavor. It is "how you eat" as in "how you think;" it is not "how much you eat" as in "how much you talk." When you talk about education you do not participate "in" education. Get back to your cell, read a book with students, write a paper, a poem, a book, and discuss ideas with others who profess. Until you can do this, "Get thee behind me!"

In another passage of *The First Circle*, Sologdin says to Nerzhin, "You ought to find out where you are, spiritually understand the role of good and evil in human life. There's no better place to do it than prison."

The life of the mind, a time to understand the role of good and evil from the inside—scientists with all their research are not educated in their lives, their "way," to understand this. They can, however, enter into education by realizing that "spiritual wealth," the nourishment of the soul, is forged in reflection over ideas and images like those Solzhenitsyn presented to Dr. Thomas Sutherland and Terry Anderson in their cell. If a man is "in education" he does not need to be in prison to be awakened to "the life of the mind." When a man studies, he voluntarily imprisons himself, he shuts off the outside world for the inside world where he reads and subjects himself to the ideas of authors, poets, and philosophers. When he focuses his mind, he communes through words filled with the spirit of souls distant from his own. And in so doing becomes, as it were, one with the word. This is not to say that he has to agree with everything that he reads, but this will prompt him to write papers, poems, and plays to respond to the ideas and, in so doing, form himself.

For the most part, the life of mind is a bloodletting; writing does not come easily, so students and faculty alike flee their cells to fill their eyes, and their pockets, with the world. There is so much to do! They often lack the discipline to subject themselves to the joy that comes from reflection, (suffering?), in a cell. This is why a scholar, who is always a student, needs contemplative time to examine the worth of his discipline and in so doing, himself.

"The unexamined life is not worth living."

On the Qualitative Differences Between Coaches and Teachers

I was recently reminded of the difference between academics and athletics at the University of Nebraska, or, for that matter, American universities in general. Mike Andersen, the baseball coach at the University of Nebraska who took his team to the College World Series where it became the first victorious team in school history, was given a 76% salary increase (from $113,531 to $200,000).

This brought to mind Socrates, who, after being found guilty of corrupting the youth of Athens and creating false gods, was given the right by Athenian law to recommend his own punishment before the Senate of Athens. Socrates thought that he ought to receive free meals at the *Prytaneum*, the town hall of Athens in which public entertainments were given, particularly to Olympian victors on their return home. Socrates' reason for asking to be treated like an Olympian victor was simple: "the Olympian victor makes you think yourself happy; I make you be happy."[1]

What Socrates said before the Senate of Athens in 399 BC is true in Nebraska in 2016 AD: the victorious Huskers make sports-minded spectators, like myself, think ourselves happy, but they do not make us be happy. However, just for making us think we are happy, the state

1. Plato, *Five Dialogues*, trans. G. M. A. Grube (Indianapolis: Hackett Publishing, 1992), Apology, 36e.

of Nebraska gives her athletes free meals at the University dining halls and her coaches are rewarded beyond reason.

I must now ask, what is the difference between a fan thinking himself happy because his baseball team won a game at the college world series and being happy? Thinking I am happy because my team has won is not so much a thought as it is a feeling that swells up in my chest and lasts for a few days. I, as every fan, am proud when my team wins and this makes me happy. Conversely, when Nebraska loses I do not think myself sad, but I feel sad. Of course, I realize that I had nothing to do with my team's successes and failures, unless I think the fans' cheering is essential to the quality of play.

Obviously Socrates thought that feeling happy was not as desirable as being happy. In his defense before the Senate of Athens, Socrates asked the Senators, exactly what he asked his fellow Athenians throughout his years as a philosopher:

> Good Sir, you are an Athenian, a citizen of the greatest city with the greatest reputation for both wisdom and power; are you not ashamed of your eagerness to possess as much wealth, reputation, and honors as possible, while you do not care for nor give thought to wisdom or truth, or the best possible state of your soul?

Socrates here is making the distinction between the goods of the body and the goods of the soul and their respective forms of happiness. Being physically fit is a good of the body but it is not a good of the soul.

Socrates tells his fellow citizens that if a person wants to be happy, he must be concerned with the state of his soul. It is not wealth, reputation, and honor that will make the soul happy. These three things will not make the soul happy because money, reputation, and honor are external to the soul. Money is an inanimate object while reputation and honor are dependent upon what other people think. This puts one at the mercy of others; if they change their minds, so goes one's reputation and honor.

The happiness of which Socrates spoke is a matter of a person's character. It is not about being a spectator and feeling happy when one's team wins, but it is about being an active participant in the virtuous development of one's own soul. It is a different form of development than the athletic development of the body which is handsomely rewarded at universities throughout America.

A teacher, especially one who is able to assist in the development of each student's character and mind by teaching him to read literature, history, chemistry, and the like and to write coherently, is not like a coach who receives monetary rewards, although his students perform on the field of life where we all are responsible for playing out our lives.

The financial rewards in universities like Nebraska's go to the coaches who cull a select few for their athletic prowess to entertain the masses of spectators who feel good about winning. Historically, it is not the business of a university to be consumed by the goods of the body to the extent of paying exorbitant salaries to those who coach games.

But would it not be something if teachers were rewarded with cash bonuses like coaches for their successes as illustrated by the performance of their students in the arena of life? We teachers at the University of Nebraska at Kearney are not evaluated on our ability to teach our subject matter to students. In fact, the students are the only ones who ever observe and evaluate what a teacher does in the classroom on a daily basis, though occasionally there may be a peer review by a colleague. No administrator ever enters a classroom to see how the students are taught or what they are being taught.

Thus, it is not surprising there is no merit pay for teachers, as this would require someone making a qualitative judgment. At this university, a professor is a professor, is a professor, etc. All things being equal, the military model of rank and years of service is used to determine each teacher's salary. For example, I have been a full professor for six years and have taught here for twenty years and anyone with the same time in rank and years of service will make the same salary. Unless, of course, the subject being taught, e. g. accounting, has a higher "market value" than, say, ethics, in which case the professor's salary will reflect the market value.

If a teacher were a teacher, universities could claim they offer a quality education to their students. However, there are different degrees of teachers who are known by their approach. Before listing the categories of teachers, it is important to note that this classification of teachers is not determined by their levels of academic degree, academic rank, or time in rank. In fact, it may well be the case that there are adjunct teachers who are among the best teachers in today's universities, just as there may be full professors who do not belong in a classroom. Furthermore, in these times of quota systems prevailing in universities where administrators are committed to the idea that the faculty of a university ought to reflect the ethnic and sexual demographics of the general population, it is not the case that the most qualified people are being hired to fill the academic positions in universities.

The classification of teachers is similar to that of the classification used by teachers in the evaluation of students; that is, from the highest to the lowest: from those who are demanding, stimulate thought, and garner respect to those who do not work themselves, stymie the intellect, and are forgotten by students the moment they leave class. These following four classifications may be applied to the faculty of a university by using a system of evaluations to test the rigor and level of the subject matter being offered to students. For example, at a weak university the general studies curriculum will be a repetition of high school courses which are textbook based, demand very little reflective writing, much memorization and multiple choice exams.

First are the Socrabites, those who live at the heart of a university waging a battle to know the truth and approach it from their respective arts or sciences. They are the spirit of learning, persistent in questioning and seeking answers. Like Socrates, they are not deterred by the demands of politicians, nor adhere to political movements and ideologies that are fashionable at the time. Such teachers are lifelong students whose passion for and subjection to their discipline are known and remembered by their attentive students years after leaving the university.

Second are the Scholarbites. They are not neophytes but have spent much time in the university testing in the fraternal line of scholarship in the single battle of accuracy in their research. They are well-educated in their disciplines and are like hermits who can be left alone with their research, only needing students to advance their study just as a car maker needs assembly-line workers to the assemble the pieces of his design.

Third are the Detestabites. They are unschooled in any discipline, untested, as gold is by fire so they are as soft as lead, living around a university as parasites. They are openly hostile to the authorities of any discipline and their only rule is the pleasure of their desires. In Socrates' day they were known as sophists, who used their intellect to deceive people with clever sounding but flawed arguments. They will never be heard outside of class discussing ideas, reading papers (except on some far away campus or conference) or publishing their thoughts on any subject. They live in constant fear for their positions and are ardent supporters of teachers' unions (their chief concern being for their salary, they are against merit pay) desiring the life-long security of their positions through tenure. (Students who think a college degree is the end of learning are attracted to such types, who are little more than talking text-books, staying one page ahead of the students and known to have their multiple choice exams on file in at least one of the fraternity houses.)

Fourth are the Gyrobites. All their lives they wander from class to class. They cannot focus on any subject long enough to gain the proficiency required of a Doctor of Philosophy in an academic discipline. They are restless servants to the seduction of their appetites, who use the position of a teacher to parade before students, some of whom are immature and easily seduced into thinking that such quasi-instructors are worthy of honors. They are opposed to all rules, even punctuation. It is better to be silent as to their deplorable teaching than to speak.

Unlike the coaches of the University of Nebraska who stand before the general public in stadiums, teachers remain cut off from the general population who are outside of their classrooms and laboratories. Thus, the aforementioned categories of teachers are only known by the students and fellow colleagues who are capable of qualitative judgment. Ironically, the teachers adamant against merit pay because there is no one who can fairly determine who is a competent teacher are the same ones who are adamant about evaluating their students' work and assigning a grade for their performances. Obviously, this assumes such teachers do in fact use qualitative judgment to evaluate students and do not just hand out grades. Evaluation is possible and desirable, for without it there is no growth for the teacher nor respect for the university, as it has long been the case that the unexamined university is not worthy of life.

In all of this we do well to remember, just as there is a difference between being a spectator who thinks he is good because his team wins and being one who is an active participant in the moral development of his own soul, so too there are differing qualities of education being offered to students by the faculty at various universities which cannot be measured in dollars but in sense.

"How are you as far as sex goes...?"

How are you as far as sex goes, Sophocles? Can you still make love with a woman?" "Quiet, man," the poet replied, "I am very glad to have escaped from all that, like a slave who has escaped from a savage and tyrannical master." I [Cephalus] thought at the time that he was right, and I still do, for old age brings peace and freedom from all such things. When appetites relax and cease to importune us, everything Sophocles said comes to pass, and we escape from many mad masters. In these matters and in those concerning relatives, the real cause isn't old age, Socrates, but the way people live. If they are moderate and contented, old age, too, is only moderately onerous; if they aren't, both old age and youth are hard to bear.[1]

These words are spoken by Cephalus in his home in Piraeus, the harbor near Athens, at the beginning of Plato's dialogue *Republic* before a group of young men and Socrates. This passage is a great ice-breaker. Most of the students who have wandered into my philosophy class are wondering what in the world philosophers do. What better way to capture the attention of youth than the mention of sex. No doubt many of the students are thinking, "On the first day of philosophy class we are talking about sex! Man, can I get into this."

This passage immediately draws students into a discussion on the perennial dilemma of the internal torments of man, the creature with two butting heads: the upper-head led by right reason focused upon virtue and the lower-head led by the swell of erotic love. Rest assured

1. Plato, *Republic*, trans. G. M. A. Grube, (Indianapolis: Hackett 1992), 329c.

the question which is being asked is not as harmless as it seems; after all it has been reserved for a poet of great stature—Sophocles—who gave the Greeks in this dialogue the character of Oedipus the King, accursed in the sight of all men, for he had unknowingly committed the unthinkable crimes of both heads, parricide and incest, rendering him an outcast in any human society. Imagine if Cephalus could ask this question to Oedipus? "Oedipus, how are you as far as sex goes?"

(Only a few students in the class have heard of Sophocles, so it is necessary to give a brief summary of Oedipus the King.)

"Young man—yes, you in back row—tell me, could you still make love to a woman upon finding you had unknowingly made love to your mother?"

No response.

Why is Sophocles, who lived twenty-four centuries ago, glad that he had escaped from thinking his manhood was measured by his ability to make love to a woman? Obviously, the times have changed. Can we even imagine someone asking such a question of one of our prominent national figures? How would President Clinton respond to this question, "President Clinton, tell us how are you as far as a sex goes. Can you still make love to a woman?" Would he say, "Quiet man, I am very glad to have escaped from all that," like a slave who has escaped from a savage and tyrannical master. Or would he say, "I have given that question some thought, and, try as I might, the act of making love to women keeps popping into my head. Whenever I see some supple young intern walking down the hall in the White House or am answering questions at a press conference and a babe in the front row crosses her long legs and her pantyhose swoosh as she adjusts her bottom in the chair, my mind is quickened as if by a rush of warm blood."

The students do not think President Clinton would say sex is a form of slavery from which he cannot escape. He would not have called himself a slave ruled by the mad tyrannical masters of sex. Though he did admit he made an error in judgment and did something that was "inappropriate," he did not admit that *he* was a slave who was at the mercy of a "mad master."

One of the male students pipes up from the back row that Clinton's hypothetical response could be true, "I mean, Man, that's what it's like, you know."

Yes, that is how it is. Instead of Sophocles writing plays about a King who is rationally innocent yet doomed to suffer from his sin in loneliness and neglect, conscious all the while, consumed by the despicable nature of his sins, we will have journalists report stories of leaders who are idolized by the majority of voters for letting an intern perform fellatio upon him in the oval office while he talks with a congressman on the phone. Oedipus, when he found out he had committed parricide and incest, saw himself as the source of pollution which had come across his land:

> In the unnumbered deaths
> of its people the city dies;
> those children that are born lie dead on the naked earth
> unpitied, spreading contagion of death; the gray haired
> mothers and wives
> everywhere stand at the altar's edge, suppliant, moaning....[2]

So he took the brooch from the garments of his dead wife's body, who was also his mother, and repeatedly stuck the pin in his eyes so they could not see his crime,

> and the bleeding eyeballs gushed
> and stained his beard—no sluggish oozing drops
> but a black rain and bloody hail poured down.[3]

And then Oedipus exiled himself from his own land.

2. David Grene and Richmond Lattimore, eds., *Sophocles I* (New York: Random House, 1942).

3. Ibid., 79–80.

Oedipus was fated to kill his father and sleep with his mother, and yet he takes responsibility for the pollution that has come across his kingdom, a moral pollution.

Could it be that President Clinton reigns over a cloud of moral pollution that has descended upon his nation? When the majority of American men approve of the job Clinton is doing as president and do not think he should be impeached for disgracing his office, could it be that the majority of American men's vision is clouded because they muse about having women half their age? The president, the father of his nation, repeatedly fulfills his sexual fantasies at the taxpayers' expense and gets away with it.

(In the background the chorus is singing, "When you can't be with the one you love/ You gotta love the one you're with.")

But the question remains, is the lure of sex a savage and tyrannical master from which a man may not be freed until old age relaxes its grip? If it is, then man is not free nor responsible for his actions when he is gripped by erotic desire. Perhaps this explains why the majority of Americans approve of the job President Clinton has done and think that a man's private life has nothing to do with public affairs. He cannot help himself. And neither can we.

Even the Greek gods are known for being under the tyrannical power of erotic love. Zeus, when all the other gods were asleep, was so overcome by the sight of Hera that he did not even want to go inside but wanted to possess her there on the ground. Can you imagine yourself desiring someone so much you would fall to the ground to play the two-backed animal instead of waiting to get indoors?

"I can imagine it," says a young man in the second row, "but I know I would not do it. I can control myself and am not a slave to the tyrannical master of erotic love."

So, do you think slavery still exists in America?

"Yes, because, if by slavery you mean someone or something being in control of you, I think we could be slaves to sexual desire."

Even though you can control yourself and you will not act like Zeus, can you control your thoughts about sex when your eyes are loose on the modern panorama? What do you think the television producers are after when they stock prime-time television with long-legged vixens in push-up bras on sitcom after sitcom, and, over on MTV, babes and dudes are bumping and grinding to the beat of pelvic rock? Then to add fuel to the fire, why does the liquor store across the street have a poster on the front door of a blond with bright red lips and breasts a milk cow would be proud of lounging up against a bottle of Tequila?

"They do not want you to think; they want you to feel," says a student.

So we moved from the higher head to the lower head, from reason to erotic love. Here your desires will be fueled by the modern gods and goddesses paraded before your eyes. The mass of men are still polytheists. They do not believe in Zeus or Athena but in the characters on television who are like men but not human. These characters do not suffer diets or pay off credit cards. Their hair is always in place, and they live in outlandish homes and seldom work (but if they do, it is exciting, and never lasts more than an hour).

Did you not know that the mass of mankind is very simple and can be easily led? Remember the first principle of marketing: "Appeal to their sensuality!" Get them to feel that they are incomplete, that they are missing out on the best times of their lives, and that their inadequacies can be remedied by a few adjustments to their image. You are the image you project! Whether it be a red, four-wheel drive Cherokee, Silver-Tab jeans, moussed-back hair, or bath oils, there must be something you can apply or wrap around your body which will accent your appeal to the opposite or same sex. What a dish. (Chorus: "I can't get no satisfaction/ I can't get no girlie action.")

It is not enough to place the sting of longing in the soul, but any of man's beliefs that are thought to be good or that might cause him to be ashamed must be removed and transfused with imported madness. This will enable him to justify his actions and keep him from self-reflection and the haunting conscience.

Moral pollution? Back to Sophocles:

> In the unnumbered deaths
> of its people the city dies;
> those children that are born lie dead on the naked earth
> unpitied, spreading contagion of death; the gray haired
> mothers and wives
> everywhere stand at the altar's edge, suppliant, moaning....[4]

Does this verse apply to our times? Have we lost count of the unnumbered deaths, of the children sucked like eggs from shells or scraped from the walls of their mothers' wombs, unpitied by their fathers who have fled. Does the contagion of death spread over this land such that these spring-like girls are to be left gray haired, weeping for their children who never saw the light of day?

"How are you as far as sex goes? Can you still make love to a woman?"

4. Ibid., 23.

The Sexual Harassment and Gender Equity Climate at UNK

At the October meeting of the staff of *The Examined Life*, the Assistant Director of Meteorology brought to our attention the recent "climate survey" sent out by Chancellor Douglas Kristensen. The cover letter opens with:

> Enclosed is the climate survey announced earlier this week. Campus climate is defined as "behaviors within a workplace or learning environment... that can influence whether an individual feels personally safe, listened to, valued, and treated fairly and with respect." (Campus Climate Network Group 2002)

The Chancellor assures the faculty and staff that testing the climate of our university was not his idea, but he is following the "recommendations" of the Regents, the North Central Evaluation team, the Affirmative Action Commission, and the Chancellor's Committee on Gender Equity.

The Assistant Director of Meteorology noted that the instrument used to determine the climate on campus differs from the barometers, hygrometers, pyrometers, rain gauges, thermometers and wind speed indicators used at weather stations. In fact, in order to determine the climate at our university, a new instrument was crafted to determine "whether an individual feels personally safe, listened to, valued, and treated fairly and with respect."

Credits for constructing the "instrument" to determine the campus climate are given to Ms. Kay Payne, Director of the Center for Rural Research and Development, and Ms. Cheryl Bressington, Director of the Affirmative Action/Equal Opportunity and Assistant Director of Human Resources, with the assistance of the Chancellor's Committee on Gender Equity, the Affirmative Action Commission, the Faculty Senate Executive Committee, the Staff Senate Executive Committee, and the Administrative Council.

The *Examined Life's* Assistant to the Assistant Director of Staffing, Suburban Climatology, Inhumane Resources, and the Executive Senior Chairman of the Committee on Committees, estimated that approximately one hundred faculty and staff members were involved in developing the new meteorological instrument.

> 1. At this point of the meeting, the Adjunct Director of Construction gave a brief synopsis of the survey "instrument." Unlike the meters, gauges and indicators with which meteorologists are familiar, this instrument is a simple sheet of paper with a series of questions on both sides—better known in the pseudo-sciences as a "survey." This "instrument" is meant to reveal how faculty and staff "perceive their experience at UNK in the areas of gender issues, diversity and general work environment." [There are also several "demographic" questions so the good people who crafted this instrument can find out a series of things, including the faculty and staff's "sexual orientation" or, which way do you go? —more on that later.]

The Assistant Director of Clarity of Thought asked to be recognized noting that what a person "perceives" to be the case is not necessarily what "is" the case. Thus, in the realm of perception, all perceptions are treated equally, as they are neither true nor false but simply a personal opinion of what "seems" be the case for them. So it does not matter if the perceptions being compiled from the "instrument" are from the secure or the insecure, the mature or the immature, the malcontent or the content, the slothful or the diligent, given that all perceptions are equal. Oh well.

The Assistant Director of Clarity of Thought then proceeded to examine the first statement of the campus climate instrument:

1. In my department, I am treated as an individual rather than as a representative of my gender.

The fallacy in this statement is that it is a general statement which does not ask how a specific colleague from the faculty or staff might have acted, but how the department, which is all its members, treated the member—as an individual or as if he were a "representative of [his] gender." Keep in mind, a department is an inanimate object which cannot act; therefore, it cannot treat a person as an individual or a representative of a gender. It is only individuals in a department who may act and treat a person in a specific way.

At this point, the Assistant to the Senior Director of Classification noted that the term "gender" is not to be confused with the term "sex" which is used to classify the biological nature of a human being. "Sex" is a what a person is by nature while "gender" is a grammatical term, used since the fourteenth century to refer to the classes of nouns in Latin, Greek, German and other languages designated as masculine, feminine, or neuter. Now, however, "gender" is a term being used by materialists to define how a culture teaches females and males roles and responsibilities that change over time and vary among societies and cultures. In other words, people learn the roles of being men or women by the culture in which they are raised. In effect, as Karl Marx stated, "... circumstances determine consciousness." So, it is not the conscientious actions of a person that determine his being; on the contrary, it is the social milieu that determines his consciousness. In short, man is not made in the image of God; he is a social animal, the product of his environment. Thus, for social determinists a person can be classified by sex as male and by gender as "transgender," which means a man who is by nature is a man can perceive himself to be a woman by the roles he plays, and, conversely, the same may be perceived by a biological woman who "behaves" (operative term as opposed to acts, which denotes a free will) in the role of man. Therefore, it is difficult if not impossible for the members of a department to know how to treat anyone without each person declaring his gender. This raises the question on whether or not the members of a department ought to be required to make their gender known periodically—given it is subject to change—to their colleagues so they may be treated accordingly. (No doubt a committee will be established which will soon be reporting to the Staff and Faculty Senates on the daily gender status of faculty and staff members.)

The Associate Director of Socratic Studies, upon examining the instrument, noted that the "survey" commits the fallacy of looking outside one's self and not looking within one's self in making a judgment about the nature of the "climate" at UNK. He asked the faculty and staff to notice the nature of the following statements and questions. (The directions noted that "[t]hese questionnaires are read by a scanner, please darken your bubbles completely." The bubbles are labeled: strongly agree, agree, neutral, disagree, strongly disagree, and do not know or not applicable.)

1. In my department, I am treated as an individual rather than as a representative of my gender.

5. In my department, if I felt I had been discriminated against, I could easily resolve the problem at the department level.

These are examples of statements for externally-minded thinkers, and not internally-minded thinkers. The nature of external statements and questions directed at the faculty and staff is to have them look outwardly at their "general work environment" to "perceive" how their department treats them. The nature of internal statements or questions is directed to what a person does, as opposed to what a person "perceives" others doing to him. For example, an internal statement would be:

1. In my department, I treat my colleagues as individuals and not as a sex objects.

2. In my department, I discriminate against others, and my chairman ought to reprimand me.

Here are some more questions from the survey for the externally-minded:

Questions 37–41 ask:

At UNK in the last 5 years, have you been sexually harassed by a:

    Faculty member

    Member of the administration

    Non-faculty employee

    Non-employee on campus

    Student

Questions 42–49 ask:

At UNK in the last 5 years, have you experienced a prejudicial remark or behavior tied to your:

    Gender

    Race

    Ethnicity

    Age

    Sexual orientation

    Religious beliefs

    Physical disability

    Socioeconomic status

Questions 50–51:

At UNK, in the last 5 years, have you experienced a prejudicial remark or behavior by a:

    Faculty member

    Member of the administration

    Non-faculty employee

    Non-employee on campus

    Student

The faculty and staff were not asked to look within themselves and truthfully answer the following internal questions:

At UNK in the last 5 years, have you made sexual remarks to or had such thoughts about a:

> Faculty member
> Member of the administration
> Non-faculty member
> Non-employee on campus
> Student

At UNK in the last 5 years, have you made prejudicial remarks to or had thoughts about someone because of their:

> Sex
> Race
> Ethnicity
> Age
> Sexual orientation
> Religious beliefs
> Physical disability
> Socioeconomic status

At UNK, in the last 5 years, have you acted in a prejudicial manner to a:

> Faculty member
> Member of the administration
> Non-faculty employee
> Non-employee on campus
> Student

Notice the difference between external questions and internal questions, between your perceptions of the "workplace or learning environment" (psycho-babble terms for school or university) in which a person works, as opposed to the thoughts and daydreams that may wander through the mind of the faculty and staff at any given moment, as they look upon colleagues, students and strangers.

Answer the first of the internal questions on whether or not you have ever had any thoughts or feelings of a sexual nature about anyone on campus. How did you answer, yes or no? If the answer is "no," you are of a nature other than human.

Thus, it is easier to answer the external questions of how you "perceive" (operative word) other people to be behaving towards you than the internal questions of how you "think" about and "act" towards other people.

Now imagine if a person could know another person's thoughts by simply looking into their eyes. Would knowing another's thoughts make "an individual [feel] personally safe, listened to, valued, and treated fairly and with respect?" Campus climate: hot, stormy, hurricane on the horizon.

Keep in mind the people in the Campus Climate Network Group 2002 have defined campus climate as "behaviors within a workplace or learning environment... that can influence whether an individual feels personally safe, listened to, valued, and treated fairly and with respect."

Notice the language used is that of a behaviorist who thinks human beings do not act from free will but respond to their environment and thereby "behave" as the result of stimuli in their "learning environment." Thus, if a person "feels [operative word, as opposed to "thinks"] personally safe, listened to, valued, and treated fairly and with respect," he will reflect a "learning environment" where one feels "personally safe, listened to, valued, and treated fairly and with respect" and all will go well with the world.

> 7. Administrators/Supervisors are more supportive of males than females.

The creators of this instrument do not state the converse: Administrators/Supervisors are more supportive of females than males, which shows a bias on their part. Furthermore, since "male" and "female" are genders and not a specific sex, it could be the case that biological males have a female gender and, conversely, biological females have a male gender, or at least "perceive" themselves so.

> Internal question:
> Do you think you were hired because you are a woman?
> Do you think you were hired because you are a man?

Do you think there are females in administrative positions who were given their position because they are female?

Do you think there are males in administrative positions who were given their position because they are males?

Demographics:

4. Marital Status:

Married

Partnered

Single/divorced/widowed

"Partnered!?" The Associate Senior Grammarian noted that being "partnered" is not a category which fits under marital status, e. g., I'm partnered as opposed to I'm married, I'm single, I'm divorced or I'm widowed. The more specific terms for "partnered" would be "fornicating," "licentiously involved" or "shacking-up" if, that is, the partnership is more than a touch and go relationship. The Assistant Director of Inhuman Resources raised the question as to how many partners anyone person might have in a partnered relationship, two? ten? fifty?

The Assistant to the Director of Waste Management predicted that if the concocters of the instrument to determine the levels of gender equity and sexual harassment had their way, we would see residence halls for students who were partnering, which would be "perceived" to be an added feature to the new apartment-style resident halls which the regents are clamoring to build on campus. Wouldn't this impress our students' parents!

9. Sexual orientation:

Heterosexual

Gay, lesbian, bisexual, transgender

The Adjunct Director of Covert Actions asked, "Why Ms. Payne, Ms. Bressington, and all the members of the various commissions and committees [whose members we do not know] want to know the "sexual orientation" of the faculty and staff members?" Much discussion followed, as to the propriety of those wanting to know the "sexual orientation" of the members of the staff and the faculty. It was agreed that a personal question such as this should not be asked by using an impersonal instrument; instead, the administrators of the instrument, Ms. Payne, Ms. Bressington, all the faculty and staff from the commissions and committees ought to personally ask each campus member whom they are probing with their meteorological instrument, the nature of his "sexual orientation" and before doing so, tell us their own sexual orientations. This is obviously necessary so others will know how to "behave" toward everyone.

The Director of Illogical Studies interrupted briefly noting the inconsistency in the use of the classification "bisexual" with the previous marital category of "partnered" as a partnership is not limited to a relationship between two people. Therefore, the terms "trisexual," "quadsexual," "cincsexual," "sextsexual," and (for those who can't keep count) "multisexual" ought to be used if the instrument to determine the climate on our campus is to be an accurate account of the orientation of sexual activity among the faculty and staff.

The Assistant to the Assistant of Socratic Studies asked to be recognized and raised the question of whether man is orientated by sex, or is sex orientated by man? This led to a discussion of man as an animal instinctively driven by sexual desires as Freud would have us believe or of man, though one above the animals, being a creature made in the image of God with the function of sexual organs being one of a procreative act. (This discussion lasted well into the night and the Assistant to the Assistant of Socratic Studies assured our members the minutes of our ad hoc discussion would be presented at the next meeting.)

The Associate to the Assistant Director of Morality noted the prejudicial nature of the sexual orientation question, referring us to the previous questions 42–49 which ask:

> At UNK in the last 5 years, have you experienced a prejudicial remark or behavior tied to your:
> Gender

Race
Ethnicity
Age
Sexual orientation
Religious beliefs
Physical disability
Socioeconomic status

It is well known, the Associate to the Assistant Director of Morality noted, that sexual relations outside of the sacrament of marriage is a sin for Catholics. Muslims, also, though not holding marriage as a sacrament, see homosexuality as a sin. Thus, the instrument that has been crafted by the members of this committee show their prejudice, and this "instrument" is an affront to Muslims, Catholics, and perhaps even people of other Christian denominations. Furthermore, the use of the term "partnered" as a marital category is newspeak for fornicating as it separates sex from the procreative act of marriage. This is what is to be expected from a Marxist materialist or a Freudian who thinks man is simply a social animal.

The Assistant to the Associate Director of Popular Culture Climatology, better known as "Whaz Happenin' Now," noted the survey is based on the jargon of the adherents of multiculturalism who feel that the "diversity" of all "life styles" must be "tolerated." A culture is defined as those commonly held values of the members of a group (as small as two), and a value is defined as whatever a person values is a value to him. Basically, it is the relativistic doctrine holding that all values are relative to a person or a group and no one has the right to judge, or for that matter is capable of judging, another's values. In fact, the supporters of relativism expect others to accept relativism as a principle to which all people ought to adhere unless they wish to be considered intolerant, which would disrupt the climate of our campus and the possibility of an individual feel[ing] personally safe, listened to, valued, and treated fairly and with respect."

And so it goes.

The Soul of the Democrat

He lives on, yielding day by day to the desire at hand. Sometimes he drinks heavily while listening to the flute; at other times, he drinks only water and is on a diet; sometimes he goes in for physical training; at other times, he's idle and neglects everything; and sometimes he even occupies himself with what he takes to be philosophy. He often engages in politics, leaping up from his seat and saying and doing whatever comes to mind. If he happens to admire soldiers, he's carried in that direction, if money-makers, in that one. There's neither order nor necessity in his life, but he calls it pleasant, free, and blessedly happy, and he follows it for as long as he lives.

You've perfectly described the life of a man who believes in legal equality.[1]

These words are from Plato and are found in book eight of *Republic*, in which the constitutions of the democratic city and the soul of the democratic man are described. Of the five constitutions of the city-states in *Republic*, and the individuals housed within each, which are presented in descending order from the highest to the lowest, the democratic state is fourth from the top, one step away from tyranny, in which the city state and man are ruled by erotic love.

Plato understands the soul as tri-part: reason, spirit and desire. Reason and desire are understood as the rational and irrational parts of the soul; the former part "calculates," and the latter part "lusts, hungers, thirsts, and gets excited by other appetites" (439d). Man by nature

---

1. Plato, *Republic*, trans. G. M. A. Grube, (Indianapolis: Hackett 1992), 561d.

has an end, telos, at which he may aim if he is to be fulfilled. Man's end is known by reason, and he is a creature who lives by ideas. A just man, a man in full, is governed by the rational part of his soul which directs him to act in a virtuous manner, such that every part of him performs its proper function while reason controls the inferior parts of his nature. The just state is realized when a person is performing his proper function and not meddling where he does not belong.

The just state in *Republic* is the ideal state, which is created by Socrates' dialectic discussion with Glaucon, Polemarchus, Adeimantus, Thrasymachus and the other young men who are present for the discussion of how justice works in the soul of man. (The reader, obviously, is present, if, that is, he is engaged.) The ideal state, the Aristocracy, has never existed, but the virtues on which it is founded, justice, wisdom, courage and moderation, are grasped by reason and do exist in the souls and actions of man. This state serves as a point of reference from which to set the extreme constitution of tyranny, its opposite, as well as the intermediate states of the timocrat, oligarch, and the democrat.

It is helpful when reading Plato to remember that man is not an animal by nature, but part of him is like an animal. Let me explain. A Gordon setter is by nature a soft-mouthed dog, ideal for retrieving birds because it does not sink its teeth into the bird. The Gordon setter is very alert, interested and aggressive. It is a responsive gun dog, and an eager-to-please dog in the home. A Gordon setter will not naturally retrieve birds, but it can easily be trained to do so because it is within its potential to do so—if, that is, the Gordon setter has a trainer.

Man is like an animal in that he also needs instruction to reach his potential. Man, like a dog, comes in a variety of breeds; however, being well-bred for a man is different than having the pedigree of a Gordon setter. Man's pedigree is revealed by the performance of his function, which has been handed down to him in the stories of his virtuous ancestors. Unlike a Gordon setter, man does not inherit his pedigree; it is something he achieves by performing his function.

Each person has a variety of functions. If he is a cobbler (obviously, an ancient example as cobblers have gone the way of the bare feet that stomped the grapes), he makes shoes, and if he is a virtuous cobbler, he makes good shoes. A cobbler has the various functions, of a husband, father, soldier, neighbor, friend and like relationships in which he finds himself. Man as a cobbler is a creature who becomes himself—or not—in his relationships with the leather and his community.

Being a virtuous human is a question of being well-ordered. In this case, order is a word which signifies a harmonious arrangement, first, in the soul, which is the moral order, and then in the city-state, which is the constitutional order.

Reason is the ruling element in the soul which grasps moral principles, the enduring standards, and the moral norms of man's nature which are necessary for self-examination. In as much as the moral principles are enduring, they are divine and not the creation of man.

Which brings us back to the soul of a democrat, a free spirit whose soul is not guided by moral principle; he lacks the ability to distinguish higher from lower, right from wrong, and good from evil. In the democratic soul, reason is the handmaid of desire, the inferior part of man's nature; thus, he lives on, yielding day by day to the desire at hand. This democrat uses his intellect to rationalize whatever his desires crave at the moment; he cannot truly discriminate between his necessary and unnecessary desires. In effect, each desire has a say, and all desires are treated as equal. This is a soul Plato ironically describes as being "a pleasant constitution, which lacks rulers but not variety and which distributes a sort of equality to both equals and unequals alike" (558b).

The democratic city state is similar to the democratic soul: everyone is treated equally. At first glance it seems to be a fine constitution, "like a coat embroidered with every kind of ornament" because it has every kind of character type. With such diversity, could it be anything but wonderful? However, in the city and the souls which live by the idea of treating equals and unequals as equal, condemned criminals walk about freely and foreigners have the rights of citizens, but the obligations of the citizens to vote or serve on juries and in the military are such that they may do so if they *feel* like it. The democratic soul turns inward and neglects its public responsibility; in fact, it does not have a sense of community. It has nothing in common with those within its city, other than being guided by desires which cry to be heard and feel the need to be satisfied.

Thus, the democratic soul, as well as the democratic city, lacks "rulers" and is opposed to any form of authority other than the pressing momentary urge. So, "he drinks heavily while listening to the flute; at other times, he drinks only water and is on a diet; sometimes he goes in for physical training; at other times, he's idle and neglects everything; and sometimes he even occupies himself with what he takes to be philosophy."

His mind is not led by moral principles (an example of a principle given at the beginning of *Republic* is "you should not return a harm with a harm") and he cannot focus upon an ideal and use it as the point for his actions. The democratic father, for example, refuses to accept a guiding principle into his soul, as it would be an infringement upon the equality of his children's right to fulfill their immediate desires. Thus, "a father accustoms himself to behave like a child and fear his sons, while the son behaves like a father, feeling neither shame nor fear in front of his parents, in order to be free"(562e).

The democratic soul sees freedom as being "free from" as opposed to "free to," so he is "free from" responsibility and does as he *feels* at the moment. It is important to notice that the father *behaves* like a child; the emphasis is on behave, as the father does not "act," for to act one needs to "know" what he is doing, making him the author of his act. The democratic father *behaves* because he is motivated by desire and not by principle. He exercises until it becomes painful, boring, or another desire clamors to be satisfied. The son *behaves* like a father; he does not *act* like a father but becomes like a father because of the demanding nature, or authority, of the adolescent desires rising up in his soul at any moment. As the son is defiant of authority, all tradition, the way of his ancestors, is denied as being outdated and confining to his freedom to serve his desires.

The democratic teacher, next in line in the tradition of authority over the young, fairs equally as well as the father because "[a] teacher in such a community is afraid of his students and flatters them, while the students despise their teachers..." (563b). The teacher is afraid of students because he has no right to impose his knowledge—all opinions being equal—upon students. Furthermore, the student despises his teachers for presuming to think that they know more than the students. It is best for students, in the words of Bob Dylan, to let their teachers know what they have told their parents,

> Come mothers and fathers
> Throughout the land
> And don't criticize
> What you can't understand
> Your sons and your daughters
> Are beyond your command.

The democratic ruler, ascending in authority, in order to gain his position, need only tell the citizens "that he wishes the majority well" (558b). Which means the citizens in the democratic state will be free to continue doing whatever they desire, be it reading Milton or looking at website pornography, being faithfully married or committing adultery, paying taxes or not, having children or aborting babies, helping the sick and aged or euthanizing them—it is all the same. Thus "the person who is honored and considered clever and wise in important matters by such badly governed cities is the one who serves them most pleasantly, indulges them, flatters them, anticipates their wishes, and is clever in fulfilling them" (426c).

The soul of the democratic man is in turmoil as reason is subservient to a multitude of desires, unrestrained by the virtue of moderation, and above authority. The words which correctly name the virtues have been distorted by this character.

Doing battle and controlling things themselves, won't they call reverence foolishness and moderation cowardice, abusing them and casting them out beyond the frontiers like disenfranchised exiles? And won't they persuade the young man that measured and orderly expenditure is boorish and mean, and, joining with many useless desires, won't they expel it across the border... they proceed to return insolence, anarchy, extravagance, and shamelessness from exile and give them fine names, calling insolence good breeding, anarchy freedom, extravagance magnificence, and shamelessness courage. (560d–561a)

What we now have is an uncontrollable adolescent, refusing authority and revering nothing. The distortions of his head visit the body and, as he ages, lacking self-control, his health deteriorates, so he thinks the function of physicians is to restore that which he abused. All the money spent on healing is of no use, so he ends up blaming the abysmal quality of physicians as the source of his feeling ill.

And isn't it amusing that they consider their worst enemy to be the person who tells them the truth, namely, that until they give up drunkenness, overeating, lechery, and idleness, no medicine, cautery, or surgery, no charms, amulets, or anything else of that kind will do them any good? (426b)

The democratic soul is obsessed with the idea of tolerance, which becomes a virtue, so it naively treats all desires as deserving equal attention. This is the intellectual position; however, when desire has replaced right-minded reason in the soul, what the head thinks to be the case is secondary to the demands of the body. So, while the head is tolerant of all desires being equal, the depraved desire of erotic love, the antithesis of philosophy which is the love of wisdom, consumes the soul. The element of authority is impotent in the soul of a democrat so "he's idle and neglects everything; and sometimes he even occupies himself with what he takes to be philosophy."

The perversion of a democrat's attempt at philosophy is seen when Glaucon, Polemarchus, Adeimantus, Thrasymachus, and the other young men of the dialogue, as "reasonable men," distort the ancient proverb "Friends have all things in common" to deduce that women and children are possessions and friends ought to share their possessions.

Under the spell of erotic love, they further decide that the best men (which they all assume themselves to be) ought to have sex with the best women as frequently as possible. To keep the women from becoming attached to their children (which is the natural way to act), the women are treated as equals and now share occupations alongside the men. Their children of the best men and best women are housed in "rearing pens," the ancient equivalent of day-care centers, to ensure that no mother knows her child. True to form the children of the worst parents are left outside the rearing pen to die. The father is oblivious to his children, as those driven by erotic love feel no responsibility for the offspring of their actions. (This is decided upon, obviously, without the young men consulting the mothers, sisters, or women of the state.)

The final descent into the tyrannical nature of erotic love is seen in the confrontation between Socrates and Glaucon, the pedophiliac, to show how the egalitarian soul is caught in a swoon before the object of its depravity which consumes its insatiable lust.

> But it isn't appropriate for an erotically inclined man to forget that all boys in the bloom of youth pique the interest of the lover of boys and arouse him and that all seem worthy of his care and pleasure. Or isn't that the way you people behave to fine and beautiful boys? You praise a snub-nosed one as cute, a hook-nosed one you say is regal, one in between is well proportioned, dark ones look manly, and pale ones are children of the gods. And as for a honey-colored boy, do you think that this very term is anything but the euphemistic coinage of a lover who found it easy to tolerate shallowness, provided it was accompanied by the bloom of youth? In other words, you find all kinds of terms and excuses so as not to reject anyone whose flower is in bloom. (474e–475a)

Such is the destructive nature of erotic love; first it destroys the love between man and woman, then it turns women into common possessions and resolves the dilemma of unwanted children by lodging them in "rearing pens," and finally erotic love accepts the sterile act of fornicating with the same sex as in Glaucon's homosexual passion for any boy in "the bloom of youth."

At this point the descent of the democratic soul is complete. "Extreme freedom can't be expected to lead to anything but a change to extreme slavery, whether for a private individual or for a city" (564a). This type of democracy is not a virtuous form of government in as much as it is one step away from tyranny. Lacking self-restraint and transfixed by the idea of the equality of both equals and un-equals alike, the soul is fractioned, each appetite having a will and clamoring to be heard. Ultimately, the strongest desire of erotic love gives license to mad sensuality having its way in the soul that is a slave to its "mad masters."

And so it goes.

Those Heartless Social Scientists

A man can understand astronomy only by being an astronomer; he can understand entomology only by being an entomologist (or, perhaps, an insect); but he can understand a great deal of anthropology merely by being a man. He is himself the animal which he studies.[1]

There are two ways for man to understand himself, and both involve going home. He may get home by staying home, or he can walk around the whole world until he comes back to the same spot. Moving from the general to the specific: he may understand himself subjectively, through self-examination, by studying himself in his home; or he may study himself objectively, by gathering facts about the whole of Man to understand himself as a part of man.

A home is different from a house; a home is the oldest of communities—it comes before politics! The adages about the home are many, but it is best explained as a place of the heart. In this respect the home is like a garden where different plants have grown, receiving the same amount of sunlight, tillage, and fertilization, all mysteriously connected by the same root. (The community is the outgrowth of families—forever sons and daughters on a common ground where neighbors go in communion to make their daily bread.)

The home is a kingdom unto itself. My home is such a kingdom. It has a population: 6; and comes with a budget, a nutritionist, a foreign policy, a garden, agriculture, transportation, literature, music, builders, quarrels, games, births, picnics, funerals, livestock, water policy, reli-

1. *Collected Works of G. K. Chesterton* (San Francisco: Ignatius Press, 1990), vol. I, 115.

gion, technology, laundry, sewing, a fence, a few gallons of milk a day, and loyalty.

In the confines of our home we leave our world by staying in our world. There is a television that presents the outside world as a series of sound bites, and there is literature, music and art. Within our boundaries we watch the fictional world created by television personalities, and we read stories, tales, and verse. The children play Mozart, Beethoven, and Joplin with their hands and M. C. Hammer and The Beach Boys with the touch of a finger, while Van Gogh, Michelangelo, and Galahad, by an unknown artist, hang on the walls and crayon drawings line the kitchen.

Though we are members of the same family, we are as distinct in our appearance as a finger is to a toe; in fact, each of us is a curious creature to the other. So there are disputes, forgiveness, joy, rebellion, comedy, debate, authority, song, dance, and love. It is here that we live in our imperfection made wonderful by a love that is long suffering, kind, and almost free from jealousy. The home is a place of the heart where I subject myself to my children and my wife, and the ancestors from which we came. It is here we are cultivated as a daughter, a sister, a wife, a mother, a son, a brother, a husband, and a father.

These are trying relationships because they are moral categories where each one of us might fail. Necessarily then, we are becoming a son, a brother, a husband, a wife, a daughter, a sister, a grandson, and a granddaughter. More importantly, in these relationships we are becoming ourselves. Here we are responsible to each other for our ways. In this kingdom, we are formed differently according to our relationships. A daughter is not a son, any more than a wife is a husband, or a daughter is a mother, or a son is a father. These relationships can never be taught; they have to be voluntarily entered into. You cannot teach a child to love his parent any more than a parent can be taught to love a child.

In our kingdom, there is no "Affirmative Action," "Equal Opportunity," "committees," "establishment," or "civil rights" needed to establish justice. This is a place of the heart. There are no laws or policies that can make a member of the family care for the others. If the family is ever reduced to the legalistic level of creating by-laws and policies for matters of the heart, it is doomed. The same may be said of the community, the congregation, and the nation. Love is not in the province of government, any more than teaching is in the province of administrators.

From the outside, our house is not unlike other houses in Kearney; from the inside it is our home, a land where Martins are the only citizens—though we welcome visitors. Be this as it may, there is much I can learn about myself by simply being a member of my family. I am my own subject, subjected in the solitary world of reflection to literature, verse, art and music. Here the ideas and images are woven into my being before I am subjected to the members of my family and my community. In these internal and external worlds I have found Iagos, Claggarts, and Madame Defarges as well as Virgils, Kings, and Mother Teresas. I have found them in thought and in the flesh and have, therefore, come to be leery of all acts involving baser motives and welcome all acts involving the heart, my own as well as those of others.

My home extends beyond the lawn to a town measured in blocks. The geography of my life, for days on end, is no larger than a planted field in comparison with the state of Nebraska. By worldly standards my world lacks diversity. I am insular within the harness of my home where I live amongst the strangest of people. But it is here that I understand the family in its fullest by paying attention to its members: Linda, Zachary, Seth, Katherine, and Rachel. I have found that a family lives precisely by virtue of its differentiation united in loving servitude.

In all of this I have found that I cannot care for Woman any more than I can care for Man any more than I can care for Humanity. I cannot "care" for an abstraction. I can care for Linda, Katherine, Rachel, Zachary, Seth in my home and my neighbors Esther, Julie, John, Jessie, Barb, Fran, etc., etc.

This leads me to consider the other way a man might go home: He can walk around the whole world until he comes back to the same spot. In contrast to staying home and trying to understand himself by forming himself in his family, his literature, his art, his religion, his music and his neighbors—you will call me blind!—he will turn his eyes outward so he can be objectively "informed" about Man by gathering information about him. This is the professional way of studying man known as anthropology, where man becomes a scientific object to be examined like a frog in a biology class. Anthropology is a study that professes to be a "science," not a natural science studying nature, but a social science studying Man as a member of a culture. Of course, the "observer" pretends not to be a part of what he is observing (the price of objectivity). It is a study that leads away from home, neighbor, and community to other lands and houses where the social scientist will learn by standing at living room windows, as it were, and looking in on without partaking. Such a method will result in "findings," e.g., the functions of the family may be grouped into four categories: (1) sexual, (2) reproductive, (3) economic, and (4) educational. It will find that human beings are "phenomena" that behave in observable ways. It will result in a system of classification. He may start with *Size*: Endomorphic-soft, fat, round; Mesomorphic-muscular, athletic, strong; ectomorphic-tall, thin, fragile. Next might be *Race*: Caucasoid, Negroid, and Mongoloid; followed by *Region*: distant or proximitous to the equator. These findings will then become quantifiable data about Man, the object.

We would do well to remember Plato's argument against the Sophists, those who think being human is a matter of technique perfected through the acquisition of "social skills." In the following passage, Plato is describing a social scientist, centuries, mind you, before anyone would dare to study man objectively. When you treat man as an object, you deny that he has a soul and end with little more than a socially conditioned beast, or some material object caught in the perpetual class struggle between the oppressed and the oppressor.

It is as if a man were acquiring the knowledge of the humors and desires of a great strong beast which he had in his keeping, how it is to be approached and touched, and when and by what things it is made most savage or gentle, yes, and the several sounds it is wont to utter on the occasion of each, and again what sounds uttered by another make it tame or fierce, and after mastering this knowledge by living with the creature and by lapse of time should call it wisdom, and should construct thereof a system and art and turn to the teaching of it, knowing nothing in reality about which of these opinions and desires is honorable or base, good or evil, just or unjust, but should apply all these terms to the judgments of the great beast, calling the things that pleased it good, and the things that vexed it bad.[2]

Sound familiar? Read it again. When the beast called Man is observed from the outside the result will be a list of "behaviors" or "roles" that a beast would exhibit. These roles are supposedly learned. How exactly, no one knows, or else the same breeding and environment would result in a similar beast. But with Man this simply is not so. The findings of the study will be used to determine a theory, which freshmen will think a fact. There will be no good and evil actions, no right and wrong actions, honorable or dishonorable actions, nor will there be any truth. In fact, there are not any actions; there are just behaviors. The social scientist cannot make a value judgment in his objective study. The social scientist is not concerned with good and evil, honor and dishonor, justice and injustice, or beauty and ugliness as a science; although when he goes home, he may be concerned with reputation, character, truth and art.

The anthropologist, under the pretense of using the scientific method, measures man with an objective eye, and pretends not to be the object he studies. In so doing, the world of God, free will, love, honor, evil, virtue and vice—the subjects of the soul!—are not his province. When a man becomes an anthropologist, he denies all that

2. Edith Hamilton and Huntington Cairs, eds., *Collected Dialogues of Plato* (Princeton: Princeton University Press, 1961), 493a–c.

is not quantifiable. Science cannot find freedom and, unless it is operable, it has nothing to do with the heart. When he tries to be scientific about man, perhaps the most noted failure of the twentieth century, the social scientist negates the soul, where literature, verse, art and music are the formative means of expressing the heart. In by-passing the language of the heart for information about Man, the social scientist ends in eliminating virtue.

It is tragic enough that such a means of study ends up treating human beings as objects, but it is a catastrophe when the matters of the heart and the home are taught as courses. At the university where I teach, we offer a variety of courses: Space for Family Living; Lifespan Development and the Family; Infant Development; Child Development; Housing and Family; Organization of Home; Family Life Education; Marriage and Family Relationships; Parent Education; Early Childhood Education: Administration, Parents, Community, and Family Life and Functions. Imagine majoring in the family.

When man wanders away from his home to understand his family, he ends up locking himself out of his home. Once outside he finds he is lost and in need of theories to unlock the secret of the family, the community, and the nation, as though he did not belong to a family or a community or a nation. The price of membership in a family, a community and a nation is freely given to those who actually participate. To be open-minded and objective about communal relationships is to be heartless, and to be heartless is to be homeless.

This is the age of the homeless.

Shacking-up at UNK

Our Assistant to the Assistant Director of Waste Management noticed the following missive floating about on the campus e-mail system and brought it to our attention at the monthly meeting of the staff of *The Examined Life*. Last year's rumors of a "trailing spouse" policy has come to fruition in the form of yet another university program to be funded by the taxpayers of Nebraska under the heading of "The Dual Career Program."

We all admitted the new program's title is niftier than "The Trailing Spouse Career Program," which sounds as though a person's spouse is tracking him down for having run off with the children or for back alimony payments. And with language working as it does these days, this could become yet another government program for some lost child of the sixties who is still seeing trails. To clarify such dilemmas, the new program has put forth its objectives:

> The Dual Career Program will offer a wide range of career assistance services to help relocating partners of UNK employees plan and execute an effective job search.

Partners! We barely made it to the end of the sentence before the questions started to swarm. Are we working with law firms, medical groups, plumbing contractors, and other such firms known for operating as partnerships?

So we asked around to see who exactly at this university was involved in a partnership, only to be finally enlightened by our Assistant to the Assistant Director of Newspeak that "partner" means the person with whom the new hire is currently having a relationship. Knowing that a partner could be either a spouse or whoever is shacking-up with the potential hire, let's, for the sake of clarity and precision in language, call the program "The Shack-Job Career Program."

In all of this the Assistant to the Assistant Director of Inhumane Resources wondered how much time a new hire has to spend with another person for their encounter to qualify as a partnership. Could it be six months, three months, three days or three minutes? Furthermore, how many partners is a new hire allowed? May the new hire have a spouse as well as an additional partner? May the new hire hook up with a student upon arrival and would the student qualify as a partner? Do children qualify as partners? Do pets qualify as partners? Is the Shack-Job Career Program obligated to assist all partners in finding a job. Is the Shack-Job Career Program obligated to assist partners who are no longer actively engaged in the partnership?

Anyway, just when the questions were swarming before us, the minutes from the Faculty Senate were clicked to our Office of Waste Management. Perhaps this will answer some of our questions. Here goes:

> Dual Career Program. Ms. Michelle Fleig-Palmer, the coordinator of the Dual Career Program, gave a presentation [to the Faculty Senate] on the nature of the program and described its current initiatives. The program was created because there have been problems in the recruitment of employees because the candidates' 92 partners were in need of appropriate employment.

There you have it. It seems our little university is having problems hiring faculty, staff, and administrators because at least 92 partners were in need of "appropriate employment." So now the administrators of the university are resurrecting a private employment agency known in Governor Wallace's Alabama as a "Good Ol' Boy System," for the wards of the ward of the state.

So new-hire, you are moving to Kearney and you are wondering if your tag-along will find an "appropriate job." Welcome to the adventures of moving. For years people have moved to Kearney with members of their families who were not promised "appropriate employment," but most, if not all, who were willing to work found a job in Kearney. Finding work depends upon whether or not your education is broad enough so you can adapt to any circumstance into which you have landed. Life is not a vacation in which you, as a tourist, can call ahead for reservations, always expecting a clean room with cable T. V., two queen size beds, a chain restaurant like Country Kitchen, and no surprises.

Our Assistant to the Assistant Director of Clarity in this Time of Smoke and Mirrors thought there is something everyone applying to UNK ought to know: You have applied for a position at UNK which is along the Platte River in the middle of a cornfield called Nebraska. Kearney is the fifth largest city in the state and has a population of 30,000. The population of the town is smaller than the university at which you did your graduate work. The major sources of employment are a hospital, the university (which is really an institution that is somewhere between a community college and a college), several manufacturing plants (valves and filters), a Super-Walmart, Morris Press (which specializes in church cookbooks,) chain motels, and restaurants aplenty as we are on Interstate 80. Do not be frightened when you are driving around and the locals lift a finger off their steering wheel. They are not flipping you off; it is their way of waving. If you have a flat and the first or second passing car stops and the driver gets out, do not fear mugging but welcome his offer to help. The pie or cake your neighbors bring to your house when you move in is not laced with arsenic or a laxative; it is their way of welcoming you to the neighborhood. And, when you and your family are walking about the town, if the strangers greeting you act like they care, they do.

More from the Faculty Senate:

On September 15, the Dual Career Program's office will host a reception for accompanying partners with members of the administration and potential employers from the community. This will provide an opportunity for them to network and develop professional contacts. The reception is from 5 to 6 p.m. at the Alumni House. Ms. Fleig-Palmer will also offer a series of workshops on job search skills. These workshops will also provide the opportunity for accompanying partners to network.

Unfortunately by the time you read this, you will have missed the Shack-Job Career Program office reception and opportunity to "network" with the local schmoozers. Not to worry. There are other ways to find work without the assistance of the wards of the state. You will find your neighbors will be more than happy to assist you in finding a job. Don't be surprised if they introduce you to their friends who may run businesses or know of people or companies that are looking for someone with your talents.

And so it goes.

The Flightless Birds of Academe

When the wild ducks or the wild geese migrate in their season, a strange tide rises in the territories over which they sweep. As if magnetized by the great triangular flight, the barnyard fowl leap a foot or two into the air and try to fly. The call of the wild strikes them with the force of a harpoon and a vestige of savagery quickens their blood. All the ducks on the farm are transformed for an instant into migrant birds, and into those hard little heads, till now filled with humble images of pools and worms and barnyards, there swims a sense of continental expanse, of a breadth of seas and the salt taste of the ocean wind. The duck totters to the right and left in its wise enclosure, gripped by a sudden passion to perform the impossible and a sudden love whose object is a mystery.[1]

Robert Frost thought a student ought not be allowed to graduate from college until he could read metaphor. There is more to the world than meets the eye. To perceive the truth, we require images. All life is allegory, and we can understand it only through parable. A boy with a birch tree can vault beyond the confines of the place and time in which he is housed to "climb black branches up a snow-white trunk / Toward heaven."

Imagine being a domestic duck or goose cooped up in Nebraska, the heart of the central flyway, hearing and feeling the pull of migratory Canadian geese, mallards, Sandhill cranes, herons, plovers, sandpipers, gulls, terns, and pelicans. The marrow in your bones quickens to your wild brethren. Stretching your neck, you flap your wings with the yearning to rise out of the confines of the coop to join the trian-

---

1. Antoine de Saint-Exupery, *Wind, Sand and Stars*, trans. Lewis Galantiere (Harvest Book 2002), 212.

gular triumphant, only to be stopped at the chicken wire, gasping, "I don't have it in me."

Further, imagine your despair, once the birds have passed, at being left among the barnyard fowl pecking cracked corn in a dung heap of your own making.

Looking out my window over the plains of Nebraska, between the Oregon and Mormon trails, I remember that beneath the houses and roads lies the ground the immigrants once tread upon while overhead the geese and ducks of today are still calling, still calling....

Back to earth. I received my health insurance package today; it looks more like a looting. Paying $230, in 2005, a month with an $850 deductible translates to $3,560 before a penny is reimbursed. Drop it? I totter to the right and left in my wise enclosure, reminded that in centuries past, immigrants did not have health, house, life, dental, or even wagon insurance. How did anyone make it without insurance for the unforeseeable acts of nature? Surely the pioneers fretted the day away, what with the wind, rain, brushfires, buffalo stampedes, dysentery, depression, fatigue, and a wagon full of children asking "when are we going to get there," knowing all the while that all they had might be lost in the blink of an eye.

"Might"?!

There are various forms of confinement. We are bound by our abilities, age, family, occupation, community, state, institutions, time, place and death. Even further, we can be confined by disease or confined in a mental asylum.

Which brings us to the university. The university has become a barnyard of sorts, a collection of birds, cocks and hens, who roost to teach pullets a diversity of things, ranging from the traditional academic disciplines in the Arts and Sciences to the use of the latest technological advancements in office equipment, as well as exercise physiology, airway science, music business, and a seemingly limitless variety of occupations, attempting to ensure the students will make a living while confined in the coop of the daily grind.

The modern university is but a dropping of what she once was. Universities were founded to sustain faith by reason and to maintain order in the soul. Universities have fallen to being secular rather than universal, no longer providing students with the whole picture: faith is not in the province of the mundane and that there was ever order in a man's soul has been forgotten. Remember, "university" comes from the Latin *universitas* which means "the whole." However, they have sunk further and further into the provinciality of place and time. A university which does not present her students with the ordered knowledge of the sciences and the flight of the spirit in the arts, "the call of the wild," leaves her students featherless in the world, grounded to scratch out a living as computer scientists, accountants, teachers, graphic artists, counselors, lawyers, physicians, and the like, without any higher sense of purpose to their lives. We are prudent, practically-minded people, interested in attaching ourselves to the means of making a living but not in addressing the ends of living.

Back to the wilds.

Geese and ducks are symbolic of freedom and order. Given they are birds, they are not free to choose to migrate but do so by instinct. It is normal for geese and ducks to order their flight in a pattern when migrating. However, their freedom may be taken by cooping them up in pens or by clipping their wings. Though geese and ducks are innately wild, their freedom is lost when they are domesticated and fattened for market.

Human beings are also born to be free; it is normal for humans to be free. However, it is not an instinctual freedom; in other words, if left to themselves to do whatever they like, people might go wild, but they would not be free. Likewise, humans were born to talk, but if left isolated from each other, our talk would be babble and the free expression of our minds would be unintelligible.

While it is normal for man to be free, he more frequently denies than accepts his freedom. (It is here important to remember the word *normal* does not mean "average" or "generally accepted:" it means "enduring standard," taken from the Latin *norma* which means "carpenter square.")

It is normal for man's intellect to migrate to the truth, to move from principle towards principle. One of the fruits of a developed mind is the ability to make qualitative distinctions, to tell what is just or unjust, what is beautiful or ugly, what is clumsy or graceful, what is good as opposed to what is evil and what is a virtue versus what is a vice. Such a mind involves us in our own birth because, by our own free choosing of what is the good, we are at liberty to become ourselves.

The last thing any student needs is to be domesticated like a pet, tamed to use his intellect to be the handmaiden of his desire for comfort and security within the confines of institutions—to be fattened in a coop. The birds overhead are wild but they are not chaotic when they are "magnetized by the great triangular flight." Paradoxically, birds are wild but stay the course and, though science may chart the flight of the birds, it is a mystery as to what prompts the birds to migrate—which is best answered with the simple explanation that they can.

Psychologists and neuro-philosophers can study both the human brain and the phenomenon of intelligence, but neither is a step closer to understanding an intelligent human being. Imagine trying to understand man's intellect by looking at how the brain works instead of looking at the works of the brain the intellect and you will have an idea of what has happened in modern education.

Man cannot be understood objectively by a man standing outside of himself, the family of man, like an entomologist studying insects by using a systematic categorization of organisms to place them into a coherent scheme. Applying the scientific method to man by classifying him according to the material conditions of sex, gender, race, body type, height, weight, economic class, years of education, and IQ ends with talking about man in the general terms of abstraction, as some composite of parts, and does not bring a person one step closer to understanding himself as a person.

The person is irreducible; this is why he cannot be fully explained in terms of his nature and history: the person is rooted in transcendence. The way to understand intelligence is by letting intelligent people enter your intellect. Pick up the *Odyssey*, *Phaedo*, *The Brothers Karamazov*, *Nicomachean Ethics*, *Inferno*, *Job*, etc., and let the images, ideas, and metaphors work their way in your mind so you can transcend yourself. Going beyond the confines of your immediate existence is a means of measuring and forming your soul through the enduring standards of humanity as found in the works of poets, authors, philosophers, artists, and musicians. This is the way of literacy, and in this way, a living soul is quickened by the words of other living souls while in the creative act of wrestling with the circumstances of his own existence to make something of himself in creation. In the words of Richard Weaver, "Cultural life depends upon the remembrance of acknowledged values, and for this reason any sign of a prejudice against memory is a signal of danger."[2]

We live in a dangerous age in which the qualitative judgment of morality necessary for the development of character and the formation of culture has been overshadowed by the relativistic judgments of public opinion surveys, which spin a statistical analysis on the results to come up with a norm based on what the majority hold regarding abortion, same-sex marriage, assisted-suicide, etc. However, what is morally right is not determined by social scientists taking opinion polls and informing people of the "norm" (meaning what the majority hold to be "generally accepted") as if it were therefore "correct."

Remember normal does not mean "average" or "generally accepted": it means enduring standard.

Russell Kirk reminds us of the tenets of the "great triangular flight" when he says, "Human beings have the power either of observing the norms of their nature, or of violating them."

---

2. Richard Weaver, *Visions of Order* (Wilmington: Intercollegiate Press, 1995), 40.

There is no surer way to dampen a person's spirit than to separate him from the enduring standards of his intellectual ancestors. There is no surer way to keep a student domesticated, cooped-up in the static confines of ignorance, than to place him in a school system which censors the books and the language of the spiritual adventures of his intellectual ancestors.

Which brings us back to Saint Exupery, who looks at the Europe of 1930s and sees:

> There are two hundred million men in Europe whose existence has no meaning and who yearn to come alive. Industry has torn them from the idiom of their peasant lineage and has locked them up in enormous ghettos that are like railway yards heaped with blackened trucks. Out of the depths of their slums these men yearn to a be awakened.... Once it was believed that to bring these creatures to manhood it was enough to feed them, clothe them, and look to their everyday needs; but we see now that the result of this has been to turn out petty shopkeepers, village politicians, hollow technicians devoid of an inner life. Some indeed were well taught, but no one troubled to cultivate any of them.... Of course any science student can tell us more about Nature and her laws than can Descartes or Newton,—but what can he tell us about the human spirit?[3]

Exupery might well look over America in 2004 to see nearly three hundred million people whose existence appears to have no meaning beyond getting the means of existence. Out of the depths of the modern ghetto of sanitized suburbia these men yearn to be awakened from the idleness of being tethered to television and computer screens. Once it was believed that to bring these creatures to fulfillment, Lyndon Johnson's Great Society was enough because it fed, clothed, and looked to man's everyday needs; but now we see that the result of providing their basic desires has left them docile, subservient, hollow wards of the state, devoid of an inner life, to be entertained by televi-

3. Ibid., 219.

sion shows which seldom rise above the comprehension level of eight-year-olds. In effect, modern men have become like house pets. I am reminded of assistant-professors in universities who are afraid to speak their minds until tenured, when in effect, fearing to speak negates that the first principle of being mindful is the freedom to speak when one disagrees with what one sees.

Sure we may think Exupery's vision of Europe harsh, but he writes a few years before Hitler and Stalin's enforcement of their vision on the world. Europe had become a prison house for the human spirit, as created by the materialistic philosophies of Rousseau and Freud, while Marx's idea of a classless society was having its way with the Russian people. These futuristic thinkers were instrumental in robbing men of their moral imagination and replacing it with an idyllic and utopian vision of a pseudo-scientifically-minded will to power which, having removed God from man's psyche, was free to make a new man through political legislations and institutions designed by social engineers to strip man of his freedom and to "turn out petty shopkeepers, village politicians, hollow technicians devoid of inner life."

It is time to fly the coop.

Exupery joined the wild geese when he enrolled in flight school for Airopostale (now Air France) in 1926, to fly cargos of passengers and mail between Toulouse in southwestern France and Dakar in French West Africa. In the early days of aviation "the motor was not what it is to today. It would drop off." The instrumentation on a cloudy day in the mountains of Spain consisted of a compass and "flying blind" through cloud-packed mountains. A man alone with the elements, he felt "ill-prepared" for this responsibility.

> A man cannot live a decent life in cities, and I need to feel myself live. I am thinking of aviation. The airplane is a means, not an end. One doesn't risk one's life for a plane any more than a farmer ploughs for the sake of the plough. But the airplane is a means of getting away from the towns and their bookkeeping and coming to grips with reality.... Flying is a man's job and its worries are a man's worries. A pilot's business is the

wind, with the stars, with night, with sand, with the sea. He strives to outwit the forces of nature. He stares in expectancy for the coming of dawn the way a gardener awaits the coming of spring. He looks forward. to port as to a promised land, and truth for him is what lives in the stars ... I am not talking about living dangerously. Such words are meaningless to me. The toreador does not stir me to enthusiasm. It is danger not love. I know what I love. It is life.[4]

It is not life in general that Exupery loves; it is the life of the individual, his life that he loves. His writing demonstrates his love for life by showing that it is not just life that he loves, for the domesticated duck loves it as much, but a certain kind of life that is worth living, that is worth loving.

He gives us the basis for life in the first four chapters of *Wind, Sand and Stars:* "The Craft," "The Men," "The Tool," and "The Elements."

His craft is flying an airplane in the early days of aviation before sophisticated instruments existed when a pilot would fly in an open cock-pit and stretch his neck around a rain-splattered windshield to get his bearings. These early pilots were charged with charting the airways as well as the geographical sites of importance, such as mountain passes and emergency landing strips to be found in farmers' fields, for future pilots. They flew through foggy nights, around mountain faces and over vast expanses of deserts. As in all crafts there are masters and apprentices.

In "The Men" Exupery, himself a novice, gives us Mermoz whose job it was to survey the division between Buenos Aires and Santiago de Chile. He was given a plane with an absolute ceiling of sixteen thousand feet and asked to fly over a mountain range that rose more than twenty thousand feet into the air. Mermoz and his mechanic, while trying to maneuver the mountain passes, were forced down on a twelve

4. Ibid., 166.

thousand foot plateau and for "two mortal days" they hunted a way off only to realize they were trapped.

So, they played their last card by rolling the plane over the edge and falling straight down the precipice where the plane picked up enough speed to respond to the controls. Mermoz was then able to tilt the nose in the direction of the peek and sweep over it; however, all the water in the pipes burst because of the cold and the ship was again disabled in seven minutes. Fortunately, the plains of Chile were beneath them by this time. The next day they were at it again.

Finally, after a dozen years of service, Mermoz, having taken off from Dakar bound for Natal, radioed that he was cutting off his right engine. Silence. Never to be heard from again.

From his master Mermoz, Exupery extracts the following:

> This, then is the moral taught us by Mermoz and his kind. We understand better, because of him, that what constitutes the dignity of the craft is that it creates a fellowship, that it binds men together and fashions for them a common language. For there is but one veritable problem—the problem of human relations.... We forget that there is no joy except in human relations. If I summon up those memories that have left with me an enduring savor, if I draw up the balance sheet of the hours in my life that have truly counted, surely I find only those that no wealth could have procured me. True riches cannot be bought. One cannot buy the friendship of a Mermoz, of a companion to whom one is bound forever by ordeals suffered in common.[5]

"The Tool." For Exupery his tool is the aircraft, produced as all of man's industrial efforts, by his computations and calculations, after nights spent over drafts and blueprints, after the experimentation of several generations of craftsmen. He admonishes moralists who have attacked the machine as the source of all man's ills for having created the "fictitious dichotomy," as if the mechanical civilization could be the enemy of the spiritual civilization.

5. Ibid., 27.

The central struggle of men has ever been to understand one another, and to join together for the common good. Technology, especially sixty years after Exupery's insights, has brought men closer together. However, he cautions that men are being driven into the service of the machine, instead of building machines for the service of man.

Which brings us to "The Elements." Every airline pilot in Exupery's group had flown through tornadoes, through the revolt of the elements which the pilot seemingly had mastered.

Exupery's tornado comes when he is flying down to Comodoro-Rivadavia, in the Patagonian Argentina. He takes off in a pure blue sky. "Too pure," he says. His troubles start with a slight tremor, but every pilot knows "there are secret little quiverings that foretell your real storm." Then everything around him blew up, he was standing still, making no headway and the "plane was skidding as if on a toothless cogwheel."

He found himself imprisoned in a valley, "There was no longer any horizon, and he was in the "wings of a theatre cluttered up with bits of scenery." He was wrestling with chaos. He discovered he was not struggling against the wind but the ridge itself, the crest, the rocky peak of Mt. Salamanca. What happened next is best told by Exupery:

> I who for forty minutes had not been able to climb higher than two hundred feet off the ground was suddenly able to look down on the enemy. The plane quivered as if in boiling water. I could see the wide waters of the ocean. The valley opened out into this ocean, this salvation. — And at that very moment, without any warning whatever, half a mile from Salamanca, I was suddenly struck straight in the midriff by the gale off that peak and sent hurling out to sea.[6]

If ever a man felt like Jonah, Exupery did, at least until he realized he was several miles out at sea facing winds of one hundred and fifty

6. Saint-Exupery, 54.

miles an hour. In the next twenty minutes of struggle, he moved a hundred yards towards the shore.

How he got back and the rest of the book are well worth reading. But I will leave that up to you. He does, however, conclude "There is nothing dramatic in the world, nothing pathetic, except in human relations... the physical drama itself cannot touch us until someone points out its spiritual sense."

Until a person realizes the spiritual sense of his relations, to his craft, to the previous and present practitioners of his craft, and how he must respect the elements with which he crafts himself, he will be unable to rise out of the confinements of his coop. Every person who has lived long enough, whatever his craft, has been confronted by at least one tornado, the death of family and friends is example enough, when all seemed to be lost. The task is to rise above the storm, to craft ourselves by working with the elements which appear to hold us captive—to be involved in our own transformation. In Greek the word "wind" is the same as the word "spirit" and the spiritual sense of Exupery is that we are exiles who have not yet found our homeland. Migrating through this world, "we are crossing the great dark valley of a fairy-tale, the Valley of Ordeal. Like the prince in the tale, we must meet the test without succor. Failure here would not be forgiven."[7]

And so it goes... still calling, still calling.

7. Ibid,. 135.

Distance Education

In a recent article in the *Kearney Hub*, the Dean of Continuing Education at UNK informed us that some studies show:

> less than 25% of learners prefer to learn by our traditional teaching methods—lecture and reading. Learning theories are now being included in instructional programs so that teachers can more effectively work with their students. And technology, such as telecommunications, the Internet, and on-line courses, has the capability to address those nontraditional learning styles effectively and efficiently. We need to encourage teachers to move into the world of synchronous (same-time) and asynchronous (delayed-time) learning with brain-friendly lessons and courses.

Welcome to the "new age" of education. The university administrator and his commercial partners (Apple, IBM, Dell, the cable companies, and Microsoft) now view education as a market for their products and students as "consumers" who will sit passively before televisions or computer screens for their college credits.

The fallacy of the technological education proponents' argument is that learning can be made "friendlier," and thereby "easier," with machinery. This is like thinking parenting is made "friendlier and easier" by placing a child in front of a television or an interactive computer.

Furthermore, there is no evidence that shows education using technological modes of delivering courses is enhanced or even equal to that provided by traditional methods. In fact, it is evident that a student's imagination and attention span is deadened by television and interactive computer programs.

I am not surprised by the reports that some studies show "less than 25% of learners prefer to learn by our traditional teaching methods—lecture and reading." But I take issue when the dean suggests that because students do not "prefer" traditional means of learning (reading a book and attending class) that "teachers [need] to move into the world of synchronous (same-time) and asynchronous (delayed-time) learning with brain-friendly lessons and courses."

Without even doing a survey, I know that less than 10% of students prefer" to get out of bed at 7 o'clock, or 8 o'clock, or 9 o'clock. And on Friday mornings, after Thursday night parties, for which UNK is sorrowfully famous, 11 o'clock is too early for even more students.

If a survey were taken of football players participating in spring football, it would come as no surprise to find that fewer than 25% of athletes "prefer" having to go to spring practice at 6:30 am.

Now can you imagine convincing the football coach that in order to make practice more "brain-friendly" for the vast majority of players who do not "prefer" the traditional ways of practicing he should create work-out programs for athletes via a big screen television on the practice field?

Fortunately, all good teachers and coaches know the formation of a mind and body is different than the development of a brain. While bright colors, flutes, bells and whistles might simulate the brain, the development of the mind and body is an arduous process. In fact, it is hard work and not something most students "prefer" to do. Then again, much of life's offerings is not going to include what you "prefer" to do.

That a computer is a tool, is a tool, is a tool cannot be repeated often enough. It is like a calculator. It is a useful tool (with a built-in dictionary, thesaurus, and spell-checker) which will assist a student in his writing but it will not teach him how to write, it will not ask questions which require an immediate response to examine his knowledge of the subject, and it will not command his attention.

Furthermore, computers are expensive. With the constant advancements in computer technology, a computer purchased today is obsolete within eighteen months. The computerization of schools has resulted in a larger portion of institutional resources being spent upon technology. This means less is being spent on maintaining a qualified faculty. This adds to the decline in the quality of faculty members teaching at universities which means more adjunct faculty (part-timers) and graduate assistants are teaching college courses.

This being the case, should it surprise us when a recent article in the *Omaha World-Herald*, "Top Grads Shun State Colleges," reports

> More high school students with top ACT scores left Nebraska to attend college from 1995 through 1998 than came from outside to enroll in state colleges and universities.... In every year except 1996, more students who scored higher than 18 on the ACT left Nebraska to go to school than entered the state.

Unfortunately, universities are too often managed by administrators who are materialistic by nature, measuring their accomplishments by visible campus improvements they have made and the buildings they have built, as well as the money they have brought to the foundation. So while the public may judge that all is well at UNK when they hear about our new education building, the addition to the student union, and the hopes of a new track, they have little knowledge of the quality of the education being offered to students. Could this be the reason students are shunning our state's colleges?

We parents fall into a similar confusion when we think we can make our children happy by buying them "things" or that living in expensive houses is a means by which to demonstrate our love for our children.

In an age where children spend more time watching TV than any other single act except sleeping, to further disconnect them from their parents and teachers with the technology of "brain-friendly" telecommunications, the Internet, and on-line courses is going to foster generation of introverts—click, click, click—who expect to be constantly stimulated—click, click, click—or they will simply "prefer" to turn you—click————

Distance Administration

The university is founded upon the desire to know and, like man, is composed of two basic parts: a body and a soul. The body of a university is its buildings which are maintained by the various caretakers: custodians, plumbers, electricians, carpenters, etc. The soul of the university is its faculty who house a variety of subjects which they minister to students seeking the disciplines necessary for a thoughtful life freed from ignorance. The quality of a university depends upon the quality of its professors, just as the quality of a hospital depends upon the ability of its physicians and nurses. Both institutions are further successful if their students and patients diligently abide by the regimen of study and convalescence as prescribed by their doctors and physicians.

Since a university is a nonprofit institution created for students similar to the way a hospital is created for the sick, the university is not a business and the students are not customers. The university is more like a hospital and her students are like patients. They are not ill but they are ignorant. Fortunately, ignorance, unlike illness, is not a painful state when sedated by the bliss of living in a wealthy country. A simple test illustrates this point: if you break your arm, whom do you seek? And if you are illiterate, whom do you seek? However, when ignorance is awakened to itself, the faculty is able to rush to the students' aid, structuring their minds through various disciplines which will enable the diligent to become life-long pursuers of truth.

A minor, though necessary, component of both a university and a hospital is its administration whose function is to provide for the needs of the professors and medical staff. During the past forty years there has been a disproportionate growth in the size of administrations at universities. Using the hierarchical, corporate model has allowed the university to become bloated with excessive duplication of administrative offices on its various campuses.

Before the advent of computers and telecommunications, each campus in the state college and university systems created a campus by using a corporate organizational model which resembles a high-rise apartment building. The president of the university is positioned on the top floor above the chancellors of the three universities and the medical school. Under the chancellors are layers of executive assistants, speech writers, and directors of various sorts: alumni and athletics, affirmative action and equal opportunity, etc. All of these are followed by a cadre of vice-chancellors, for academic affairs and the not so academic affairs, university relations, business and finance, and student affairs. All of these are supported by support staff, assistant vice chancellors, and faculty assistants to the vice chancellors of administrative assistants. Beneath the various vices come the deans who also have one or two assistant deans, administrative assistants, secretaries, and work-study students. In short, when looking at the operational flow chart of a university, it looks like an apartment building in which one would descend floor after floor before locating a teacher with a room full of students.

However, we are in luck, for in this new age of voice-activated computers which allow people to talk and be seen by the person with whom they are speaking, it is possible to streamline the administration of all the campuses of the University of Nebraska system. In fact, UNL, UNO, and UNK, which are currently operating as separate but dependent institutions, can become the University of Nebraska operating under one administrative system with extension campuses. This can be accomplished through Distance Administration.

In as much as all the departments and all the faculty within the university system are linked by computers, the departments on each campus within the university system can be moved into one department. The department of English, for example, at the University of Nebraska at Kearney, Omaha, and Lincoln can be merged into one department. This will result in the Department of English of the University of Nebraska with branches in Lincoln, Omaha, and Kearney. This model can also be applied to the departments of Biology, Chemistry, Math, Physics, Philosophy, Psychology, Political Science, Sociology, etc.

The necessary forms faculty depend upon for payroll, payroll deduction, travel authorization, reimbursement, sick leave, medical leave, and the like will be accessed via computer in individual offices, and, once completed, emailed to the necessary location for approval.

Under the new system of Distance Administration, one member at each branch would be the director of his respective department, responsible for assigning teaching loads and reporting directly to the chairman of the department, who would be elected by and from the directors of the extended campuses to serve a term of four years. The same model would apply to deans, such that all the chairmen of Arts and Sciences at the University of Nebraska would report to the dean who is housed on one of the three campuses and elected by and from the various chairmen of his college. The same models can be used for the various vice chancellors and the chancellors.

Having a chancellor and the various vices, deans, directors and chairmen at each campus is like having a Governor with his entire staff in each county, treating each county as though it were a separate state within the state of Nebraska. With the technological advances of Distance Administration, it is no longer necessary to have a chancellor representing the interests of each campus as it is no longer necessary to be separate universities within Nebraska, but one University of Nebraska.

The consolidation and down-sizing of administration at each campus will result in a sizable saving for the taxpayers of Nebraska.

Go Huskers!

The Hope of America
Rests with Her Teachers

For I agree with you that there is a natural aristocracy among men. The
grounds of this are virtue and talents. Formerly bodily powers gave
place among the aristoi.... [But] There is also an artificial aristocracy
founded on wealth and birth, without either virtue or talents, for with
these it would belong to the first class. The natural aristocracy I consider
as the most precious gift of nature for the instruction, the trusts, and
government of society. And indeed it would have been inconsistent in
creation to have formed man for the social state, and not to have provided virtue and wisdom enough to manage the concerns of society. May
we not even say that that form of government is the best which provides
the most effectually for a pure selection of these natural aristoi into
the offices of government? The artificial aristocracy is a mischievous
ingredient in government, and provision should be made to prevent its
ascendancy.[1]

These words belonging to Thomas Jefferson were
written to John Adams on October 28, 1813. By this
time, both men had been President of America and had retired to their
farms. Among America's wisest men, they are reflecting on the nation
they have been instrumental in creating. Jefferson agrees with Adams
that the hope of America rests with her natural aristocracy: the virtuous and talented citizens. Both founding fathers fear that the artificial
aristocracy, the wealthy, who are neither virtuous nor talented but a
"mischievous ingredient in government," will grab the helm of govern-

---

1. Adrienne Koch and William Peden, eds., *The Life and Selected Writings of Thomas
Jefferson* (New York: Random House, 1954), 632–3.

ment with the intent of protecting the wealth of their class before the good of their fellow citizens.

Jefferson and Adams are philosophical: they see what is the case and they see what ought to be the case. Furthermore, they are capable of qualitative judgment, of discerning the higher from the lower, the virtuous from the vicious, the man who uses his talents to serve the greater good as opposed to the man who uses his talents to serve himself. Being students of history, both know principalities, kingdoms, and nations have long been led by the artificial aristocracy: tyrants and nobility, whose primary function is to maintain and increase their material prosperity at the expense of the common man's liberty and right to self-determination. Thus, it is essential that America, this land where "all men are created equal and endowed by their Creator with life, liberty, and the pursuit of happiness," be governed by the natural aristocracy who are marked by being virtuous and talented.

To ensure the rise of the natural aristocracy to positions of leadership in America, Jefferson tells Adams of a bill he has introduced to establish schools throughout the country:

> This [bill] proposed to divide every county into wards of 5 or 6 square miles.... to establish in each ward a free school for reading, writing and common arithmetic, to provide for the annual selection of the best subjects from these schools, who might receive at the public expense a higher degree of education at a district school; and from these district schools to select a certain number of the most promising subjects to be completed at an University, where all the useful sciences should be taught. Worth and genius would thus have been sought out from every condition of life, and completely prepared by education for defeating the competition of wealth and birth for the public trusts.[2]

Jefferson proposes public schools ought to be established for the public trust, and from these schools the guardians of America ought to be the best students, selected by their teachers, to be promoted beyond

2. Ibid., 262.

the elementary to a "high" school, from which the "most promising subjects" ought to be promoted to a university, in order to negate only the rich from competing for the public trust. Therefore, America's future depends upon her teachers' grading to select the natural aristocracy from the masses.

John Adams, in a letter to his wife Abigail on February 4, 1794, foreshadows Jefferson's desire for an educational system which promotes the virtuous and talented students so as to keep government out of the hands of the wealthy:

> By The Law of Nature, all Men are Men and not Eagles, That is they are all of the same species. And this is the most That the Equality of Nature amounts to. But Man differs by Nature from Man, almost as much as Man from Beast. The Equality of Nature is Moral and Political only and means that all Men are independent. But a Physical Inequality, an Intellectual Inequality of the most serious kind is established unchangeably by the Author of Nature. And Society has a Right to establish any other Inequalities it may judge necessary for its good.
>
> The Precept, however, Do as you would be done by implys an Equality which is the real Equality of Nature and Christianity, and has been Known and understood in all Ages.

Jefferson and Adams see what every good teacher knows: by nature, students are not equal in their intellectual ability or physical talents. In fact, no matter how hard a teacher works students, many will not progress beyond the basics of reading, writing, and simple arithmetic.

The hope of America being governed by the natural aristocracy rests with her teachers being responsible for selecting the virtuous and talented students by judging who is capable of superior work, regardless of their creed, their race, or their sex, and culling out the rest.

All Americans have an equal opportunity to the education Jefferson proposes, but all Americans do not have the right to be equally intelligent or to be considered equally virtuous.

Equality of opportunity is ideally placed before every person in America; however, the equality of abilities has never existed, as Alexis de Tocqueville notes in *Democracy in America*,

> No matter what efforts a people makes, it will never succeed in making conditions perfectly equal within it; and if it has the misfortune to arrive at an absolute and complete leveling, there would still remain the inequality of intelligence, which, coming directly from God, will always elude the laws.[3]

The rudiments of the university curriculum for Jefferson's natural aristocracy are outlined in a letter to his nephew Peter Carr, who is about to attend college:

> An honest heart being the first blessing, a knowing head is the second. It is time for you now to begin to be choice in your reading; to begin to pursue a regular course in it; and not to suffer yourself to be turned to the right or left by reading an thing out of that course. I have long ago digested a plan for you, suited to the circumstances in which you will be placed. This I will detail to you, from time to time, as you advance. For the present, I advise you to begin a course of ancient history, reading every thing in the original and not in translations. First read Goldsmith's history of Greece. This will give you a digested view of that field. Then take up ancient history in the detail, reading the following books, in the following order: Herodotus, Thucydides, Xenophontis Hellenica, Xenophontis Anabasis, Arrian, Quintus Curtius, Diodorus Siculus, Justin. This shall form the first stage of your historical reading, and is all I need mention to you now. The next, will be of Roman history. From that, we will come down to modern history. In Greek and Latin poetry, you have read or will read at school, Virgil, Terence, Horace, Anacreon, Theocritus, Homer, Euripides, Sophocles. Read also Milton's Paradise Lost, Shakespeare, Ossian, Pope's and Swift's works, in order to form your style in your own language. In morality, read Epictetus, Xenophontis Memorabilia, Plato's Socratic dialogues, Cicero's philosophies, Antoninus, and Seneca. In order to assure a certain progress in

3. Ibid., 232.

this reading, consider what hours you have free from the school and the exercises of the school. Give about two of them, every day, to exercise; for health must not be sacrificed to learning. A strong body makes the mind strong.[4]

Such a curriculum distinguishes the virtuous people of history, the wisdom of poets, the ideals of authors, and the ideals of virtuous Greeks and Romans. In order to draw from history, literature, poetry, and philosophy, students must be taught to read such works which will reveal those who are capable of making qualitative judgments about human actions just as a minister or priest must be educated in scripture and those who have "eyes that do not see and ears which do not hear" ought never shepherd a congregation.

Given that Jefferson is a deist, he understands the classical sense of virtue and is attracted to Aristotle, while Adams, being a Christian well-educated in Greek and Roman culture, understands the cardinal virtues as well as the theological virtues of faith, hope, and charity which are not grasped by reason alone but infused by God's grace— "Do as you would be done by" implies an Equality which is the real Equality of Nature and Christianity, and has been Known and understood in all Ages

Thus, Jefferson's natural aristocracy is reminiscent of the natural selection of the virtuous and talented students who are the guardians of Plato's *Republic* and Aristotle's students of the *Nicomachean Ethics* who know that the end of politics is the good of the state and that to be a "competent student of what is right and just, and of politics in general, one must first have received a proper upbringing in moral conduct." The natural aristocracy of the *Republic* is selected for an education meant to polish those who are marked by the virtues of justice, wisdom, courage, and moderation. The natural virtues, which are grasped by intellect, the "divine element within" for Aristotle, are the transforming qualities which make men God-like. The virtues of Aris-

4. *Thomas Jefferson*, 374.

totle, known as the cardinal virtues, which reason grasps as the principles of just action, are wisdom, courage, magnificence, generosity, gentleness, high-mindedness, moderation, and truthfulness.

Aristotle classifies virtue into two categories: intellectual and moral. Intellectual virtue "owes its origins and development chiefly to teaching, and for that reason requires experience and time."[5] Moral virtue is formed by habit, and man by nature is equipped to receive them. Man is not by nature virtuous, but it is in his nature to be virtuous. The same holds true for speech; man does not by nature speak, but it is in his nature to speak. Inherent in the development of moral virtue, as it is formed by habit, is the importance of a good upbringing by parents who teach their children civility, for virtues are acquired by "first having them put into actions." To explain this point, Aristotle states,

> For the things which we have to learn before we can do them, learn by doing: men become builders by building houses and harpists by playing the harp. Similarly, we become just by the practice of just actions, self-controlled by exercising self-control, and courageous by performing acts of courage.[6]

Wealth, for Aristotle, is not a good in itself but only useful as a means to something else. To treat wealth as an end is to worship an inanimate object, an "artificial object," and, as Midas learned, the worth of his daughter changed dramatically when she turned to gold. Wealth, when treated as a god, becomes a demon and if not the tap root of evil, it is at the very least a root of evil. This does not mean that being wealthy is a sign of a corrupt and evil man, for a rich man can do much good with his money. Money, gold, diamonds, stocks, etc., are inanimate objects that lack a will, as do all inanimate objects, to act; they are, therefore, incapable of being virtuous or vicious.

Aristotle notes, the average person may exercise the virtue of generosity with his money, giving what little he has to aid others; however,

5. Nicomachean Ethics, 1103a15.
6. Ibid., 1103a30.

the rich man may be magnanimous, giving things of substantial worth, libraries, colleges, scholarships, hospitals, museums, and parks to serve the greater good of the community and nation long after his death. So, Jefferson does not see virtue and money as an "either/or," as though a wealthy man could not be virtuous. Nor are they equivalent; virtue is not wealth.

Jefferson would see the cardinal virtues not only exemplified in the life of Socrates, but especially in his apology, addressed to the senators of Athens before his execution, "Wealth does not bring about excellence, but excellence makes wealth and everything else good for men, both individually and collectively."

And so, neither Jefferson nor Adams ascribes to the economic theory of History: that all politics and ethics are the expression of economics. It is up to the virtuous and talented citizens to battle the artificial aristocracy to preserve America, whose people have been endowed by "their Creator with certain unalienable Rights [and] that among these are Life, Liberty and the pursuit of Happiness." The fundamental maxim of government for Adams is "never trust the lamb to the wolf."

In order to preserve America, it is essential for the natural aristocracy to understand that Liberty is a virtue and not a freedom to do whatever makes one happy. Liberty is what sailors are given when they go ashore in uniform; they are not free to define liberty as whatever they please and to act accordingly, but in accordance to being representatives of the United States Navy.

Levi Hart, in a tract written in 1775, addresses the different senses, moving from the lower to the higher, of the virtue of Liberty,

> Civil liberty doth not consist in a freedom from all law and government,—but in freedom from unjust law and tyrannical government.... Religious liberty is the opportunity of professing and practicing that religion which is agreeable to our judgment and consciences, without interruption or punishment from the civil magistrate.... Ecclesiastical liberty, is such a state of order regularity in Christian society, as gives every member opportunity to fill up his place in acting for the general

good of that great and holy society to which the true church of Christ.... Finally, there is another kind of liberty and bondage, which deserves particular attention in this place, only as they are especially pointed to in our text, but as being of principle concern to men, they be denominated spiritual liberty and bondage: —This liberty is spoken of by our Lord, "Ye shall know the truth, and the truth shall make you free, —if the Son make you free, ye shall be free indeed.[7]

Being liberally educated, Jefferson and Adams both understand that Liberty is as necessary to the protection of a people from tyrannical government as a good teacher is necessary to the formation of students' minds, which must be sharpened on the long and hard reading of the best minds. It is this pursuit of truth which reveals the natural aristocracy, those who are capable of sound moral judgment.

There will be teachers who do not like the idea of grading students according to their abilities, who think that an education in a democracy entitles all students to be equally rewarded regardless of a student's ability to demonstrate the rudiments of a thoughtful mind. Teachers who think a student's development of a "positive self-esteem" is more important than actually knowing history, literature, poetry, science, or the ideas of even one philosopher are responsible for dummying-down America's schools, colleges, and universities to levels unacceptable even for tech schools. Today there are college students lacking even a tech-school craft who graduate without ever having read even one of the historians, poets, authors, or philosophers on Jefferson's reading list and without even understanding that this is essential to being educated. Such students have suffered a textbook education and have learned to highlight and parrot essential points upon which they will be tested with multiple-choice questions and perhaps a few short written answers. It is the difference between being able to navigate a ship with a sextant as opposed to being a galley slave rowing to the lash of a whip.

7. Hyneman and Lutz, eds., *American Political Writing during the Foundation Era, 1760–1805* (Indianapolis: Liberty Fund, 1983), 310–11.

Such teachers in America give the artificial aristocracy exactly what they want: mindless wage slaves, subserviently working in chain stores, universities, government agencies, superstores, fast-food joints, or convenience stores where they operate a fuel truck or cash register for the oil cartel or perhaps sit cow-eyed before computers.

As much as Jefferson hopes for America, he also sees America as a country taken over by "timid men who prefer the calm of despotism to the boisterous sea of liberty."

The hope of America rests upon the best students being "sought out from every condition of life and completely prepared by education for defeating the competition of wealth and birth for the public trusts," and thereby refusing to allow the artificial aristocracy ever to be the guardians of those public trusts.

In closing, I have seen Jefferson's natural aristocracy in Nebraska surfacing from towns like Aurora, Amherst, Anselmo, Bridgeport, Central City, Columbus, Dannebrog, Elgin, Gretna, Holdredge, Kearney, Minden, Ralston, St. Paul, McCook, Wallace, and Wayne and entering into this university. They step back into the world as computer programmers, bank-tellers, physicians, nurses, ministers, priests, nuns, carpenters, heavy equipment operators, truck drivers, lawyers, teachers, housewives, farmers, engineers, bartenders, painters, soldiers, social workers and artists. Such students are the leaven in the bread, the honest hearts and knowing heads, who in the words of the American historian David McCullough, know that "trying to think without knowing the classics is like trying to plant cut flowers."

Come, Let Us Cut the Budget and Build Skyboxes

This year at our small university on the plains of Nebraska, some of our administrators are all a bubble because of the new building for the College of Education and the addition to the Student Union. The first was paid for by the taxpayers of Nebraska, the second by tacking a fee of $50 a semester on our students for the next twenty years. Both buildings are heralded as "state of the art." This translates, in the first building, to truckloads of computers and distance learning pods for the teachers willing to transmit education to the hinterland and, in the second, to a new "food court" complete with a snack shop, Starbucks coffee shop, Shear Madness Salon, Taco Bell Express, computer store, student government offices, and a variety of meeting rooms, the two quintessential of which are located on the "skinny" third floor of the new addition.

Upon entering the two meeting rooms, which comprise the entire third floor, you will notice that the windows start at the floor. Now walk over to the windows while focusing on the floor. When you are approximately two feet from the windows, stop. Look up. What do you see? Lo and behold, the meeting rooms look directly over the football field.

(Regrettably, due to lower than expected tax revenues, the Dean of Fine Arts and Humanities suggested we cut the German professor, which means our Modern Language Department would be down to two languages: French and Spanish. Fortunately, the Chancellor, because of support around the campus for German, did not accept the Dean's proposal, and German is safe till next year when the next round of budget cuts get under way.)

Does anyone suppose the meeting rooms, to which students have access throughout the week, will be accessible to the students for home games when these rooms are—SHAZAM!—transformed into sky-boxes, for which students will be paying for twenty years? Want to bet the sky-boxes will be reserved for our university patricians, who will feast on a variety of finger foods, assorted drinks (liquor if the chancellor is present), all in climate-controlled boxes at the Circus Maximus Kearnicus?

Anyway, some of our administrators become downright effervescent when explaining the impact these building are going to have on recruiting students. Never mind the fact that during the last ten years, which saw the building of dormitories, dining halls, a coliseum, and food courts, and the renovation of the entire west end of campus and Bruner Hall of Science, our enrollment has continued to declined.

(If our administrators were serious about attracting students with buildings, they ought to consider transforming the sky boxes into a student health club. Place elliptical exercise machines, stationary bikes and stair steppers in front of those windows; fill the middle of the room with weight machines and line the walls with free weights. Then turn the other room into an aerobic workout room. Stand back and watch it fill up!)

It is a mushy-minded materialist who thinks that because the state is spending tax dollars and student fees on buildings, students will be attracted and will stay at this university. Buildings do not command or hold a student's attention enough to keep him from transferring or dropping out of college any more than the size and décor of his parents' home will keep him at home.

The people who are drawn into transforming the campus into a country club are probably the same people who live in 4,000+ square foot houses and think people admire them because of the size of their abodes, big screen televisions, and luxury cars.

Well-educated people have always known there is more to a university than its square footage and buildings crowned with satellite dishes. Thomas Carlyle reminds us of this in his advice to students when he was installed as the Rector of the University of Edinburgh, April 2, 1866:

> The main use of Universities in the present age is that, after you have done with all your classes, the next thing is a collection of books, a great library of good books, which you proceed to study and to read. What the Universities can mainly do for you,—what I have found the University did for me, is, That it taught me to read, in various languages, in various sciences; so that I could go into the books which treated of these things, and gradually penetrate into any department I wanted to make myself master of, as I found it suited me.... the clearest and most imperative duty lies on every one of you to be assiduous in your reading. Learn to be good readers,—which is perhaps a more difficult thing than you imagine. Learn to be discriminative in your reading; to read faithfully, and with your best attention, all kinds of things which you have a real interest in, a real not an imaginary, and which you find to be really fit for what you are engaged in. Of course, at the present time, in a great deal of the reading incumbent on you, you must be guided by the books recommended by your Professors for assistance towards the effect of their predilections. And then, when you leave the University, and go into studies of your own, you will find it very important that you have chosen a field, some province especially suited to you, in which you can study and work. The most unhappy of all men is the man who cannot tell what he is going to do, who has got no work cut-out for him in the world, and does not go into it. For work is the grand cure of all the maladies and miseries that ever beset mankind,—honest work, which you intend getting done.[1]

1. Inaugural Address at Edinburgh 2D April 1866, on Being Installed as Rector of the University, 2nd April 1866.

There you have it! The main use of Universities is not in entertaining the eyes with buildings, of which a far grander scale exists in other locales, nor in accommodating administrators and faculty in the lifestyle to which they have grown accustomed, nor in students feasting on junk food or gathering in meeting rooms overlooking the football field. A student will discover the main use of his university when he is finished with his classes and has gone to his library to study and read so as to "penetrate into any department [he]wants to make [himself] master of."

The mark of a good university is built in the souls of her students who have been taught to "read in several languages, in various sciences;" and after 5, 10, 20, 40, 60 years of having left of our classrooms, having their own library of good books to which they refer for their own improvement. Sounds simple? Thomas Carlyle knows learning to read is "a more difficult thing than you imagine" because it takes time to understand not only several languages but also various sciences and to accumulate a library of one's own. But he also knows the student will come to find himself through this very effort in "some province especially suited for [him]."

Conversely, the mark of a bad university is weakening the souls of her students who have not been challenged to read in several languages or in various sciences and who, when the 5, 10, 20, 40 or 60 years have passed after having walked out of our classes, do not have a library of books to which they can refer for their improvement nor a purpose beyond the job they received through our training.

The best way for a student to select his classes is by walking through the bookstore to find out which books are being read in each class. Avoid classes which substitute textbooks for primary sources. You do not want to read about anthropology, sociology, psychology, biology, philosophy and literature. You want to read anthropology, sociology, psychology, biology, philosophy and literature.

We have all suffered teachers who distill lectures from textbooks, passing information like gas that dissipates outside the classroom. It is an old adage: give a man food and he is dependent upon you for life; teach a man to farm and you have seen the last of him. The student who is taught to read in various languages and sciences has a mind that is free to explore the depths of his soul in literature, philosophy, and poetry, and the worlds of biology, chemistry, astronomy, as well as mathematics. Train a student to sit through lectures and parrot the information he has absorbed, and you have a slave who, being denied a liberal education, is only fit to be a clerk.

There is more to a university than spending wads of money on buildings and the latest technology. We now have "smart classrooms" which may work for people who need to click pictures and charts upon screens but which are simply inconsequential to understanding a sentence of Darwin, Rousseau, or Max Weber.

Last Friday I was in a smart classroom in which there was also a discarded overhead projector and a television on a cart with a VCR in the corner. I was standing behind a computer on the only table in the room which really wasn't a table but a cabinet housing a VCR, DVD player, CD player, "Elmo," and various amplifiers, and a remote which looked to be for the projector hanging by metal straps from the ceiling. We were reading Descartes in a technological museum. The overhead projector against the wall is twenty years old, the television and VCR are ten years old and every bit of the gadgetry in the cabinet will have to be replaced in four years. The "smart classroom" of today will be antiquated in five years and obsolete in ten. The writing of Aristotle, Marx, Machiavelli, Einstein, Dante, Darwin, Jung, Freud, Jefferson, Chaucer, Descartes, Rousseau, Hamilton, Newton, Weber, Bacon, Voltaire, and even Hitler will be new to the students who, if liberally educated, will see them for the first time.

In closing, a "smart classroom" is a misleading metaphor. An inanimate object is not smart. What we need are not "smart classrooms" but professors smart enough to start a student collecting his library.

However, with the cost of replacing technology and maintaining buildings constantly on the rise, what almost happened to the German professor at our small university on the plains will happen to the French, philosophy, English, art professors, etc. (unless they use computers) as we continue our spiral into a tech school producing unreflective graduates ready to do the work some corporation or some government agency has cut out for him.

And so it goes.

College Seniors Taught
Right and Wrong Is Relative

Three quarters of all college seniors report that their professors teach them that what is right and wrong depends "on differences in individual values and cultural diversity," a poll conducted for the National Association of Scholars (NAS) reveals.

Only about a quarter of 400 college seniors randomly selected from campuses around the country said their professors taught the traditional view that "there are clear and uniform standards of right and wrong by which everyone should be judged."

The poll was conducted in April by Zogby International and has a sampling error of plus or minus 5 percent.

A large majority of students also report that they've been taught that corporate policies furthering "progressive" social and political goals are more important than those ensuring that stockholders and creditors receive accurate accounts of a firm's finances, the study said.[1]

The article "College Seniors Taught Right and Wrong Is Relative" was clicked my way last week. Whoever sent it to me did so, I suspect, because he or she knows I teach Introduction to Ethics to college students. The article is by Lawrence Morahan, a Senior Staff Writer for CNSNEW. Surprise, surprise, surprise! The poll conducted by the National Association of Scholars does as most surveys do: it states the obvious. The students in American universi-

---

1. College Seniors Taught Right and Wrong is Relative. CNS News.com, 7/08/02, Lawrence Morahan.

ties are relativists; they think morality is a matter of opinion, that right and wrong depends "on differences in individual values and cultural diversity," which is as it should be, given the vast majority of college students are the products of school systems where "cultural diversity" is the politically correct pablum fed by the teachers of the state to the youth of America.

Cultural diversity rests on the doctrine of cultural relativism which any high school or college student will recite like a talking doll when you pull her string. Cultural relativism states that all men live in cultures; a culture is a common belief and value system which a group of people pass on to their offspring. Cultures are composed of subcultures. A subculture is a similar value system held by a small group of people who inhabit a similar environment. Examples of subcultures are Hell-Angels, fast-food workers, Wal-Mart employees, Corporate CEO's, working moms, soccer moms, university administrators, service-bay lube jockeys, etc. A person may belong to more than one subculture. People who are members of a particular culture or subculture cannot understand people who are not in their culture or subculture. No culture or subculture is superior to any other culture or subculture. People must be tolerant of people in other subcultures and cultures.

Anyone who swallows the dogma of cultural diversity thinks that whatever they value is valuable to them because they value it. This does not mean that their values are superior and right or that another person's values are inferior and wrong. It just means that there are no standards and that different people have different values which change from generation to generation and place to place.

Back to teaching Ethics. I asked a student if Jeffrey Dahmer, the man who was convicted of murdering people, cutting off their heads and eating various parts of their bodies, was wrong in valuing the taste of human flesh?

I think he was wrong.

Did Jefrey Dahmer think that what he was doing was wrong?

No, Jefferey Dahmer did not think he was doing anything wrong.

So, he was right?

What he did was not right to me.

But it was right for him?

Yes.

So you are both right?

Yes, but the majority of people would agree that what he did was not right.

O. K. Now, if you were in the German military in 1944, would the majority of soldiers agree that gassing the Jews was right?

Yes, but that would not be the right thing to do now.

That is not the question. Would it have been the right thing to do for a Nazi?

Yes.

So, thinking the Nazi soldiers are wrong in gassing the Jews is right for you, and the Nazi soldiers thinking gassing the Jews is right was right for them?

Yes.

So you are both right?

We are both right in our own minds, but the majority would no longer think the Nazis were right.

What is right changes with the times? So, you may think cannibalism is wrong today, but someday you might value the taste of human flesh and that will then be your value?

Yes.

So, some day the majority may side with Jeffery Dahmer in thinking it right to be a cannibal?

That's right.

If, in fact, "three quarters of all college seniors report that their professors teach them that what is right and wrong depends, on differences in individual values and cultural diversity," then the majority of professors are sophists and are incapable of moral judgment with regard to human actions, their own as well as others.

Sophists are not new to the academy. Plato in *Republic* character-
ized a sophist as a private teacher who, working for pay, discerns what
man is by observing his behavior and keeping a record of his observations. A sophist has no idea of what is good or evil, right or wrong,
just or unjust, but he does know from observation what pleases and
displeases man. Here is how Plato depicts the sophist:

> It is as if a man were acquiring the knowledge of the humors and
> desires of a great strong beast which he had in his keeping, how it is to
> be approached and touched, and when and by what things it is made
> most savage or gentle, yes, and the several sounds it is wont to utter on
> the occasion of each, and again what sounds uttered by another make
> it tame or fierce, and after mastering this knowledge by living with the
> creature and by lapse of time should call it wisdom, and should con-
> struct thereof a system and art and turn to the teaching of it, knowing
> nothing in reality about which of these opinions and desires is honor-
> able or base, good or evil, just or unjust, but should apply all these terms
> to the judgments of the great beast, calling the things that please it
> good, and the things that vexed it bad, having no other account to ren-
> der of them, but should call what is necessary just and honorable, never
> having observed how great is the real difference between the necessary
> and the good, and being incapable of explaining it to another. Do you
> not think, by heaven, that such a one would be a strange educator?[2]

The sophist claims man to be an animal. His man does not have a
soul, a will, a conscience, or the ability to grasp the principles of morality to live a virtuous life by exercising his free will in choosing the rational virtues of being just, wise, courageous, and moderate and the theological virtues of faith, hope, and charity.

Sophists are private teachers "who work for pay." They are not to
be confused with philosophers, with those who are concerned with
knowing the truth. Philosophy is defined as the love and pursuit of
wisdom by intellectual and moral self-discipline seen best in the life of

---

2. Edith Hamilton and Huntington Cairs, eds., *Collected Dialogues of Plato* (Princeton: Princeton University Press, 1961), Republic, 493a–d.

Socrates. Imagine being a teacher of philosophy, of biology, of chemistry, of music, of mathematics, of sociology, of political science, or of English who worked solely for the pay, who taught solely for the money. This is not to say that a teacher should not be paid for teaching; however, the reason to teach is "not for pay" but out of love for truth. A teacher is a philosopher, a PhD (Doctor of Philosophy) who teaches his discipline as truth. He is dogmatic in that he has a doctrine he teaches which is true. This is not to say that all philosophers have to be in agreement about the truth, as though we would expect a Marxist would agree with a Wittgensteinian. But it is to say that anyone who professes to be Marxist must believe what he is teaching is true. No one belongs in the ranks of professors at universities who is not teaching the truth as he sees it.

The sophist is not a philosopher, but he does, ironically, have a truth that he teaches. Here it is: there are no moral absolutes. The sophist arrived at his truth, he supposes, by using the scientific method to observe man's behaviors in order to understand his nature. This frees the sophist from the study of art, music, literature, poetry, philosophy and religion. It is, after all, easier to observe man "calling the things that please it good, and the things that vex it bad" than it is to study what has been written, painted, and played by authors, poets, philosophers, musicians, and theologians.

The sophist is an unnatural scientist (he is the object of his own study) who pretends to be objective and removed from making value judgments regarding the nature of man, the beast he is observing. In fact, the sophist does not think there is any absolute value to human life and that anything a human may value is an opinion, a view, or a perception. In the words of sophist Protagoras (481–411 BC), "Soul is nothing apart from the senses and everything is true."

Given that everything man knows is by the senses, then everything he knows by the senses is true to him. They are after all *his* senses! However, if everything is true, then nothing is true. The sophist knows, "nothing in reality about which of these opinions and desires is honorable or base, good or evil, just or unjust, but should apply all these terms to the judgments of the great beast, calling the things that please it good, and the things that vexed it bad." In short, the sophist is a cultural relativist; he only knows what he perceives and he does not have any idea of what he *ought* to think. Thus a sophist will never attach moral terms to his observations, e. g., fidelity, fortitude, perseverance, honor, dignity, generosity, love, greed, sloth, lust, or decadence. He admittedly is incapable of making qualitative judgments about human actions. He does, however, hold that whatever feels good is good at the moment to the man who experiences the pleasure of the moment. So he can, when shopping for a car, select a Lexus over a Ford Escort, a double latte over truck-stop coffee, a leather couch over a futon, human flesh over beef, etc.

The sophist in today's modern University is the same as the sophist Protagoras in fourth century BC Greece. They are the same because they are both thoroughly modern. The word "modern" comes from the Latin *modo* which means "just now"—hence the word "modish," that is, being in or conforming to the prevailing or current fashion. Being modern has always been sensible: a sensible person can grasp what is the object of his senses at any particular moment. A sophist is a sensible person having only the object of senses to tell if the current sensation is pleasurable, painful, or somewhere in between. Being incapable of judgment, he does not think but he *feels* the moment and goes with the flow of the now, floating from one impression or fad to the next. He is a mindless creature who does not discriminate whether his perception is "fine or shameful, good or bad, just or unjust."

The man of modish mind has an open-mind through which everything flows like grass through a goose. To be open-minded, in this sense, is the same as having no mind at all, lacking the ability to discriminate or to make qualitative judgments about human actions, his own as well as others. Such a mind is democratic: it treats all ideas as equal thereby putting "his pleasures on an equal footing."

In Plato's words,

Sometimes he drinks heavily while listening to the flute; at other times, he drinks only water and is on a diet; sometimes he goes in for physical training; at other times, he's idle and neglects everything; and sometimes he even occupies himself with what he takes to be philosophy. He often engages in politics, leaping up from his seat and saying and doing whatever comes into his mind. If he happens to admire soldiers, he's carried in that direction, if money-makers, in that one. There's neither order nor necessity in his life, but he calls it pleasant, free, and blessedly happy, and he follows it for as long as he lives.[3]

A sophist is carried away by his senses which leave him utterly senseless in questions of morality. He "perceives," and this is the operative word, that when it comes to ethics and morality everything is a matter of his perception (What other perception could you possibly have?) and there are no moral absolutes. A social scientist as a social scientist will not talk about moral principles and argue for the right and true course of action. A social scientist will take a survey and after he has gathered a pile of "evidence" (data), he will do a statistical analysis of the situation and offer up as truth the norm, what the majority of people perceive to be the case at the moment.

A social scientist does not go beyond stating the obvious, what is the case, and he will not state what ought to be the case, for to do so would bring the charge of imposing a value judgment upon his sensory mode of observation.

It is not surprising that the students in universities think morality is a matter of opinion. At my university the students are required to take 12 hours of social sciences (history is a social science) and only 3 hours of humanities, which include, among its offerings philosophy.

Finally, while all our students are required to take Economics 100, only the nursing students are required to take ethics. I suspect this is because when we are sick or dying, we do not want someone watching

3. *Republic*, 561d.

over us who is incapable of moral judgment and ready to do what feels good at the moment.

And there you have it.

Literature No Longer Matters

The day when fiction had a central role in American culture, when novels piqued the public imagination, are long gone. I think that, for good or bad, whether it was a delusion or not, there was a sense among us, to put it very squarely, that literature mattered. Society (today) is informally ignorant of this aspect of life: literature. It doesn't care. It's just a tiny distraction, and not an interesting one. [Now] we have "the screen." First, the movie screen, then the TV screen, then the computer. The human mind prefers the screen.

— Phillip Roth

In my Introduction to Ethics class last summer, we read the first five books of Aristotle's *Nicomachean Ethics* and *Cancer Ward* by the Russian author Alexander Solzhenitsyn. It is, as Russian novels are, long—536 pages to be exact. The last week of the semester I congratulated the 25 pupils who had read their way through Oleg Kostoglotov's story of World War II, imprisonment in a Soviet Gulag, cancer, radiation therapy, impotency, love, and eternal exile. Then I asked them to truthfully answer two questions with a show of hands: how many of you have ever read a novel of this length before; and, is this the first novel you have read? Their answers, respectively, 4 and 21. The students are mostly juniors and seniors. "How did you get through high school and college without reading a novel?" "Cliffnotes," the bright-eyed young lady in the front row responded.

Phillip Roth is right about one thing: "the day when fiction had a central role in American culture, when novels piqued the public imagination, are long gone." While it is comforting to know that 21 students have read their first novel, whether or not these students will ever read another remains for them to tell. They may all fall back into the various screens to which they were affixed before we read and discussed each chapter in *Cancer Ward*.

"The human mind [which] prefers the screen," however, is an immature mind, undeveloped and held captive by the world of appearances. Most of what is on television is mind numbing. It is, after all, a medium established to market products. We switch it on to get away from our individual worlds. Next to sleep, there is no other activity on which America's children spend more time. This tapers off in adult life; work does get in the way, but, with Direct TV, over 500 channels are accessible, calling us like sirens to retreat into entertainment. There is nothing better for us guys than a one-hour football game stretched over a three-and-a-half-hour psychedelic period, set to This Bud Belongs to You, complete with Tostitos with salsa, beckoning us to lease a Ford tough truck each year to drive us into old age when we can peter out before the screen along with ex-presidential, Viagra popping, candidate Bob Dole who gets a rise off of Brittany Spears strutting her thing for Pepsi.

Literature may be "long gone" for Phillip Roth, but fiction survives and is doing quite well on the various screens which hold the modern mind captive.

Never have there been more reading lamps, wing-back chairs, couches, bookstores (with a Starbucks), libraries, presses, and access to books on the internet among more people who are illiterate. This is not to say Americans cannot read. The vast majority do read street signs, job applications, directions for installing video games and can be seen flipping through *Sports Illustrated*, *People*, and *Time* while waiting to have their oil changed at Jiffy-Lube. But, sad to say, most Americans do not read literature.

So much for the linear view of history where each generation is fueled by technological advancements to progress beyond its ancestors. We have cycled back to the dark ages. The reason the students have not read a novel is because no one has sat down with them to read one. So, now, surrounded by electric lights they live in darkness and lack interior light. They are filled with information but lack insight.

While it may be the case that "the human mind prefers the screen," it does not follow that those who choose the screen have a mind worthy of a human being. The first screen which held its viewers captive was created twenty-four centuries ago in the allegory of the cave by Plato. The allegory depicts prisoners who are chained so that they can only look forward at a wall in the cave. There is a fire behind the prisoners, and in between the prisoners and the fire are people who cast shadows on the wall by holding up objects. The prisoners do not have a say in the shadows nor do they know their source. However, they think the objects are real; they further think themselves free. Plato uses this allegory to depict the education of those who cannot think their way out of the dark, being solely dependent on what they have been shown. It was the first television—some people had control over what others could see.

The human intellect, however, is not satisfied with shadows any more than a free man is satisfied with what others would force him to see. The human being is meant for truth and to seek the truth by telling the truth and doing what is right in each situation.

G. K. Chesterton observed that students would much rather read a novel than math or chemistry. "The reason is very simple; it is merely because the novel is truer than most subjects are. This is because our lives are never mathematical or scientific, but they are always novel.

The Lord of the Rings is a popular movie because ordinary moviegoers think it is true: we humans are in an adventure, a mystery, in which each one of us longs to be the hero or the heroine, who, in spite of all the inconveniences placed upon us by cavities, braces, pimples, ACL tears, roommates, biology, calculus, English, conjugating verbs, meetings, headaches, backaches, marriage, children, neighbors, cancer, enemies, friends, winter, suffering, and death, will see each inconvenience in the light that goodness always prevails over evil, and our novel is meant to end with "… and I lived happily ever after."

So we sit and watch the cinematographic marvel of Frodo Baggins as he repeatedly overcomes the power of evil in his soul. He isn't a complete man; he is a halfling, a hobbit, who preserves goodness, holding fast to it and not the power of evil longing to lord over him and the world. Frodo has been entrusted with the source of evil, a ring which he sets out to destroy by casting it back into the molten lava of Mt. Doom where it was forged by the dark lord Sauron. To add to the excitement, Frodo is pursued throughout his quest by evil forces who want the ring so they can rule the world.

As good as the movie is, my fourteen-year-old daughter Rachel said the book is better. Why? "Because the book has the characters' thoughts." That is right: the mind is quicker than the eye and the reader's imagination is richer than a movie producer's images, which take months to form on the screen for the viewer.

By casting images, a movie producer hopes to chain his audience to the seats of a movie theater. Though entertaining, the word in literature goes deeper and is more inspiring than a moving picture. A picture which moves is fleeting, but a painting by remaining still lasts longer, and the longer it lasts the richer it becomes.

Good fiction is heroic, revealing the struggles of a contemplative soul overcoming himself and his environment. Bad fiction is anti-heroic, depicting sociological characters who lack imaginations and will, being simply reflections of society, cheap products of their environment. Imagine reading a novel about a character whose movements are determined by his genetic makeup and his chemical reactions to the environment. The only possible deviation from his necessary behavior would occur if he were injected with a foreign substance allowing for a foreign reaction. It would be as edifying as watching a colonoscopy.

Remember your Aristotle:

For our character is determined by our choosing good or evil, not by the opinions we hold.[1]

When an individual has no ulterior motive, he speaks, acts, and lives his real character. Falsehood is base in its own right and deserves blame, but truthfulness is noble and deserves praise.[2]

Can anyone imagine Dostoyevsky, Hugo, Shakespeare, Dante, Eliot, Dickens, Chaucer, and whoever wrote *Beowulf* agreeing with Phillip Roth's statement "I think that, for good or bad, whether it was a delusion or not, there was a sense among us, to put it very squarely, that literature mattered"? Literature a delusion? Bah humbug!

Compare Phillip Roth's statement to Alexander Solzhenitsyn's statement to his fellow authors in his Nobel lecture acceptance:

> My friends! Let us try to be helpful, if we are worth anything. In our own countries, torn by differences among parties, movements, castes, and groups, who for ages past has been not the dividing but the uniting force? This, essentially, is the position of writers, spokesmen of a national language, of the chief tie binding the nation, the very soil which the people inhabit, and, in fortunate circumstances, the nation's spirit too.... Who, if not writers, are to condemn their own unsuccessful governments (in some states this is the easiest way to make a living; everyone who is not lazy does it) as well as society itself, whether for its cowardly humiliation or for its self-satisfied weakness, or the lightheaded escapades of the young, or the youthful pirates brandishing knives?... We will be told: What can literature do against the pitiless onslaught of naked violence? Let us not forget that violence does not and cannot flourish by itself; it is inevitably intertwined with LYING.... The simple act of an ordinary courageous man is not to take part, not to support lies! Let that come into the world and ever reign over it, but not through me. Writers and artists can do more: they can VANQUISH LIES! In the struggle against lies, art has always won and always will. Conspicuously,

---

1. *Ethics*, 1112a.
2. Ibid., 1127a25.

incontestable for everyone. Lies can stand up against much in the world, but not against art.[3]

Solzhenitsyn is like Frodo Baggins, an ordinary courageous man who will neither take part in nor support lies. Any novel without such characters is not worth reading.

In *Cancer Ward* Solzhenitsyn portrays life in Russia under the rule of Soviet leaders, bureaucrats, military, KGB, and clerks as being like a cancer feeding on the Russian people. The novel opens with the admittance of Pavel Rusanov, a minor Soviet official, into a cancer hospital in a remote province of the Soviet Union. He is insulted at having landed in a ward with common citizens—soldiers, shepherds, political exiles, teachers, prison guards and farmers—who are the proletariat, the same people he theoretically worshipped from his comfortable apartment where he and his family were physically separated from these commoners who live with two, three, and four families in similar-sized apartments.

On his admittance to the ward, Pavel is immediately met by Yefrem who says, "Well, what have we here? Another nice little cancer!" To which Pavel responds, "I have cancer of nothing. I have no cancer whatsoever." Yefrem gets the last word, "Stupid fool! If it's not cancer, what the hell d'you think they put you in here for?"

Death serves as the great equalizer; it comes for us all and respects neither a person's wealth nor rank. The petty Soviet official is thrown in with the People. The immediacy of death serves to intensify the lives of those in the ward who are at the edge of life hanging on to whatever they hold sacred as the reader watches in the wings to see whose lifeline takes him past death.

Yefrem is a bull of a man, the Russell Crowe of the Soviet Union: virile, hair like a fox, chiseled arms, drinker of vodka without missing stride. Ironically this man who dooms Pavel to death has cancer of the

---

3. Alexander Solzhenitsyn, *Noble Lecture*, trans. F. D. Reeve, (New York: Farrar, Straus and Giroux, 1972), 31–3.

tongue and is recovering from surgery in which his tongue has been shortened and narrowed. Ironically, this is the same tongue which "lied" him through life.

> In fifty years he'd given it a lot of exercise. With it he'd talked his way into pay he'd never earned, sworn blind he'd done things when he hadn't, stood bail for things he didn't believe in, howled at bosses and yelled insults at workers. With it he piled filth on everything most dear and holy, reveling in his trills like a nightingale. He told fat-ass stories but never touched politics. He sang Volga songs. He lied to hundreds of women scattered all over the place, that he wasn't married, that he had no children, that he'd be back in a week and they'd start building a house. "God rot your tongue!" one temporary mother-in-law had cursed him, but Yefrem's tongue had never let him down except when he was blind drunk.[4]

I asked the class who would want to go out with such a man? The bright-eyed young lady, schooled on *Cliff Notes*, without a moment's hesitation said, "I would; sounds like a good time."

Back to the story.

Yefrem has defiled language by using it to lie to get his way at work and to have his way with women by the hundreds. He has no idea how many children he has fathered. Now we find him stomping down the aisle of the ward, his neck in the noose, heavily bandaged, constantly reminding the other men about death. In the face of death, he is terrified; this man whose whole life has been a free exercise of his tongue realizes cancer has a will of its own and is feeding on his healthy cells the way he has fed on women. Yefrem is a sensualist, "the whole of his life had prepared [him] for living, not for dying."

Oleg Kostoglotov, the protagonist of the novel, tired of Yefrem's ranting in the face of death, confronts him with Tolstoy's *Twenty-Three Tales*, "Yefrem! That's enough of your whining! Here, read this book!"

---

4. Alexander Solzhenitsyn, *Cancer Ward*, trans. Nicolas Bethell and David Burg, (New York: Random House, 1983), 97.

To which Yefrem, obstinate like a bull, responds, "Read? Why should I read? We'll all kick the bucket soon." The following conversation ensues:

"That's the point! If you don't hurry you'll have kicked the bucket before you've read it. Here you are, quick!"
He held out the book, but Yefrem did not move. "There's too much reading here. I don't want to read."
"Are you illiterate or something? said [Oleg], trying halfheartedly to talk him in to it.
"What do you mean? I'm very literate. When I've got to be, I'm very literate."
"Don't be afraid," he murmured, " they're nice, short little stories. Here, just these few here—try them. I'm fed up with your whining do you hear? Read a book."
"I'm not afraid of nothing!" Yefrem took the book and tossed it on the bed.[5]

"Are you illiterate of something?" Well, no, Yefrem has read booklets on production experience, descriptions of hoisting mechanisms, operating instructions, administrative orders and some short histories, but he never saw any purpose in reading literature or it being anything more than an amusement—like television—to pass the day. Oleg knows better, there are some books a man needs to read before he kicks the bucket.

Yefrem, have you ever read any literature that spoke to your soul, that made you wonder if there was anything you ought to do with your life? Are you more than an animal moved by sensual passions only kept in check by the mores of your society, like an animal in a cage? Are you a biological accident, or have you been assigned to existence to fulfill a purpose as Socrates thought he had been? Is death the degeneration of you to dust or will you pass on to judgment in the afterlife and be held responsible for your actions? Do you have a conscience where the

5. Ibid., 14.

truth is admonishing you for your trespasses, vanity, pettiness, fornication, desertion...?

Who can answer these questions for Yefrem? Science? Sociology? Would it help to take a survey to see what the mass of men in the ward opine? What would count as evidence for a man's own corruption? Would you have someone else lead your life and do your thinking for you before death? At this moment Yefrem is alone amongst the other patients.

Yefrem turns to Tolstoy. For the first time in his life he sits and reads literature. He would never have opened the book if Oleg had not challenged him, nor would he have read this book if it had been a novel. Tolstoy's book is a collection of short stories;. Yefrem looks at the table of contents: "Work, Illness and Death," "The Chief Law," "Neglect a Fire and It Will Overmaster Thee," "Go Into the Light While the Light There Is" "What do Men Live By?" Yefrem understands immediately that the book means business. He picks the shortest story and goes on to the next. He feels like thinking; the pain is shooting through his neck as he continues to read and to think.

Life in the cancer ward continues around him, but Yefrem no longer stomped up and down the aisle between the beds; he just read.

The book was talking to him. It was unlike any he had ever read.... He had lived his whole life without such a serious book ever coming his way.... Still, it was unlikely he'd have ever started reading if he hadn't been in a hospital bed with this neck shooting pain through his head. These little stories would hardly have got to a healthy man.[6]

Modern man is too healthy for literature; he is too busy pursuing his sensual satisfaction, affixed to the screen, hoping medical discoveries will lengthen his life so there might be time to reflect on goodness, or the lack thereof, in his life.

The story of Tolstoy which speaks to Yefrem is "What Do Men Live By?" In fact, he asks this question to the other patients in the ward,

6. Ibid., 102.

and here is how they respond: "Their rations. Uniforms and supplies;" "By their pay, that's what;" "In the first place, air. Then—water. Then—food;" "Professional skill;" "Your homeland." The Soviet administrator has the last word, the politically correct answer, "Remember: people live by their ideological principles and by the interests of society." One of the prisoners wants to know the answer to the question, and Yefrem gives a summary:

A cobbler, with his wife and children lived as peasants owning neither land nor home.... Anyway, the shoemaker started hitting the bottle. One night he was going home full of drink when he ran into a guy called Mikhilo who was freezing to death and took him home. His wife scolded him. "What? Another mouth to feed?" she said. But Mikhailo started working for the shoemaker for all he was worth, and learned to sew better than the shoemaker. One winter's day the squire came to see them. He brought a piece of expensive leather and gave them an order—one pair of boots that wouldn't warp or rip. And if the shoemaker spoiled the leather, he'd have to replace it with his own skin. Mikhailo gave a strange smile because he'd seen something over there in the corner behind the squire's back. The squire had just gone out of the door when Mikhailo went and cut the leather and spoiled it. It wasn't big enough now for a pair of welted stretch boots, only for something like a pair of slippers. The shoemaker clapped his hand to his head. "You've ruined me," he said, "You've cut my throat. What have you done?" Mikhailo said, "A man lays down stores for a year, and he doesn't even know whether he'll be alive that evening." Sure enough, the squire kicked the bucket on the way home. And the squire's wife sent a boy to the shoemaker to say, "No need to make boots. But we want a pair of slippers as quickly as you can. For the Corpse." Which is exactly what Mikhailo had cut the leather to make.[7]

Immediately Pavel Rusanov exclaims, "Good God, what nonsense! What does it say there that men live by?"

7. Ibid., 102.

"It says," Yefrem replied, "that people live not by worrying only about their own problems but by love of others."

"Love?... No, that's nothing to do with our sort of morality."[8]

Yefrem, however, is not concerned with what the other men in the ward live by, nor does he accept Pavel Rusanov's politically correct response. Yefrem has seen himself in the story. He, like the squire, had demanded the skin of others; he had spoiled hundreds of women. He had never thought of women as his equals but more like shoes for his use. He would have been amazed if anyone had tried to tell him that he treated women badly. Nevertheless, Yefrem is starting to see he is to blame for everything.

It turns out that while cancer feeds on his healthy cells, requiring a medical diagnosis and treatment to battle its advance and hopefully push it into remission, the cancer that feeds on Yefrem's soul is revealed by reading Tolstoy, and it would take a hand much greater than a doctor's to administer a cure.

Tolstoy has shown Yefrem a part of himself he refused to accept when he was having his way with women. No one could have told Yefrem directly that he was to blame; a direct attack, Kierkegaard noted, "only strengthens a person in his illusion, and at the same time embitters him." No one can tell us directly that we are to blame. No one likes to be judged; to be spoken down to is a direct confrontation and would only serve to toughen Yefrem's stand. However, by means of the indirect confrontation which Tolstoy's story provides, Yefrem sees himself as a cancer to women, the author of lies whose word is as short-lived as the momentary pleasure women provide him.

Yefrem's insight marks the beginning of his transformation and even the students who had never read a novel, who disliked Yefrem for taunting the other patients and abusing women, see this as an improvement in his character. Yefrem, however, realizes it is too late to ask forgiveness from the women and the children he has defiled. He no

8. Ibid., 107.

longer stomps; he sits quietly immersed in thought. Within a week he is discharged from the cancer ward, goes to the train station, collapses, and dies.

If he had not been stopped by cancer, Yefrem would have continued on his way; he would not have had the time nor thought it necessary to read literature nor have seen himself for what he truly was.

Literature matters: to hold council with the best authors in the self-examination of conscience makes for a life worth living. If we vanquish the lies in our own lives, we can stand against the lies that are being cast at us from the various screens we do not control.

Hopefully the bright-eyed young lady in the front row, schooled on *Cliff Notes*, will see beyond the images before some healthy Yefrem finds her.

All Men are Created Equal

We hold these truths to be self-evident, that all men are created equal; that they are endowed by their Creator with certain unalienable rights; that among these are life, liberty and the pursuit of happiness.

— Declaration of Independence

That we the people are endowed by God with unalienable rights is a point of contention for Americans who profess to be atheists, and rightfully so; for if being an American were reserved for those who believed in God, then only those who believed in God would be Americans. This would be a violation of a citizen's liberty and, thereby, his freedom to accept or refuse God as his creator, the source of equality and the unalienable rights of life, liberty and the pursuit of happiness.

However, by refusing to recognize God as the Creator of man's rights, does it not necessarily follow that all men are not created equal?

It is obvious to anyone who has taught, or been a student, that students are not equal in their intellectual capacity. It is equally noticeable to anyone who coaches, participates in or is a spectator of sports, that athletes are not equal in their physical talents. Finally, it is evident to anyone who works for a living that all men are not of equal market worth nor do they have an equal accumulation of material goods.

Now imagine if Thomas Jefferson had written, "All men are reproduced equal; that they are endowed by Nature with certain unalienable rights; that among these are life, liberty, and the pursuit of happiness." And further imagine that "to secure these rights of Nature, governments are instituted among men, deriving their just powers from the consent of the governed; that, whenever any form of government becomes destructive of these ends, it is the right of the people to alter or abolish it, and to institute a new government." It would then be the function of government to insure that since all men are reproduced equally by Nature, they ought to be so treated. Schools would ensure that all students were equally educated, sports would establish rules to equalize the level of play, and government would ensure the equal distribution of material goods to all.

I am here reminded of the office of the "The Handicapper General" in the short story "Harrison Bergeron," by Kurt Vonnegut, Jr. It is the year 2081 and everyone is equal. Those who are born unequal—with superior ability—are handicapped to ensure the equality of the human race. Anyone who is perceived to be beautiful must wear a hideous mask, strong people are required to wear weights, and those with superior intellects are hampered by loud noises in their minds when they try to think.

Thomas Jefferson and his fellow signers of the Declaration of Independence, however, were not simply divorcing themselves from the King of England to establish a government of the people, by the people, and for the people; they separated from the English crown to establish a nation. They founded this nation upon the ideal "That all men are created equal."

That all men are created equal is a theological claim. It is God who has created us as equals before Him in that all men are equal in their claim for justice, thereby necessitating government to ensure all are treated justly.

A nation is not a club established for a select group of people who share some common interest they wish to preserve through a governing body which excludes anyone who is not like them. A nation is a family whose members are united under a moral idea as brothers and sisters in a common cause.

In an analogous sense, God loves His creation and what makes man lovable is that God has first loved man. It is not man loving his neighbor that makes him lovable; it is not the government forcing people to celebrate the diversity that makes man tolerable. It is God that makes our neighbor lovable and we are free to love our neighbors or not.

Recently, a freethinking college professor noted that when Thomas Jefferson wrote, "All men are created equal" he meant only white males. Such a claim reduces Jefferson's universal claim to an exclusive claim. This means that Thomas Jefferson did not know how to use an adjective to qualify his statements. "Man," as it is used in the Declaration of Independence, is an inclusive term, meaning mankind, male and female, and it is not until the most recent creation of politically correct grammar that anyone who could read English would have thought it otherwise.

Given that all men are created equal, anyone who discriminates against a person because of his race, sex or creed fails at being an American.

Martin Luther King, understanding exactly what Thomas Jefferson meant, delivered his speech of August 28, 1963, on the steps at the Lincoln Memorial in Washington D. C., saying, "I have a dream that one day this nation will rise up and live out the true meaning of its creed: 'We hold these truths to be self-evident, that all men are created equal.'" Thus Martin Luther King ends with:

> And when this happens, and when we let it ring from every village and every hamlet, from every state and every city, we will be able to speed up that day when all God's children—black men and white men, Jews and Gentiles, Protestants and Catholics—will be able to join hands and sing in the words of the old Negro spiritual: "Free at last! Free at last! Thank God Almighty, we are free at last!"

Unless, of course, we are just animals. And that would mean the end of America.

The Madonna, the Harlot, and the Modern Woman

Beauty! I can't bear the thought that man of lofty mind and heart begins with the ideal of Madonna and ends with the ideal of Sodom. What's still more awful is that man with the ideal of Sodom in his soul does not renounce the ideal of the Madonna, and his heart may be on fire with the ideal, genuinely on fire, just as in his days of youth and innocence. Yes, man is broad, too broad. I'd have him narrower. The devil knows what to make of it! What to the mind is shameful is beauty and nothing else to the heart. Is there beauty in Sodom? Believe me, that for the immense mass of mankind, beauty is found in Sodom. Did you know that secret? The awful thing is that beauty is mysterious as well as terrible. God and the devil are fighting there and the battlefield is the heart of man.[1]

These words belong to Dmitri Karamazov in Fyodor Dostoyevsky's novel *The Brothers Karamazov*. We have been reading this book for the greater part of the semester in Introduction to Ethics. There is nothing quite like a novel by Dostoyevsky to quicken the level of discussion in an undergraduate class, or any class for that matter. If you have ever read Dostoyevsky, you will have a difficult time being captivated by other modern literature as the characters never reach the point of thinking beyond the level of a child. The latest novels I have read, *Plainsong, A Man in Full, Angela's Ashes*, and *The Shipping News*, read more like case studies than novels. The

---

1. Fyodor Dostoyevsky, *The Brothers Karamazov*, trans. Constance Garnett (New York: Random House, 1995), 118.

characters are never to blame for their faults given that they are from "dysfunctional" families. The reader is subjected to pages of characters mistakenly trying to find themselves in a meaningless world where nobody ever rises beyond being a victim of circumstances. There is never a mention of God or a soul, which severely limits self-reflection and the pangs of conscience and renders the characters incapable of any judgment beyond the level of strong sentiment. Unlike with Dmitri you will not find a character in these novels able to speak twelve sentences from the depths of his soul.

Which is not to say that in Dostoyevsky's novel there aren't characters from "dysfunctional families." His characters are from broken families. Dostoyevsky would never call his families "dysfunctional" because this word is a biological term, denoting a disordered or impaired functioning of a bodily system or organ, and the human being is beyond being an organ whose life is determined by the larger system. Using this biological term denies free will and reduces the individual to being a product of his environment, one who simply reacts to circumstances. Such characters are not creatures worthy of creation; they even fail at being pathetic characters because they do not grow by their sufferings to overcome the victimization of environment. They lack, in the common expression, "blood and guts" and are so squeamish that such books read like newspapers, never to be read twice.

Dostoyevsky's characters rise out of broken homes. They are fallen creatures who are or are not involved in their own transformation before God. Dmitri's father Fyodor, for example, has four children by two wives and the rape of Stinking Lisaveta, the village idiot. Fyodor is all a father should not be; he does not abandon his children but simply forgets them in the backyard. If it were not for his servant Grigory, his children would have starved to death. He is a lecherous buffoon who proudly tells his grown sons, "I never thought a woman ugly in my life—that's my rule! You've milk in your veins, not blood. You're not out of your shells yet. My rule has been that you can always find something interesting in every woman that you wouldn't find in any other."

A few pages later he tells Alyosha that the "wenches" won't come to him in his old age, so he is saving all his money for prostitutes, "For sin is sweet. All abuse it but all men live in it. The only difference is that others do it on the sly and I do it openly."

With this in mind, Dmitri's words at the beginning of this essay are addressed to his nineteen-year-old brother Alyosha. Dmitri tells Alyosha he is battling with two contrary ideas of woman, the Madonna and the harlot, and the battlefield is in his heart. He is not the author of the image of the Madonna, nor of the harlot; these are not natural images of woman, though they appear in the world. The world, God's creation, is the battleground where God and the Devil are fighting, and Dmitri recognizes the battle rages within him in his desire for Beauty, set in the contrary images of the sacred Madonna and the sensual harlot.

Dmitri, an ex-army officer, is twenty-four years old and currently engaged to Katerina, his former commander's daughter, but he is presently captivated by the vamp Grushenka. Grushenka flirted with Dmitri enough to fuel his lust to the pitch of a fever-heat and then turned a cold shoulder his way. Dmitri, at the beginning of the novel, is in the grips of a fury. To add fuel to the fire, Fyodor Karamazov is also pursuing Grushenka ("whose figure suggests the line of Venus de Milo") and is willing to pay 3,000 rubles for her attention. Katerina, who knows of Dmitri's passion for Grushenka, swears she will always remain faithful to Dmitri. Grushenka, meanwhile, is not interested in Dmitri, Fyodor, nor anyone in particular. Thus, we have Katerina's faithful love for Dmitri, who in turn desires, along with his father, Grushenka, who does not want either one of them.

Dmitri sees that no one is going to understand man unless realizing that "for the immense mass of mankind, beauty is found in Sodom."

Look around! Dmitri states the obvious. The young woman exercising on the stair-stepper next to me at the university gym this morning knows what interests Dmitri. She did not come right out and say it, but the title of the lead article on the magazine cover propped on her exercise machine said it for her, "Want the Perfect Body?" Can anyone say "no" to such an offer? I wanted to point to the article and say, "I do," but, in these times, when words are easily misunderstood, she might think I was trying to work myself into that shape. I am years beyond wanting to have a perfect body in that sense. However, to look at perfect bodies, heavenly bodies, well, that is another matter.

Anyway, the sirens on the cover of the magazine "strutting their stuff" in their push-up-bras and short dresses, torment young girls and modern women with the image of the "perfect body." I did not have the heart to tell the young woman that Cher was older than I; that she used to have a nose (a regular honker, way larger than her current cookie-cutter nose), that her breasts are silicone, and that one more face lift would probably draw her face so tight she would not be able to close her mouth or shut her eyes when she slept. In all of this, a woman must remember there is nothing complete in the perfect body Dmitri desires that will hold his attention any longer than a workout on a stair-stepper. In his own words:

> Today it would be a lady; tomorrow a wench out of the streets. I entertained them both. I threw away money by the handful on ladies, too, for they'll take it easily, that must be admitted, and be pleased and thankful for it. Ladies used to be fond of me; not all of them, but it happened, it happened. But I always liked the side paths, little dark back alleys behind the main road—in the dirt.... I love vice. I love the dishonor of vice. I love cruelty.[2]

He loves vice; he loves to dishonor women. Dmitri's dishonoring of woman is possible only because of his contrary ideas of woman. He cannot dishonor a woman without also being able to honor a woman. Without the Madonna, the image of the complete woman as a sacred being honored by God, there is not an image of the dishonorable woman, a way to defile the perfect body meant to house a child of God.

Imagine a young man in 2015 using the words Beauty, riddles, soul, ideal, Madonna, Sodom, devil, God, and battlefield all in one para-

2. Ibid., 118.

graph with the conclusion that God and the devil were fighting for his heart. If a modern young man spoke this way, he would undoubtedly be committed to a variety of therapists for observation and diagnosed as suffering from a chemical imbalance, being the product of a dysfunctional family, of abusive, cult-oriented parents, or of some equally traumatizing activity, like too many hours of playing video games resulting in hallucinations of spirits fighting in his heart, of all places. In short: a victim.

Imagine a modern young man being tormented like Dmitri, battling between the image of woman as Madonna and as harlot. The only Madonna most young men and women know of is the siren who wears her underwear in public for shock effect. The harlot's perfect body bombards man at every turn, from his multi-channeled, pay-for-view television to thousands of pornographic websites; from the racks of air-brushed babes on magazine covers at convenience stores and supermarkets, to the packets of condoms in men's rooms; from coquettes wrapped around tequila bottles in liquor stores and advertising manual shavers, to young beauty queens too pretty to be taken seriously in the television roles of doctor, detective, and lawyer.

The images of woman being sold to women at check-out counters range from Cosmopolitan's, which advertises "Land that man, ace your job, and look your sexiest ever," to Glamour's recent discovery of a "new technique for satisfying your lover while not feeling guilty having an affair." Tom Wolfe, in his previously mentioned novel *A Man In Full*, characterizes the image of modern woman as a "boy with tits," a fitting result of the current push for equality between the sexes; women now are treated as men. Equality means sacrificing womanhood to be recreated in the image of man.

Dmitri's lust for "dark back alleys" is modern man's desire for the procreative act without creation. Make women equal to men and the love between them will be no higher than man's desire for man, a woman created in a man's image, a narcissistic love. It is the desire for a sexual union which, though fertile by nature, denies the reproductive act. The end of the procreative act becomes the gratification of sexual desires freed from the responsibility of children. It is the image of woman as a sterile object, unproductive and clouded by the desire for self-gratification.

The back alleys Dmitri loves to frequent in the 19th century have become our super highways in the 21st century. What was once a toll-road has become a freeway littered with unwanted children.

Back to the stair-stepper and the next article in the women's magazine: "Are You Sexually Normal?" Who would ever float such a question through a young woman's mind? Would her parents or grandparents ever trouble her with such a concern? Dmitri at least has the sense to know that this question is a temptation meant to dishonor and defile women. This question is older than the author who wrote the article. It is a question that exists in the darker side of Dmitri's soul, floating through his mind and our minds as well. How is such a question to be answered? With a survey? A test? Once the norm is established, obviously the Madonna will be a deviant. And who wants to deviate from the norm?

In all of this, the question before the reader remains the same, "Who is winning the battle for my soul?"

And so it goes.

A Wife is Like a Fire

The wife is like a fire, or to put things in their proper proportion, the fire is like the wife. Like the fire, the woman is expected to cook, not to excel in cooking, but to cook; to cook better than her husband who is earning the coke by lecturing on botany or breaking stones. Like the fire, the woman is expected to tell tales to the children, not original and artistic tales, but tales—better tales than would probably be told by a first-class cook. Like the fire, the woman is expected to illuminate and ventilate, not by the most startling revelations or the wildest winds of thought, but better than a man can do it after breaking stones or lecturing.... Women were not kept at home in order to keep them narrow; on the contrary, they were kept at home in order to keep them broad. The world outside the home was one mass of narrowness, a maze of cramped paths, a madhouse of mono-maniacs.[1]

During our end of the year cleaning feast, the Associate Assistant Waste Management Specialist found this passage in an envelope marked, "Too Hot to Handle." Our associate does not know to whom these words belong so he asked the folks at the editorial desk. They were also at a loss. Anyway, much discussion followed and everyone agreed, the idea of a wife being like fire sounds primitive. Who but a pre-Socratic philosopher looking for the primary stuff, the Urstoff, of all things, would compare a wife to one of the four basic elements? Everyone knows fire lives by feeding on, by consuming

---

1. *Collected Works of G. K. Chesterton* (San Francisco: Ignatius Press, 1990), vol. III, 115.

and transforming into itself heterogeneous matter. A fire springs up, as it were, from a multitude of objects. If a fire were a wife, she would consume and seek to transform those around her into herself, and without this supply of material (her husband and children), she would die down and cease to exist. (The very existence of fire depends on this "strife" and "tension.")

Furthermore, it does not seem right to compare a wife to fire, since the home has been electrified and wives have been spared the wood stove and the cauldron for the microwave and the crockpot. Nor would the wife of the technological age, who is bent on finding herself outside the home as a professional, be thought the source of illumination to her children. This is an age filled with drugs and wangling techniques promising to eliminate the strife and the tension, the *stress*, from the "super-mom's" life. The only form of illumination most children receive, after being picked up at the day care pen, is from the light of the 40+-inch non-stop storytelling machine plopped in middle of the family room.

All this aside, however, it does seem reasonable to compare a wife to fire, as the establishment of the relationship of wife to husband has its origin in the same source as fire. For example, the Pawnee Indians, who are under the ground upon which we at *The Examined Life* have been tromping for the last decade, offer the following as the beginning of the relationship of woman and man:

> After Tirawa had created the sun, moon, stars, the heavens, the earth, and all things upon the earth, he spoke, and at the sound of his voice a woman appeared upon the earth. Tirawa spoke to the gods in the heaven and asked them what he should do to make the woman happy and that she might give increase. The moon spoke and said, "All things that you have made, you have made in pairs, as the Heavens and the Earth, the Sun and the Moon. Give a mate to the woman so that the pair may live together and help one another in life." Tirawa made a man and sent him to the woman; then he said: "Now I will speak to both of

you. I give you the earth. You shall call the earth "mother." The Heaven
you shall call "father."[2]

As the Heavens are to the Earth and the Sun is to the Moon, so too
is a man to a woman. They have been set down together on Earth by
Tirawa to "live together and help one another in life." A woman cannot
be thought of without her mate any more than a man can be thought
of without his. Together woman and man are the parts of a whole. If a
young Pawnee were to ask why are men and women different, his parents would answer with the story of Tirawa's creation of woman and
man being made for each other, halves of a whole. In telling their story
they would include the task set before them: "live together and help
one another in life on the earth which is your mother."

The creation story of the Pawnee is similar to the Biblical account
of the creation of man and woman:

> And the Lord God took the man, and put him into the garden of Eden
> to dress and to keep it.... And the Lord God caused a deep sleep to fall
> upon Adam, and he slept: And He took one of his ribs, and closed up
> the flesh instead thereof; and from the rib, which the Lord God had
> taken from man, made He a woman, and brought her unto the man.
> And Adam said, this is now bone of my bones, and flesh of my flesh: she
> shall be called Woman, because she was taken out of Man. Therefore
> shall a man leave his father and his mother, and shall cleave unto his
> wife: and they shall be one flesh.[3]

Although in the Pawnee story woman comes before man and in
the Biblical account woman comes from man, in both stories they were
made for each other, woven together, "bone of my bones," as one flesh.
The relationship of woman and man is an essential part of the universe,
standing as the Heavens to the Earth and the Sun to the Moon. In this
respect all women are created to be wives, and all men are created to be

2. *The Pawnee*, George A. Dorsey, curator (Washington: Carnegie Institution of
Washington, 1906), 13.

3. Genesis 2: 15–25.

husbands. In other words, no person can exist unto themselves, single, severed from their other half. Although it is not the case that a woman or a man must marry, it is the case that each must marry in order to be complete.

Thus it is the case that in Spanish, for example, the gender of the land, the home, the school, and the church is feminine (*la tierra, la casa, la escuela, la iglesia*) and, like mother earth, are places of nourishment, nursing, growth and salvation. These are all places a person may marry and be called into a relationship, as a servant. Without such a relationship man would be isolated and unable to fulfill himself as a human. Aristotle saw that only something inferior or superior to a human could live outside the family and the community: a beast or a god. Thus, man marries the land and becomes a husbandman; he involves himself in the propagation of trees and other plants in a nursery; he leads a school of children, becoming their master or mistress; and he can marry the church to become a servant of God as priest or nun.

The author of the passage that compared a wife to a fire and then, to balance the perspective, compared a fire to a wife, could surely have carried the analogy further by comparing a husband to the wind, and concluded, like Tirwara and the author the Bible, by weaving the two together in one flesh. When woven together, "Fire lives the death of Air, and Air the death of Fire." Without the wind, the fire cannot feed and without the heat of the sun, the earth would be a windless, cold, and barren planet.

From the primordial relationship of woman and man comes the moral relationship of a wife to her husband and a husband to his wife. From both, joined in the creative act of love, comes a family, a unit as basic to the world as the four primary elements of earth, water, wind and fire. In this respect, the benevolent rule of the father and mother over their children was ordained in the creation of woman and man and is therefore a royal position among the Pawnee. Even among tribal people today, we still find kings and chiefs ruling over their people.

Then again, every home on every block is a kingdom unto itself, and one hopefully governed by a philosopher King... and Queen.

Today there is much talk about a woman's right to be self-sufficient by landing a job outside the home, as though leaving home were a form of emancipation granted previously only to men. The idea that the wife had been discouraged from leaving home and the work of housewifery presupposes the husband had been liberated by leaving home for a job alongside other men. However, this is a lie because leaving home for a job under a complete stranger was not a moment of liberation for our ancestors but a form of wage slavery.

Before the electrification of America most people were farmers and their people before them were serfs, peasants and commoners much like the *campesino* currently immigrating from Latin America. Our American ancestors left, or lost, their farms for a variety of reasons: war, the Depression, drought, tuberculosis, and the lure of the city.

It was not a glorious day when the first husband, in a long line of husbandman, replaced the crow of the cock with the ring of a clock, and, showering before work, put on clean clothes to impress the strangers. Nor was it a great moment in history when the electrified husband started his day by listening to the news (which is forever the same thing being made to seem quite new) while eating cereal out of a box, and then packed a lunch, all before punching a clock which calculates "hours worked" to be multiplied by x number of cents to be received at the end of the week. Conversely, a husbandman never had a job; he worked, but he did not have a job. No husbandman ever woke and said, "I have to go to my job." Nor did he dream about retirement, the day when his job would be finished. There is no end to the "work" on a farm, as there is no beginning point in the cyclical movement of the seasons.

No longer are there husbandmen who "dress and keep" Mother Earth with their wives and their eight children (the average on my mother's side of the family from the Revolutionary War till the beginning of the 20th century.) Now there is the husband who works at one job; whereas before, he had been a jack of many trades (laying brick, logging, blacksmithing, cutting ice, husbanding animals, and mastering an assortment of tools from spades to picks, hammers, saws, planes, files, braces, chisels, belt punches, and tongs), now he has become a monomaniac: doing one job the entire day, whether it be driving a bread truck, delivering milk, laying bricks, operating a lathe, stocking shelves, working in a mill, climbing telephone poles, or selling suits. Once in town the husbandman lost his need to know carpentry, agriculture, animal husbandry, or fashioning a hinge on an anvil. Here he concentrated on a specific job determined by a complete stranger he learned to call his employer. With this job skill, the former husbandman became narrower and narrower and was called a specialist. But though the husband became narrower, his wife remained broad in the keeping of the kingdom at home.

The home is meant to be a place of schooling which begins on the first day of life with the baptism of a name and rises to the comfort of a parent's lap. It is in the home where the children learn their mother tongue and noble ways, through tales which warn against the witches, wizards, dragons, and demons who feed on the innocent. A good mother raises her children in work, study and play: from feeding animals to weeding the garden; from peeling potatoes to baking bread; from churning butter to plucking chickens; from drawing out letters to reading Scripture; from pressing leaves to decorating cakes; from nature walks to sack races; from stitching clothes to sowing shut wounds; from bathing children to washing the bodies of her dead to be placed before the community in the front room of her home. Such a wife is ruler of the home, fueling her children with a love which understands the work of housewifery and motherhood as all-consuming because it involves the transformation of the children.

No doubt such thoughts will be labeled romantic, a glorification of a past that never existed. However, that wives or husbands at home, who, as Aristotelians, teach morals, manners, theology, and hygiene to their children, are broader and their work more important than that of their spouses narrowed in the shop cannot be denied. And there will be those who argue that although there was such a time, there is no going back. But it is not the case that because we cannot go back that we have gone forward. We have traded our cyclical life for a linear view of progress. We are being pushed down corridors into "one mass of narrowness, a maze of cramped paths, a madhouse of monomaniacs." All at the expense of being broad.

Cultural Diversity

For a first-year student to depart from that established path [the Eurocentric perspective] will be a bold undertaking requiring the election of a curriculum that promotes an equitable study of the cultures and contemporary issues of the national non-white citizenry. This prickly path will require the pursuit of courses of study such as African American, Chinese American, Native American, Japanese American, Puerto Rican American, Women's Studies as well as other studies of the pluralism of America.

These are the words of one Vivant Verdell Gordon who wrote the article, "Multicultural Education: Some Thoughts from an Afrocentric Perspective," which someone shot my way in campus mail. In the article she laments the plight of "African American, Chinese American, Native American, Japanese American (etc. etc.), who are not a part of the dominant culture when faced with the absence of their presence among the Greco-Roman tradition." She further assumes that the "study of contemporary issues of the national non-white citizenry" is essential for an "equitable study of cultures."

Vivant Gordon is using a material sense of culture that defines a culture as the mores, values, customs and race you happen into and a subculture as an association where every two or three are gathered in name. In order to have "cultural diversity" at the institutions of higher learning, the Vivant Verdell Gordon's of "higher learning" argue that there needs to be an assortment of "studies" from the "perspective" of each race and cross-race to properly infect what has hitherto been a "Eurocentric male point of departure which imposes a presumed

Greco-Roman and male point of departure for all world people, especially Americans."

All in all, this is a superficial approach spoken by someone measuring with her eye by dividing the world into male and female, white, black, yellow and all shades in between and concluding that each has a "culture" with "contemporary issues" that must be discussed in Academia. I will not argue against this idea; rather, I will point out that there is another sense of culture which does not as readily meet the eye, nor is it about "contemporary issues," but it is about an everlasting issue facing us all: the sense of culture whereby a person "cultivates" his soul in the moral struggle to be a good person throughout all the days of his life.

An American, or a Japanese, or an Indian is born into a history, literature, art and religion of a people who have a recorded story of the beginnings of their spiritual journey till the present day. This struggle involves stories of individual attempts to cultivate a soul and, thereby, to become a member of his people. (A Zulu is not a Zulu by birth but becomes a Zulu by a series of trials which test his worthiness.) There are other forms of "self-improvement" in history such as the economic gains and losses of a people. Ronald Reagan spoke to simple economics in his re-election campaign when he asked Americans, "Are you better off than you were four years ago?" while pointing at their wallets. But this is an all too "contemporary issue" which is not the currency necessary for those concerned with moral development. It would be like confusing Christ's command, "Be ye therefore perfect" with a motto for a health club.

Belonging to a culture is different from being cultured. Not everyone who belongs to a culture is intent on cultivating a soul by struggling to be moral. But for the people who are, it is like being awakened to the realization that one's life is like the growth of a plant in a garden. The garden is one's culture, the soil in which one has been planted. After the soil is turned over, disked, raked, and planted it seems the work is over; however, the task has just begun. If one wishes to reach maturity, the morning glories and horseweeds must be hoed as they sprout.

Those who work in the soil are awakened to the ways of their ancestors who have persevered to the end in their struggle to be moral. However, these people are no longer present to defend themselves. They have turned to dust. All that is left is their spirit, in word, in deed, and in images which have been handed down. Hoe and uncover Thales, who when asked, "What is difficult?" replied, "To know oneself" and when asked, "What is easy?" replied, "To give advice to another." Hoe again and uncover, "For whosoever exalteth himself shall be abased; and he that humbleth himself shall be exalted." Hoe further and find Socrates, "But I suggest gentlemen, that the difficulty is not so much to escape death; the real difficulty is to escape from doing wrong, which is far more fleet of foot." Hoe and run into Martin Luther King, "I have a dream that one day every valley shall be exalted, every hill and mountain shall be made low, the rough places will be made plain, and the crooked places will be made straight, and the glory of the Lord shall be revealed, and all flesh shall see it together."

If this seems too noble, move to another land and hoe. Try India. Hoe into her past to unearth *The Bhagavad Gita* and find,

> But contacts with matter, son of Kunti,
> Cause cold and heat, pleasure and pain;
> They come and go, and are impermanent;
> Put up with them, son of Bharata!
> For whom these (contacts) do not cause to waver,
> The man, O bull of men,
> To whom pain and pleasure are alike, the wise,
> He is fit for immortality.[1]

Who is fit for immortality?

1. *The Bhagavad Gita*, trans. Franklin Edgerton (Cambridge: Harvard University Press, 1944), 10.

If the Vivant Verdell Gordons are interested in the moral development of students by using their literature, art, music and poetry, I am all for them. I suspect, however, that when they look out over the campuses of America and "see" a population of "African American, Native American, Puerto Rican American, Chinese American, and Japanese American students," they think students cultivate themselves by reading "about" other cultures. This type of reasoning assumes we are educated by simply being exposed to "international students" and "students of color." (Notice the language has gone full circle: is a "student of color" any different than a "colored student?")

If, however, the hyphenated American students—to which all Americans belong—wish to cultivate their souls to the ways of their ancestors, they will have to do more than just sit at the smorgasbord of "Multicultural education." They will have to subject themselves to self-examination under the supervision of their ancestors.

In conclusion, let us look at the words of Alexander Solzhenitsyn, who was fortunate enough to have escaped the "Eurocentric male point of departure which imposes a presumed Greco-Roman and male point of departure" by being walled up in the Soviet Union:

> The people is not everyone who speaks our language, nor yet the elect marked by the fiery stamp of genius. Not by birth, not by work of one's hands, not by the wings of education is one elected into the people.
> But by one's inner self.
> Everyone forges his inner self year after year.
> One must try to temper, to cut, to polish one's soul so as to become a human being.
> And thereby become a tiny particle of one's own people.[2]

2. Aleksandr Solzhenitsyn, *The First Circle*, trans. Thomas Whitney (New York: Harper & Row, 1968), 389.

The Age of Isms

In Germany, relativism is an exceedingly daring and subversive theoretical construction (perhaps Germany's philosophical revenge which may herald the military revenge). In Italy, relativism is simply a fact.... Everything I have said and done in these last years is relativism by intuition.... If relativism signifies contempt for fixed categories and men who claim to be the bearers of an objective, immortal truth... then there is nothing more relativistic than Fascist attitudes and activity.... From the fact that all ideologies are of equal value, that all ideologies are mere fictions, the modern relativist infers that everybody has the right to create for himself his own ideology and to attempt to enforce it with all the energy of which he is capable.[1]

These are the words of one Benito Mussolini, who joined Hitler to sow discord, to say the least, on the planet. Benito and Hitler are dead and gone, but like all writers, their ideas still linger over the firmament, exhausting their emissions upon the rest of us. With this in mind, let us air out Mussolini's idea to see where it leads, and, who knows, maybe even cleanse the air.

Benito saw that all ideologies—all isms—are of equal value, in that they are fictions; creations, (as fictions are) of men, who think they can create an image of man, and enforce it by means of legislation, if they are peaceful, or by force, if they are fascist. Benito and the adherents of relativism have contempt for the idea of an "immortal truth," a greater and a lesser, a good and an evil, virtue and vice; in short, a way

---

1. *Diuturna* [The Lasting] (1921,) as quoted in *Rational Man: A Modern Interpretation of Aristotelian Ethics* (1962) by H. B. Veatch, 20.

of discriminating between the goodness and the wickedness of one's own actions, or another person's actions, or between the merits of two novels, philosophies, or works of art. In effect, a relativist says there is no way that a person "ought" to think or act, thereby granting himself permission to think and act any way he chooses.

For the relativist, everything he "thinks," "feels," or "sees" is a matter of perception, of how it appears to him. If he goes outside and it is twenty below zero and it appears to be warm, it is. If he reads "Hamlet" and perceives it to be trite and boring, it is. In ancient Greece this was known as, "Man being the measure of all things," which quickly reduces to, "I am the measure of all things." Each "thinking being" may have his own idea of what appears to be valuable, hence a multitude of ideologies, ideas, and theories of what appears to be the case. That is why Benito says, "all ideologies are mere fictions." And he is right. The logic of "man being the measure of all things" makes each individual his own god. Once all men are gods, there is no God, and everything in the realm of moral judgment becomes fiction.

How did the relativist arrive at such a position? Relativism results when those beneath the firmament deny that there is an "immortal truth," and an ideology results when a relativist decides to create his own image of man. The ideologue would be harmless if he were content to let everyone be entitled to his "view," but he does not. He does as Benito and his friend did. Look at Hitler's image of man and the place of the Aryan in *Mien Kampf,* "Blood mixture and resultant drop in the racial level is the sole cause of the dying out of old culture; for men do not perish as the result of lost wars, but by the loss of that force of resistance which is contained only in pure blood. All who are not of good race in this world are chaff." This is why Benito writes, "the modern relativist infers that everybody has the right to create for himself his own ideology and to attempt to enforce it with all the energy of which he is capable."

Benito was not the first to think this way. In fact, he sounds like his ideological parents, Marx and Nietzsche, when he describes the modern relativist's hatred for authority and the will to power. Marx in the *Manifesto of the Communist Party* writes, "But Communism abolishes eternal truths, it abolishes all religion, and all morality, instead of constituting them on a new basis; it therefore acts in contradiction to all past historical experience."[2] And Nietzsche in *Twilight of the Idols* says that the free man upholding his idea must be prepared

> to sacrifice human beings for one's cause, not excluding oneself. Freedom means that the manly instincts which delight in war and victory dominate over other instincts, for example, over those of "pleasure." The human being who has become free—and how much more the spirit who has become free—spits on the contemptible type of well-being dreamed of by shopkeepers, Christians, cows, females, Englishmen, and other democrats. The free man is a warrior.[3]

The first step of an ideologue is to deny eternal truths and morality; and the second step is to take up the unbound freedom and enforce his position "with all the energy of which he is capable."

So what does all this have to do with education?

Recently a flyer appeared in the mailboxes at my end of the hall from a group calling itself "Teachers for a Democratic Culture." In an age marred by the academic relativism—all courses being of equal merit in the students' education—this is what you get. Rather than an individual forwarding an argument, you get a group, or worse yet an organization, complete with Coordinators, Gerald Graff and Gregory Jay, a P.O. box number, where they "welcome contributions of $25.00 for faculty and staff, $5.00 for students" forwarding a "view," an ideology, and for a little bit of money it can be my "view" too. (The first century philosopher Epictetus would have accused such people as singing in the chorus: "Even as bad actors cannot sing alone, but only in cho-

2. Karl Marx, *Selected Writing*, Lawrence H. Simon, ed. (Indianapolis: Hackett Publishing Company, 1994), 175.

3. *The Portable Nietzsche*, Walter Kaufmann, ed. and trans. (New York: Viking Penguin, 1954), 542.

rus; so some cannot walk alone. Man, if thou art aught, strive to walk alone and hold converse with thyself, instead of sulking in the chorus! at length think; look around thee; bestir thyself, that thou mayest know who thou art!")

On page two of their program, the "teachers" get around to defining a "democratic culture":

> What does the notion of a "democratic culture" mean and how does it relate to education? In our view, a democratic culture is one that acknowledges that the criteria of value in art are not permanently fixed by tradition and authority, but are subject to constant revision. It is a culture in which terms like "canon," "literature," "tradition," "artistic value," "common culture," and even "truth" are seen as disputed rather than given. This means not that standards for judging art and scholarship must be discarded, but that such standards should evolve out of democratic processes in which they can be thoughtfully challenged.

Notice the relativistic stance "In our view," which immediately reduces their opponent to also having "a view," and the contempt for "fixed categories and men who claim to be the bearers of an objective, immortal truth." The members of this chorus have "a view" which they take to be "a culture" with no assigned permanent fixtures placed there by an authority. Now we are in the cave of perceptions where everything is as it appears—the world of self where everything "seems" to be the case, and nothing "is" the case. In their "culture" terms like: "canon," "literature," "tradition," "truth" are seen as disputed rather than given. This follows. Once you deny there being any "immortal truths," you cease to understand that your life has been assigned to you in eternity, that you, like your ancestors, were given the task of becoming human and that now you are caught in a moral struggle to cast off the ways of a world where a man's appearance has always been more important than a man's character.

The relativist lacks a sense of the spirituality of life and the idea that education has to do with our souls, that some of our ancestors still speak as mediums in the forms of authors, artists, and poets who teach us how to live by forcing us to examine ourselves against their words and images. Have you never read a book or a poem and heard that voice speaking directly to your soul?

In the relativists' denial of there being anything beyond the nonce that is universally true, truth can only be a matter of perception, popular opinion, the current "fiction of man." Thus, they tend to immerse themselves in politics to seek the power that comes with numbers to justify their position.

What the members of the chorus do not realize is that standards do not "evolve;" they "revolve." All of our ideals are behind us, and that is why we study the past to understand the present. The nature of an ideal is that it "is" timeless, thus the past is forever present. If you do not believe me, take the works of literature, poetry, philosophy, and art of our ancestors, and place them alongside of "modern" works (notice the term "modern" assumes progress). Read Aristotle and Boethius with Sartre and Beauvoir; Homer and Dante with Sylvia Plath and Anne Sexton; Michelangelo alongside Andy Warhol, and Dostoevsky alongside Norman Mailer, and listen and look. See?

The reason that some works have been preserved through the centuries, is that it is these works that teach us to question any would-be "culture" which bases itself on the anarchy, the chaos, and the despair of those like Benito and his friends who hold up "isms" in the place of truth.

Come One, Come All

The new admissions standards are out! After months of working "diligently," a committee, that wondrous group who lives in the passive voice, has provided its "recommendations" as to what qualifies for entrance into the University of Nebraska at Kearney. Are you ready?

First there is a "core curriculum" required of the future graduates of high schools: four years of language, three years of math, two years of laboratory science, two years of social science, and four years of electives in recognized college preparatory courses. The public schools are on their way to having a curriculum that will focus on disciplines that are at the heart of a liberal arts curriculum. As a taxpayer, I am pleased to see that my children and my neighbors' children will have an education which focuses on disciplined thought. After high school is successfully completed, the student may apply to UNK, if he meets one of six "criteria."

1. He must rank in the upper one-half of his graduating class.
2. He must present a composite ACT score of 20 or a combined score of 850 on the SAT.

So far so good, it looks as though the admissions policy is set to develop an institution noted for having standards and attracting good students. Then come the qualifications.

3. If students fail to meet the criteria above, they may apply for conditional admission. Up to 20% of the freshman class may be admitted

in this category on the basis of special talent, ability or circumstances (e.g. cultural or economic disadvantage).

Now UNK has admitted 70% of the high school graduating class, 20% of which may be from the bottom of its graduating class on a conditional basis. If the freshmen class has 2,000 students, 400 of those students may have been admitted because of some "special talent, ability or circumstance." Notice why they will be admitted. What exactly is a "special talent," which would be reason to admit a student if they cannot successfully complete the high school curriculum? A forty-two-inch vertical leap? What kind of talents ought a university accept if not in language, literature, science, and history? Well, it may be a particular "ability or circumstance." Good, now we are getting specific; an ability or circumstance is a bit clearer than a special talent. Not much, but a bit. We are on our way to defining what otherwise is vague terminology. An example is given, which is always needed if you want to be specific. Ready. A "circumstance (e.g., cultural or economic disadvantage)." There you have it. If a student is culturally or economically disadvantaged, they may be admitted to UNK. How the word "cultural" is being used, I do not know, especially in an age of a thousand cultures. Hell's Angels, truck drivers, the Rainbow Coalition, Black Muslims, graduate students, all have one thing in common; they belong to a "culture" in the sense that they have a "life-style" to which they adhere. If you are a member of one, or more, of these cultures, are you insulted? You should be, you have just been told you are disadvantaged. But perhaps the committee that met for "months" to concoct this recommendation did not mean this. Perhaps by "cultural" they meant the incoming student was not cultured in the sense of being literate, of having an appreciation for the literature, art, and music accompanied by a gentle disposition. If this is what they meant, then we may be admitting the bottom half of the class and those who cannot combine a score of 450 on the SAT. They surely could not have meant this! However, maybe the student is poor. Being sensitive, the committee could not say this directly so they couched their language in terms that would not be "perceived" to be offensive, like "economically disadvantaged." Sounds better than being poor. Since most of our students are currently working thirty hours a week, they will qualify for admittance under this policy.

You might be wondering why there is such a category, and being a taxpayer, you might wonder further why your money is being used on a student who could not finish in the upper half of his high school class. Should he now be given the "opportunity" to go to a university rather than a community college. Picky. The reason students are being admitted is because this will "enable the institution to pursue its goal of a pluralistic student body." If you have successfully passed English, you immediately recognized the fallacy of the passive voice in this statement; you know that the "institution" is an inanimate object which cannot "pursue" any more than it can speak. But if it could speak, which it cannot, it would want to let people in because it wants a "pluralistic student body." Now imagine you are one of the students who has been admitted as a representative of a "disadvantaged culture." Are you thankful for the magnanimous generosity of this institution? Have you ever considered that you are a disadvantaged person?

The next category is for non-traditional students, adults over twenty-one years of age, who may be admitted conditionally "to provide them the opportunity to present evidence of ability to do college work." So anyone who is over twenty-one years of age may get into the University of Nebraska and then "present evidence of ability to do college work." What this might be, or who determines such things, I do not know, but I have a sneaky suspicion that this will be decided in the office of "Student Affairs," seeing that the committee for his policy was headed by the Vice Chancellor for Student Affairs. What is the Vice Chancellor for Student Affairs doing on a committee dealing with admissions to a university?

It is time to treat the University of Nebraska at Kearney as a university and not a community college where anyone who comes down the pike is ushered into a "student loan" and required to take "University Foundations," a course taught by some quasi-specialist in our "remedial-ed center" for which University credit is given. Did you know that at this institution you can get credit for learning to use the library?

Our Admissions Policy is an important matter because as University teachers, we must be aware that our admissions office is admitting students into our classes who have not shown they can read, write, work mathematical problems, or think scientifically at a secondary level. Furthermore, there are disadvantaged students and non-traditional students who have not necessarily successfully completed a high school curriculum, but are now in our classes to "try" to see if they can do college work. Irony of ironies, we will now have these students evaluating our teaching.

E Pluribus Unum

He dreamt that the whole world was condemned to a terrible
new strange plague that had come to Europe from the depths of
Asia. All were to be destroyed except a very few chosen. Some
new sorts of microbes were attacking the bodies of men, but
these microbes were endowed with intelligence and will. Men
attacked by them became at once mad and furious. But never
had men considered themselves so intellectual and so completely
in possession of the truth as these sufferers, never had they considered their decisions, their scientific conclusions, their moral
convictions so infallible.... All were excited and did not understand one another. Each thought that he alone had the truth and
was wretched looking at the others, beat himself on the breast,
wept, and wrung his hands. They did not know how to judge
and could not agree what to consider evil and what good; they
did not know whom to blame, whom to justify. Men killed each
other in a sort of senseless spite.[1]

The above passage is Raskolnikov's dream in Dostoyevsky's novel *Crime and Punishment*. The dream
is of a people who have lost their center, and are now living in a time
where "the falcon can no longer hear the falconer." The people are dis-
eased and the blood coursing through the "body politic" is filled with
"microbes" infecting each member, each cell, with the idea that he is an
"intellectual" who "alone [has] the truth and [is] wretched looking at
the others." No longer are these people moving towards the "new Jeru-

1. Fyodor Dostoyevsky, *Crime and Punishment*, trans. Constance Garnett (New York:
Bantam Books, 1987), 501–2.

salem;" instead, they are cut off from their heritage and are now set in an indefinite world. There are as many truths as there are people, each with a "view," an "interpretation," and chaos moves over the face of the earth, "and men kill each other in a sort of senseless spite," as what their very gossip seeks is murder.

In this age of special interest groups, campus politicians, departments fixated with generating credit hours, the on-going general studies review, multiculturalism, countless other "isms," wanting to be heard, those on the left, those on the right, those in the middle, I can but wonder if we in the academe have anything in common other than our retirement plans.

It has not always been this way.

Aristotle thought "man" a "political animal," who naturally sought happiness by fulfilling a vocation in the body politic. Man has a telos, a purpose, an end for which he is made; and government, if it is to be a good government, must ensure the right of each citizen to live according to his function, in a virtuous manner, the means by which a man is fulfilled and becomes complete, or perfect.

Aristotle was not an idealist like his teacher Plato, who thought all men equal in their ability to seek happiness. Aristotle thought some men slaves:

> The slave is not only the slave of his master, but wholly belongs to him. Hence, we see what is the nature and office of a slave; he who is by nature not his own but another's man, is by nature a slave.... But is there anyone thus intended by nature to be a slave, and for whom such is expedient and right, or rather is not all slavery a violation of nature?
>
> There is no difficulty in answering this question, on grounds both of reason and of fact. For that some should rule and others be ruled is not only necessary, but expedient; from the hour of their birth, some are marked out for subjection, others for rule.[2]

2. *The Basic Works of Aristotle*, "Politics," Richard McKeon, ed. (New York: Random House), 1254a 10.

Aristotle clearly violates "Affirmative Action" and "Equal Opportunity." But Aristotle is interested in the order of things. He is a scientist; he is not an idealist promoting equality, especially the equality of unequals. A man is a man, is a man, is a man, does not hold for Aristotle, any more than a dog, is a dog, is a dog. There are individual men: women and men, types, some of whom are capable of being ladies and gentlemen and others who will remain brutes and slaves. Those who cannot rule themselves are in every age in need of a master.

There is still more. Man, according to Aristotle, is composed of a body and a soul. The man who is to be a gentle man must use his soul to rule over his body. If the body rules over the soul, the corruptible will be guiding the incorruptible and this is simply not a good idea. If the body were to rule over the soul this would be an "unnatural condition," as it is "clear that the rule of the soul over the body, and of the mind and the rational element over the passionate, is natural and expedient; whereas the equality of the two or the rule of the inferior is always hurtful."[3]

Slavery, therefore, is the condition of the body ruling the soul, of the belly and/or the groin making decisions, as it were, which would not be based upon principles and convictions. A slave is a person who cannot restrain himself: he is harmful to himself. This form of slavery is not a condition that can be abolished by a proclamation. It is a condition that cuts through race, gender, and class because all people have the potential to fall into slavery—bank presidents, priests, garbage men, plumbers, etc. One thing is certain: a slave needs a master for his own good if he is to become a master piece.

(As members, like it or not, of the "body politic," we must have something in common, lest we amputate ourselves from the body, and, like grapes severed from the vine, shrivel and die.)

Even if we are infested with the "microbes" leading to the superiority of "our" truth, there are a great many things we still have in

3. Ibid., 1254b 5–10.

common. Aristotle understood this to be man's nature. Man cannot escape what will "naturally" happen to him any more than the planet can escape the seasons; it is his "condition." In this respect the condition man finds himself in—"the context?"—does not change. Each generation lives to repeat the drama, "the old resounding in the new." The story is as true as the statements we make about our species when we say we have two lungs, our heart has four chambers, and that there are two sexes.

Each of us is set like the seasons. We are born in a nation, in a family; we are brought up by elders, we have the potential for self-examination, the potential to be moral and immoral, the potential to fall in love, the potential to throw stones, the potential to be a concentration camp guard, the potential to be a Mother Teresa, the potential to reproduce, to worship, to doubt, to mourn, to hold our children's children. And there are some things that will unavoidably happen: we will grow old, we will suffer, and we will die and go into the earth, alone. In our climate-controlled environments, the seasons in which our ancestors lived and worked seem but a myth to the "progressively-minded," but the whirl of the past is in the present whether or not we open our windows.

We have much in common as members of the "body politic" of the same nation. A nation founded by commoners on a common belief. Lincoln thought we should read the Declaration of Independence and the Constitution each fourth of July, lest we forget who we are and fall to thinking ourselves a nation unto ourselves.

> We hold these truths to be self-evident, that all men are created equal; that they are endowed by their Creator with certain unalienable rights; that among these are life, liberty, and the pursuit of happiness. That, to secure these rights, governments are instituted among men, deriving their just powers from the consent of the governed; that, whenever any form of government becomes destructive of these ends, it is the right of the people to alter or to abolish it, and to institute a new government, laying its foundation on such principles, and organizing its power in

such form, as to them shall seem most likely to affect their safety and happiness.

We are members of a "body" founded on self-evident truths, created "equal" by God, endowed by Him with the right to life, the right to liberty, and the right to happiness. The sole purpose of government is to ensure these rights, and if our current government cannot ensure these rights then we have the "right" to alter or abolish the government and replace it with one that does. We have the same rights with regard to our schools. If they become "destructive of these ends," it is the right of the people to alter or to abolish the schools.

Notice the order of the rights. We have the right to life, then the right to liberty, then the right to happiness. These rights are in a necessary order. We are created, we are free, we are free to seek our happiness. The task of our schools is to prepare us for the "pursuit of happiness." And they do, except everything is exactly backwards in our educational institutions. They prepare us for life, but not for happiness. They prepare us for the kingdom of death, but not for the kingdom to come.

This is the new myth of the microbes, a myth fostered by our "guidance counselors" and teachers of "value-free curriculums," conjured up in our schools of education. Here it is. Man is born into a state of drudgery. He can rise up out of this drudgery through education. High school will lead to college where he may learn a skill which will guarantee an entry-level position. In ten years, he will own a house in the suburbs. There he will be saved from the drudgery of labor, and be a "superior person" who has learned to "think big," and who has a "quality of life."

The myth of the microbes denies the spiritual side of man. It encourages his physical side, asking him to seek happiness in the accumulation of material things. Such happiness is a myth because it is unattainable: there is no end to appliances and gimmicks. Man will be like a child at Christmas who remarks after opening his last present,

"That's all there is!" And this will leave him, as idols do, empty. And he will mope.

Jefferson had more in common with Aristotle than he did with the visions of politicians who measure "progress" in the physical language of the GNP and housing starts and with our administrator down at the University of Nebraska at Lincoln ("higher education"), who thinks education's sole purpose is to guarantee quality workers. Nations are not meant for unlimited growth, all nations eventually decline and give way to other nations. What is to become of a nation that prepares its people only for unbound wealth when its spiritual bounty goes dry? Jefferson wrote a spiritual declaration for a people whose happiness was meant to be the pursuit of virtue. Life is a moral endeavor, and as with all moral endeavors, there is suffering. For if you love, you must suffer as you sojourn in the trials of your land, your family, your congregation, and your fellow citizens who long for a happiness that has been endowed by their Creator.

Happiness is a "pursuit" which is not achieved by degrees. There are moments when we are happy, as there are moments when we are moral. But morality is a pursuit which involves a continual struggle with one's own soul, and only self-examination reveals how one has fallen short. Nevertheless, we are not without hope. Tomorrow we are again free to start anew to improve ourselves, prompted by the realization that in suffering, as in love, there is joy, and our happiness lies in this struggle as we work out our happiness.

Am I writing about "our" America?

Ombudsman/Ombudsperson

Which of these terms is correct? Well, perhaps, "correct" is not the right choice of words: "gender biased" is closer to the heart of the matter. Recently, at the University of Nebraska at Kearney, the Faculty Senate unanimously approved the following recommendations from the "Ad hoc Gender Bias Survey Committee." There are eleven recommendations in all. For the sake of brevity, we need only look at a few to grasp the spirit of their thoughts:

2. Administration should encourage and facilitate the creation of a warm climate for all students.
6. Departments, Colleges, and Administration should ensure equal treatment of female and male faculty.
8. Verbal harassment and language that excludes or demeans women should be discouraged at all levels of UNK's operation.

What are we to make of recommendation number two? Do they want the campus moved south, insulation added to the buildings, nesting material made available for the students, or are the faculty who ask difficult questions to stop asking questions that make students uncomfortable? Regardless of the intentions of the committee on this specific recommendation, the above three recommendations share the common fallacy committed when an inanimate object is acting as though it had a free will. Let me explain. A department, a college, and the administration cannot act. Only a human being can act. Have you ever seen the College of Fine Arts and Humanities going to the library or telling a student he could register for a closed class? A specific individual, a professor, can or cannot admit a student to a class, but a college cannot do such a thing. Neither can a college "ensure equal treatment of female and male faculty;" that is something only an individual, a professor, a secretary, a Jim, a Bob, a Betty, a Gail, a Tom, or an Al can do. So why did the ad hoc committee not say, Jim, Bob, Betty, Gail, Tom, Al, and all other faculty members and members of the staff "should" ensure that they are treating their fellow female and male faculty members equally? Was it because they wanted to avoid being specific or have been conditioned not to be so? I think so. If they had been specific, they would have been pointing a finger at the people who were not treating females and males equally, and they, in their righteousness, would have to stop them. Then again, the members of the committee do not want, by their choice of words, a confrontation.

One of the problems with politicians is that they hide behind language so as to avoid responsibility. They will not reprimand anyone. Let the policy do that. Perhaps committees have been established by chancellors, deans, chairmen, and the senators of the Faculty Senate to deflect anyone who is looking for a responsible individual. Can you imagine running your home, your life, or your business with a university committee?

The eighth recommendation is, I suspect, the reason the word "ombudsman" was recently changed to "ombudsperson" on our campus. It was obvious to whomever had read the latest policy from the ad hoc committee that the word "ombudsman," all by its lonesome, was guilty of "excluding or demeaning" women.

As rational creatures who arrive at decisions by thoughtful investigation, not blind adherence, we/I will ask, "Can language exclude or demean women?" More specifically, "Can a word exclude or demean women?" In answering this question, it is necessary to look at how a word functions. What exactly does a word do? Does every word in English signify something, refer to something, serve as a rigid designator, such that every time we speak the word we evoke the thing we have named? In answering these questions let us look at a word. Take the word "hammer" as an example. What does the word hammer mean? Stumped? You should be, there is not a context for the word "hammer." Is the word a noun or a verb? If it is a verb it will have different uses than if it is a noun. In order to be clear about its part of speech, a context is necessary. You can hammer a nail, or you can hang your hammer by its claws, if, that is, it is a claw hammer and not an air hammer. (If you were hip, or had teenagers, you would know about "Hammer-time.")In each case, the word is not being used in the same way, nor does it mean the same thing. Imagine that: a word is always spelled exactly the same can have many different meanings! In looking through my word box, I found some other words, "saw," "level," "square," "bolt," and "screw."

Does any one of these words have a specific definition so that whenever it is used, it is being used to mean the same thing? Let us look at some sentences that have been lifted from their context using the above words, one word at a time. I need a "saw" to cut the board. I used a crosscut "saw." I "saw" a sawhorse in the yard next to the see-saw. A "level" is used to tell if something is "level." John is levelheaded. We must "level" the forest in order to build our farm house. Have you seen the "square?" John is down at the "square" selling newspapers. You're "square!" Did you "bolt" the gate? The "bolt" in the rifle is jammed. A "bolt" of muslin was sitting on the shelf. I need a Philips-head "screw?" Will you "screw" or nail the boards together? He has a "screw" loose. How many other senses of these words can you think of?

If you use the English language, you can imagine a context for each of these sentences; and, you know that the context will change the sense of the word. Imagine what it would be like not to know that the word had a variety of different senses. For example: the word "bolt" means "a fastener consisting of a threaded pin or rod with a head at one end, designed to be inserted through holes in assembled parts and secured by a mated nut that is tightened by application of torque." Having this definition of bolt in mind, Jim, whose wife Martha tells him early in October she needs a bolt of muslin for a Christmas project, decides he will surprise her. He goes to the hardware store to buy a muslin bolt. He goes to the aisle seven where the bolts are and goes through the bins, 2 x 3/8, 2 3/4x 3/8, no muslin bolts here, all steel. Then he moves to the next row, 2 x 7/8, 2 3/4 x 7/8, no muslin bolts here, all brass, and on and on till sunset, without any bolts of muslin, but only steel, brass, and aluminum. The plight of a literalist!

What does the word "ombudsman" mean? We might ask ourselves this question if we heard the word being used and did not know what it meant. So we would go to a dictionary, "A government official. esp. in Scandinavian countries, who investigates citizens' complaints against the government or its functionaries. "Does this word "demean" women? If you assume that "Ombudsman" means a man, and only a man, who is an ombuds, then a woman who is hired to be an "ombudsman" could not be an "ombudsman," as she is woman, and the word specifically designates a man. So if a woman has the job of being the Chancellor's ombudsman, her title will be ombudswoman. But, there is still a problem: the last syllable is "man," so let's use the gender inclusive term, "ombudsperson." Obviously the thought police, and here I am reminded of George Orwell's *1984*, have failed to be consistent. The word "ombudsperson" demeans women because of the last syllable, "son." For the sake of consistency the word should be changed to ombudsper. However, there are still problems with the first syllable of the word. "Om" is the single-syllable Brahman in the sacred Hindu work *The Bhagavad Gita*. This is an obvious lack of religious sensitivity to Hindus, as "om" is used to focus on God—especially when it is being used to refer to someone who simply works to resolve complaints between the faculty and the administration. We could shorten "ombudsper" to "budsper," but the first syllable still poses a problem. "Buds," if, it had an apostrophe, would turn into "Bud's" which is a male's name, so the word ought to be reduced to "per," so as not to demean women, which should be "wo," so as not to offend or demean "wos."

I have intentionally committed the fallacy of accent, which results, in stressing one rather than another syllable of a word. No one for instance would be taken in by the following argument:

Mankind is not women.

The beings that compose the human race are mankind.

Therefore, the beings that compose the human race are not women.

Now, you see why I am reminded of Orwell's *1984*. I live in an age where the thought police of Ingsoc are pruning the language for the political purpose of cleaning up the language. Here is a little of *1984*:

> The purpose of Newspeak was not only to provide a medium of expression for the views and mental habits proper to the devotees of Ingsoc, but to make all other modes of also the possibility of arriving at them by indirect methods. This was done partly by the thought impossible. It was intended that when Newspeak had been adopted once and for all and Oldspeak forgotten, a heretical thought—that is, a thought diverging from the principles of Ingsoc—should be literally unthinkable, at least so far as thought is dependent on words. Its vocabulary was so constructed as to give exact and often very subtle expression to every meaning that a Party member could properly wish to express, while excluding all other meanings and invention of new words, but chiefly by eliminating undesirable words and by stripping such words as remained of unorthodox meanings, and so far as possible of all secondary meanings whatever.[1]

Sound familiar? Language cannot "demean or exclude" women. That is something only another individual or a group of individuals can do. Nor can language be sexist, rude, angry, brave, violent, or cruel. Only a specific person can by rude, angry, brave, violent, and cruel unless, of course the "sea is angry," but that is a personification. A person can use the correct terminology, so as not to offend those who are overly sensitive to words and still be a bigot, disliking all the members

1. George Orwell, *1984* (New York: Signet Classic, 1981), 246.

of a sex, race or religion. A person can also use the correct terminology in such a tone as to offend those he wishes to offend.

What is to become of us if those who misuse language, like a fundamentalist reading scripture, are let loose to police the users of language in the universities? And what is further going to happen when the thought police move from thinking that language is sexist to thinking the person who is using unapproved language is a sexist when his intent may be completely otherwise? When words or terms like "freshman," "manhole," "master key," "senior," "shuttlecock," "cocktail," "master's degree," "prick," "bachelor's degree," "cock," "masterpiece," are used, is the person who is using the words to be termed a sexist, then corrected, punished, or exiled?

It is time to remember the first amendment, "Congress shall make no law respecting an establishment of religion, or prohibiting the free exercise thereof; or abridging the freedom of speech, or of the press...." Maybe the faculty members who unanimously approved—as they so often do—the recommendations which would censor use of language on the campus of the University of Nebraska at Kearney thought they were on their way to approving a new "world-view" and fostering "mental habits" proper to a new world order by surrendering their freedom of speech. But they should not assume that everyone is as willing to surrender his rights, especially those who think that no word, all by its lonesome, can "exclude or demean" women.

Let the tea party begin.

Trust Your Eyes and Not Your Ears

A University is not a birthplace of poets or of immortal
authors, of founders of schools, leaders of colonies, or conquerors of nations. It does not promise a generation of Aristotles
or Newtons, of Napoleons or Washingtons, of Raphaels or
Shakespeares, though such miracles of nature it has before now
contained within its precincts.... It is the education which gives
a man a clear conscious view of his own opinions and judgments,
a truth in developing them, an eloquence in expressing them,
and a force urging them. It teaches him to see things as they are,
to go right to the point, to disentangle a skein of thought, to
detect what is sophistical, and to discard what is irrelevant. It
prepares him to fill any post with credit, and to master any subject with facility.... He is at home in any society, he has common
ground with every class; he knows when to speak and when to be
silent....[1]

I t is worth remembering the words of Newman regarding the "end"—the purpose—of a university education
as the administrators at my institution are once again trying to figure
out ways to attract students to a life that is worth living. We do not
have to read Newman's *The Idea of a University* to remember the end of
a university, though it would improve us all; instead, let us look at one
sentence used to identify the graduate of a University:

It teaches him to see things as they are, to go right to the point, to dis-

1. John Henry Cardinal Newman, *The Idea of a University* (New York: Holt, Rinehart and Winston, 1964), 134.

entangle a skein of thought, to detect what is sophistical, and to discard what is irrelevant.

A student who has been educated at a university can "see things as they are," which Plato deemed the ability to tell appearance from reality. It seems odd that years of study are necessary to tell appearance from reality; however, being born ignorant in a world crackling with information, hype and persuasion is not the best of possible beginnings. Furthermore, sophists and marketers are constantly convincing the youth to sell their souls to the corporate world of appearance, where a man is measured by his silk shirt collection and the sheer amount of expensive junk in his two-car garage.

The world is a wonderful place and a dangerous place, so we tell children stories as antidotes for the temptations they will encounter along the way—lest they awake in their forties to find their lives have become Hell.

"Many years ago there was an Emperor who was so excessively fond of new clothes that he spent all his money on them. He cared nothing about his soldiers, nor for the theater, nor for driving in the woods except for the sake of showing off his new clothes."

Remember? There were two swindlers who told this Emperor they were weavers and knew how to weave the most beautiful fabrics imaginable? Not only were the clothes from their cloth beautiful but they had the additional quality of becoming invisible to anyone who was not fit for the office he held, in other words, a simpleton. The King needed to hear no more; he needed such an outfit, for "he" would be able to tell those who were unfit for their post and wise men from fools. So the weavers set up their looms and wove their beautiful invisible cloth which all the ministers of the King applauded lest they be considered fools. True, there was much delay, but finally the day came for the Emperor to see his new clothes, which he couldn't, but he was no fool. Consequently, he marched through the town, buck-naked, as all the town folk oooohed and aaahhhed. Such clothes they had never seen. (Small wonder!) Then a child exclaimed, "But he has got nothing on!" Imagine the embarrassment of his parents, who that morning had cautioned the child, "Keep your mouth shut, or this will be your last parade!" But once he had spoken, the words spread like wildfire through the crowd, "He has nothing on; a child says he has nothing on!" till even the Emperor saw the obvious. Did it stop him? The Emperor writhed, for he knew it was true, but he thought the procession must go on, so he held himself straighter than ever as the chamberlains held up the invisible train.

The child acted like a university graduate when he spoke his mind, showing the crowd what stood before their eyes. This is what it is to have a mind, to witness the truth, "detect what is sophistical, and discard what is irrelevant." It has always been harder to stand with the truth than it has been to know the truth. Peter said he would stand till the end; and the cock crowed.

Imagine if the Emperor had awoken one morning and been persuaded by the swindlers that every Kingdom worth remembering had had a university. After thoughtless reflection, he decided, his kingdom ought to be known for more than its emperor's elegant clothes. It should be known for its Emperor's university. So he summoned his ministers and commanded they make him a university. The ministers, being unaware of such things, did not know what to do. Finally, the Emperor turned to the swindlers, who having become his friends, assured him if money were given, they could do it. So they constructed buildings of stone, one after the other, in quads with great archways, towers and bells. There were rooms of all sizes, to administer, to house, to feed, and even to advise. Then came the day for the Emperor to tour this Majesty U., but to his disappointment, like a bad parade, there were no people lining his way. So he called his ministers to fill the halls. This they could do; they also filled it with villagers, farmers, and merchants.

The Emperor paraded before them till all had been seen. Then, turning to the swindlers, he asked, "What more do we need?"

"They," pointing to the multitude, "are to be kept here."

"Whatever for?" the Emperor, puzzled, replied.

"Why to generate revenues. Why ever anything but."

"But what will we sell in these empty halls?" asked the Emperor more perplexed than per puzzled.

"We'll sell them the means by which they may live. To the farmers we'll sell farming where fewer do more; to the merchants a way to make the plenty'd richer by annexing vassal's lands. And if they resist we'll turn to the sportsmen, all fit from their games, into conquerors of lands, asking them to bring back jewels, spices, and more."

The King went back to his dressing room, the crowd to its classes. And the swindlers are still roaming the halls of universities in Nebraska.

Nebraska novelist Willa Cather, in the short story "One of Ours," speaks of the crowds of students that went to class in Lincoln, Nebraska, when she describes Claude:

> He had grown up with the conviction that it was beneath his dignity to explain himself, just as it was to dress carefully, or to be caught taking pains about anything. Ernest was the only person he knew who tried to state clearly just why he believed this or that; and people at home thought him very conceited and foreign. It wasn't American to explain yourself; you didn't have to! On the farm you said you would or you wouldn't; that Roosevelt was right, or that he was crazy. You weren't supposed to say more unless you were a stump speaker—if you tried to say more, it was because you liked to hear yourself talk. If you got too much bored, you went to town and bought something new.[2]

Claude was not as yet a university graduate, but he never wanted to be "caught taking pains about anything." Ernest, whom "the people at home thought... very conceited and foreign," is an example of what a university education is supposed to foster. A graduate prepared

2. "One of Our Own," in *Willa Cather: Early Novels and Stories* (New York: Viking Press, 1987), 977.

to give a biological, chemical, physical, mathematical, philosophical, poetic account, as well as "to fill any post with credit, and to master any subject with facility." Ernest is foreign to the multitude. The emperor is uncovered by the child in the tale because the child could not be dismissed as having an agenda. He spoke not from self-interest or conceit. He spoke as a foreigner. Each member in the crowd had his reason for not speaking, but his reason was not rational so much as it was the result of rationalizing, using intellect to make excuses and cover the truth for personal convenience. For Aristotle "there are many ways of going wrong; for evil is in its nature infinite... but there is only one possible way of going right." A university education takes one out of the crowd, out of the chorus mouthing clique-hype; away from the latest ideologies masquerading as principles for the social engineers.

Willa Cather looking over her Nebraska saw many Claudes but few Ernests. It is not that the Claudes cannot be like Ernest, but they are not encouraged in the art of disciplined thought. —Is there anything greater than high school sports! If our academic programs were measured like our athletic programs, where disciplined practice strives after excellence, the liberal arts would be having yet another losing season. It is a universal law that like begets like. If the incoming freshmen are ill-prepared, and they must be, as the general studies program is a repetition of high school courses, it is because their teachers went through the same college. A chairman who is aspiring to go even "higher" in administration recently told me, "philosophy is an elitist discipline because everyone cannot understand it, and while philosophy courses were attracting the better students, his department had to teach everyone." (Little did he know I had finished high school with a D average, started community college after four years of military service and was awakened to my mind by reading Descartes, Dostoyevsky, Camus, Wittgenstein—to mention a few—in my mid-twenties, and by teachers who pushed me.) Furthermore, he argued, if the standards were raised, we would lose enrollment and that would mean faculty positions. Like it or not, his department was getting them through.

Are we in the business of turning students to thought or simply turning students out? I had never thought of the University of Nebraska at Kearney as a government job program for the faculty.

This man would not be a member of Newman's University, as his words were like the Emperor's: all appearance, no substance. Willa Cather knew that not all the teachers at the University of Nebraska resembled the multitude they taught. Listen to what happened to Claude when he went to Lincoln:

> As soon as he reached Lincoln in September, he had matriculated at the State University for special work in European History. The year before he had heard the head of the department lecture for some charity, and resolved that even if he were not allowed to change his college, he would manage to study under that man. The course Claude selected was one upon which a student could put as much time as he chose. It was based upon the reading of historical sources, and the Professor was notoriously greedy for full notebooks. Claude's were of the fullest. He worked early and late at the University Library, often got his supper in town and went back to read until closing hour. For the first time he was studying a subject which seemed to him vital, which had to do with events and ideas, instead of with lexicons and grammars.[3]

This is more in line with Newman's idea of a faculty member, as reason is the faculty which enables us to see order in the universe, to see ideas and moral principles—not just "lexicons and grammars." To this day there are still such university professors, "the faculty," who reason in their disciplines, in Biology, Chemistry, Mathematics, Music, Philosophy, Literature, Poetry, History, and the like. In the age of the multiversity where countless silly things are being taught, the word faculty has lost its force. To be a member of a faculty, you must belong to a discipline. For example, teaching, in and of itself, is not a discipline any more than Education is a College. It has no subject. Chemistry, on the other hand, is a discipline with a faculty.

3. Ibid., 971–2.

It would not cost a cent to improve the education of the multitudes in Nebraska. Have the faculty from the various disciplines certify the teachers of literature, chemistry, art, biology, geography, history, math, physical science, which are the academic subjects in public schools. Some will argue that without teacher training the students will not know how to teach. This is a myth. Any graduate of a university has been watching his teachers teach for sixteen years. It is an insult to the student who graduates with an academic degree to think he lacks the energy, will, discipline, imagination and intellect to figure out how his subject should be taught. However, if he lacks these, he should not be given a degree.

In the Middle Ages, Thomas Aquinas reminded the crowd that,

> In all things which are ordered towards an end wherein this or that course may be adopted, some directive principle is needed through which the due end may be reached by the most direct route. A ship, for example, which moves in different directions according to the impulse of the changing winds, would never reach its destination were it not brought to port by the skill of the pilot.[4]

A directive principle is precisely what the disciplines of the academy offer the student who studies with a faculty who steer like a pilot through the changing winds of fashion. Willa Cather additionally knew that without receptive students, the Ernests, the most we could ever hope to offer the students in Nebraska is what appears to be an education. But what of the others? The not so earnest? "Since you never said anything, you didn't form the habit of thinking. If you got too much bored, you went to town and bought something new."

And the swindlers?, well, they are always ready to sell us "something new" when we get to town.

---

4. Thomas Aquinas, *On Kingship*, trans. Gerald B. Phelan (Toronto: Pontifical Institute of Mediaeval Studies), 3.

The Bald-headed Tinkers of Academe

Bad colleges and universities are those whose faculties bear elegant titles and at commencement appear in flashy gowns and hoods, but whose students do not learn foreign or ancient languages, the history and principles of philosophy, and the techniques of thought, but gaining their degrees by accumulating "credits" in various unrelated, and usually trivial, subjects, most of them involving the sort of current events studied in high school. Bad colleges and universities finally extrude with impressive credentials students whose essays, if any, have never received rigorous criticism requiring them to revise substantially. Bad colleges and universities consist of students (and certainly faculties) devoid of curiosity except where it can be shown to result in academic promotion.... Bad colleges and universities create students who automatically join the labor force without the capacity to wonder what they're doing or whether their work is right or wrong, noble or demeaning.[1]

These words belong to Paul Fussell, whom some of you know as the author of *Poetic Meter and Poetic Form*. They are from his book *Bad or the Dumbing Down of America* and were sent to the offices of *The Examined Life* by a former student who is off in graduate school reading, amongst other things, Samuel Johnson. Anyway, at this week's staff meeting, we set about discussing whether or not Paul Fussell was correct in his analysis of bad colleges and universities and to see if our little university of the plains qualified.

1. Paul Fussell, *Bad, or The Dumbing of America* (New York: Simon & Schuster, 1962).

The Senior Executive of Waste Management Artisan pointed out that Fussel was obviously making a sweeping generalization when he wrote that bad colleges and universities "are those whose faculties bear elegant titles and at commencement appear in flashy gowns and hoods, but whose students do not learn foreign languages, the history and principles of philosophy, and the techniques of thought, etc." The staff agreed with the Executive Senior Waste Management Artisan that Fussell should have said that "some" of the faculty instead of "whose faculty," which assumes all the faculty of a college and not just some of the faculty, are strutting about like peacocks festooned in their hoods of many colors at commencement, and who themselves do not "know a foreign or ancient language, the history and principles of philosophy, the techniques of thought, and who have gained a degree by accumulating credits in various unrelated, and usually trivial, subjects, most of them involving the sort of current events studied in high school."

In other words, a hood and a gown a professor does not make, any more than a backpack, jeans, and a T-shirt does a student make, any more than the blocks of buildings housing libraries, labs, and equipment does a university make. The reason colleges and universities are getting such a bad name is that the people who have joined the ranks of professorship are not what they appear to be. So while we enjoy putting "Dr." in front of our names on our personalized checks, office doors, and mailboxes, we do not spend the necessary hours to have our students work at levels expected of college students.

In fact, as a Junior Waste Management Artisan recalling Plato pointed out, if Fussell is right, the university is filling up with "bald-headed tinkers." This is why Fussell thinks it is important to know the "history and principles of philosophy."

Anyone who knows the history of philosophy is familiar with the distinction between a sophist and a philosopher, between one who uses reason to have *his* way and one who, being obedient to reason, has control of himself and seeks truth. In book six of Plato's *Republic*, Socrates discusses the difference between the sophists and the philosophers and why those in philosophy are getting such a bad name. The sophists are those who hire themselves out as teachers and do not teach anything other than the convictions that the majority expresses. In other words, a sophist is not interested in using reason to arrive at truth, but he does use reason to rationalize whatever is fashionable or necessary to win his part of an argument. Thus the definition of a sophist, to this day, is "a scholar or a thinker, especially one skillful in devious argumentation" and a sophistic argument is one which is fallacious. The philosophers are those who love and pursue wisdom by intellectual means and moral self-discipline.

Philosophy is the love of wisdom and begins with the act of wonder in the human soul about the meaning and purpose of one's own existence and the knowledge of the world and the universe. In this respect, anyone who wonders about what he ought to do with his life in his place in the world or about the world and the starry night is a philosopher. If you wonder long and hard about the stars, the end of your degree program is a Doctor of Philosophy in Astronomy; if you wonder long and hard about the animal kingdom, the end of your degree program is a Doctor of Philosophy in Biology, and so on throughout the liberal arts and sciences. Coming down from the middle ages, the term "doctor" is reserved for those who are so well-versed in a department of knowledge that they are able to teach.

Back to the bald-headed tinker. If the doctors of philosophy in the various disciplines of knowledge are not suited to their positions, the profession fills up with sophists, the pretenders who do not know the history of philosophy or its means of thought, and who, lacking the spark of wonder, are unable to promote wonder in the souls of their students. In the words of Plato:

> And it's a reasonable thing to say, for other little men—the ones who are most sophisticated at their own little crafts—seeing that this position, which is full of fine names and adornments, is vacated, leap gladly from those little crafts to philosophy, like prisoners escaping from jail who take refuge in a temple.... Don't you think that a man of this sort looks

exactly like a little bald-headed tinker who has come into some money and, having been just released from jail, has taken a bath, put on a cloak, got himself up as a bridegroom, and is about to marry the boss's daughter because she is poor and abandoned?... What about when men who are unworthy of education approach philosophy and consort with her unworthily? What kinds of thoughts and opinions are we to say they beget? Won't they truly be what are properly called sophisms, things that have nothing genuine about them or worthy of being called true wisdom?[2]

Fussell laments about institutions which appear to be colleges and universities but in actuality are not college and universities. They are something else, post high school centers where very few students are challenged to work themselves into the intellectual shape necessary to read and understand *The Federalist Papers*, *The Brothers Karamazov*, *On the Origin of the Species*, *King Lear*, *Nicomachean Ethics*, *The Rise and Fall of the Third Reich*, or even Plato's *Republic*.

The Assistant Senior Executive of Waste Management Artisan concluded our weekly staff meeting by comparing today's colleges and universities to country clubs. The professors are tenured pros who have been given the keys to the clubhouse lounge and bar, as well as the freedom to play as many rounds of golf as they please. They have been hired by the owners, who are the taxpayers of the state, to teach the children of the state. The sophists are those who appear to be professors in these colleges and universities but spend more time in the bar and lounge than on the course. Students are attracted to the sophists' courses because their classes require little if any effort and are as demanding as sitting in a sports bar in front of a big screen television can be. The philosophers are the professors in colleges and universities who, like club pros, spend their time on their course and drive themselves to work their students into the shape necessary to wonder and

2. Edith Hamilton and Huntington Cairs, eds., *Collected Dialogues of Plato* (Princeton: Princeton University Press, 1961), Republic, 495d.

to understand the authors, poets, philosophers, and scientists of their disciplines.

The country club is managed by administrators who evaluate their success by having the members, the university students, evaluate whether or not they enjoyed their stay at the country club. It is not surprising that the students who stumble out of the lounge think they have received a fine education.

Is it any wonder colleges and universities are graduating scads of students who automatically join the labor force "without the capacity to wonder what they're doing or whether their work is right or wrong, noble or demeaning?"

And when these students leave the colleges and universities, they will find the education they received from the sophists is to higher education what miniature golf is to the game of golf. We should not be surprised if throughout their lives, they are in the rough, far from the fair way. But will they ever even realize their loss?

And so it goes.

When Values Are Lifestyles, Pimps Will Be Saints

I came across a proposal or a policy written by either a committee or an individual. I do not know, as it, as all such things, was not signed. Nevertheless, there are several ideas worth examining in these words. We will look at it in bits. First the heading: "CULTURAL DIVERSITY OBJECTIVES." All caps (so we know this is going to be important!). Then a list of objectives:

> To teach understanding, tolerance, and appreciation of cultural diversity.
>
> If we hope to achieve a more peaceful and harmonious world, we must develop a tolerance for those whose values and lifestyles differ from our own.

I doubt if anyone is against the idea of a "more peaceful and harmonious world," especially if it can be achieved through college courses. But how will the professor teaching "tolerance and appreciation of cultural diversity" ever know if his students are actually tolerant and appreciative of others rather than just mouthing the right answer for a grade? There must be some way to tell if the course objective has been accomplished, lest the professor, hoping for a "more peaceful and harmonious world," will not be able to assess the outcome of the established objective. Obviously an instrument needs to be devised to measure the tolerance levels of a student to determine when he has crossed the line of bigotry and become tolerant of others "whose values and lifestyles differ from his own."

Until a tolerance instrument is devised we may as well tell stories. Once upon a time there was a group of people who were going to stone a woman for committing adultery. They refused to tolerate her actions because she had broken the law; not to mention upsetting at least one family in their town. And maybe she even upset some of the members of crowd who thought she might talk and expose them—who also knew her in the carnal sense. Who knows, the story does not go into detail. All we know is that they were ready to execute the law: "anyone who is caught in the act of adultery is to be stoned." They were ready to pick up stones and throw them, till they were stopped by a question: "He that is without sin among you, let him first cast a stone at her."

This question was not addressed to the mob; but to each member of the mob. They stood there for a moment thinking. The question did not ask them to tolerate the woman, or appreciate her "lifestyle," and it did not ask them to stop throwing stones. It simply asked if they were innocent. They answered with their feet, "being convicted by their own conscience."

Then the woman was asked by the one remaining man, "Woman, where are those thine accusers? hath no man condemned thee?" She said they had not. The questions may have led her to believe that her life had been spared from a death by stoning, at least from her accusers, but there was still one man who had not left. Perhaps he was going to throw a stone. Then he spoke again, "Neither do I condemn thee." Maybe she was relieved when he told her that he would not stone her; and perhaps she thought this meant that he tolerated her actions, given that he had not cast a stone. But then he finished speaking with a command, "Go and sin no more."

This story draws a line in the sand between the law, tolerance, forgiveness and love, a story forgotten, or never heard, by those who thought up the first objective. When people have reached the point where they can no longer tolerate each other, they need a strong police force, like the one in South Africa, to keep the Zulu from hacking each other to death or harnessing men in burning tires to watch them burn. Without law and its authority to protect citizens from each other, people live, as Thomas Hobbes, the seventeenth-century philosopher, described in a state of "continual fear, and danger of violent death," and such a life is "solitary, poor, nasty, brutish and short." But is this any different from a nation where parents simply tolerate their children's actions, friends simply tolerate their friend's actions, and neighbors simply tolerate their neighbor's actions, no matter how vicious or cruel? Furthermore, imagine a man who was tolerant of his own actions; who was never ashamed.

In order to be moral, a human being needs to be intolerant of some of his actions. Having a free will does not leave a person with the singular decision of whether to do right or wrong, good or evil; it is choosing amongst a multiplicity of wills fighting for control of one's soul and believing that there is one good and proper way to live. Socrates thought he would fail to be human if he placed the idols of money and honors before virtue. At the end of Socrates' apology, his speech before the senate of Athens, he tells the senators how they should care for his sons whom he will soon orphan:

> When my sons grow up, gentlemen, if you think that they are putting money or anything else before goodness, take your revenge by plaguing them as I plagued you; and if they fancy themselves for no reason, you must scold them just as I scolded you, for neglecting the important things and thinking that they are good for something when they are good for nothing.[1]

Socrates was the first philosopher in the western world to be directed by his conscience, which never told him what to do; it only told him when he was doing wrong. If Socrates' sons can pay attention to their conscience and not the idols in the market place, they will

---

1. Edith Hamilton and Huntington Cairs, eds., *Collected Dialogues of Plato* (Princeton: Princeton University Press, 1961), Apology, 41e.

become human beings. To do so they must be intolerant of the various voices which are wrestling for their souls, voices of gossip, lust, sloth, and pandering, all of which will turn their souls from the proper end.

Those who suggest tolerance and appreciation of others values and "lifestyles" think every spirit in their souls deserves to be heard, sampled and appreciated. They even go so far as to speak of values in the same breath as "lifestyles." If values were relative, they would be "lifestyles," and each person could fashion a self to his or her liking. Today it may be fashionable to marry and raise children; tomorrow it may be fashionable to father children like a bull in a field of heifers; and the next day it may be fashionable to be a pederast. When values are lifestyles, pimps will be saints.

Benito Mussolini understood the precarious position of the relativist when we wrote:

> From the fact that all ideologies are of equal value, that all ideologies are mere fictions, the modern relativist infers that everybody has the right to create for himself his own ideology and to attempt to enforce it with all the energy of which he is capable.[2]

Implicit in the logic of ideologies is that, like styles, they are relative to the person and the moment. There is no difference between some voluptuous, bestial prank and a heroic feat such as even giving one's life for the good of mankind. When a man fashions himself in his own image, he is his own measure. The member or members of the committee who suggested tolerance as a means of achieving a "more peaceful and harmonious world" have to tolerate every man's actions. They are incapable of discriminating between honorable acts and dishonorable acts, and they will find themselves having to swallow, with a hesitant smile, Thrasymachus' line in Plato's *Republic*, "I affirm that the just is nothing else than the advantage of the stronger."[3]

---

2. *Diuturna* [The Lasting] (1921) as quoted in *Rational Man: A Modern Interpretation of Aristotelian Ethics* (1962) by H. B. Veatch, 20.

3. *Republic*, 338c.

So, while advocating tolerance, we end in accepting the intolerant, lest we be accused of imposing our values, our style, on someone else. Hopefully the person or persons who thought up this idea did not realize what was implicit in this idea. They are probably good-hearted people who have an "ethic of caring"—my gosh, they're for "peace and harmony in the world!"—or then again, perhaps they are sordid people who want their "style" of life to be appreciated by others, to quell the unrest in their souls. But either way, they mistake sentimentality for virtue when they advocate tolerance and appreciation of "values and lifestyles different from our own."

Flannery O'Connor captures the logic of this idea in her essay, "A Memoir of Mary Ann":

> If other ages felt less, they saw more, even though they saw with the blind, prophetical, unsentimental eye of acceptance, which is to say, of faith. In the absence of this faith now, we govern by tenderness. It is a tenderness which, long since cut off from the person of Christ, is wrapped in theory. When tenderness is detached from the source of tenderness, its logical outcome is terror. It ends in forced-labor camps and in the fumes of the gas chamber.[4]

These words are worth repeating, "When tenderness is detached from the source of tenderness, its logical outcome is terror." Whoever wrote "If we hope to achieve a more peaceful and harmonious world" is assuming that peace and harmony are values shared by the various peoples of the world. Who would disagree with anyone advocating such a noble idea? Why it ranks right with "caring for students," "meeting the needs of students," "servicing students," and "teaching students to feel good about themselves." All this is gush. Whoever hoped for a more peaceful and harmonious world? Perhaps it is only the person who suggested the objective, or some of the members of a committee, or the majority of the citizens of Nebraska; or maybe it is a federal

4. Flannery O'Connor, *Mystery and Manners* (New York: Farrar, Straus & Giroux, 1957), 227.

policy that has to be included in the role and mission of a university to receive federal funding. Whatever, the validity of the peace and harmony is not strengthened one iota. It is a rootless ideal. "We hope to achieve a more peaceful and harmonious world" is a passive missive based on a pipedream. It has been cut from its source. It is an impersonal voice pretending to be divine while replacing the New Jerusalem with utopia.

Listen to the second objective:

> To prepare students to function in a multi-cultural world. In order to participate in today's global society, one must understand the various cultures that comprise it.

So there are values and lifestyles which a student should learn so he can "function in a multi-cultural world" and be a citizen of a "global society?" The "global society" is a euphemism for the "workers' paradise," which has been tried on the other side of the Berlin wall, and, as from a phoenix, its hard-nosed beak is now rising out of the ashes as a passive suggestion before some committee in the middle of Nebraska. How easily we forget.

The notion of there being peace on earth passed before the eyes of those who forwarded these "objectives," and it was received like our hearts hearken to it at Christmas, before it is put away with the lights and tinsel till the next season of caring. The person or committee who suggested this policy is forwarding a truth that has been cut from its source. It is like talking about "rights" and "equality" in America while forgetting their source in the Declaration of Independence: "We hold these truths to be self-evident, that all men are created equal; that they are endowed by their Creator with certain unalienable rights; that among these are life, liberty, and the pursuit of happiness." Martin Luther King referred to this exact passage before the Lincoln Memorial and then went on to say, "Now is the time to rise from the dark and desolate valley of segregation to the sunlit path of racial justice. Now is the time to open the door of opportunity to all of God's children. Now is the time to lift our nation from the quick sands of racial injustice to the solid rock of brotherhood."

All talk of having students understand various cultures so there can be peace on earth ("today's global society") is like the lady in Dostoevsky's *The Brother Karamazov* who loves mankind but could not tolerate her neighbor. The task is to understand yourself, not the globe. Now is the time for the members of America, not the "global society," to rise to brotherhood. But Martin Luther King's ideas are overlooked by the same people who are eager to honor him for being a black man. Being a black man is no more honorable than being a white man, as neither is a condition in which a person had a say. It is an accidental quality. However, the quality of his character, like Socrates' and Socrates' sons, is a different matter.

The greatest fear in the academy should be this: slogans and political agendas are blindly accepted without being examined. Do such ideas direct us in the pursuit of truth that brings us to look upon our neighbors as living souls? And if they do not? Well, maybe we should pull out our swords like Cyrano de Bergerac does at the end of his life and attack the various wills trying to gain control of our souls:

> You there—Who are you? A hundred against one.
> I know them now, my ancient enemies—
> Falsehood! ... There! There! Prejudice—Compromise—
> Cowardice (Thrusting)
> What's that? No! Surrender? No!
> Never—never!
> Ah, you too, Vanity!
> I knew you would overthrow me in the end—
> No! I fight on! I fight on! I fight on![5]

---

5. Edmond Ronstad, *Cyrano de Bergerac*, trans. Carol Clark (New York: Penquin Classics, 2005), 224.

Upon Nothing

When at last the veil is lifted, we perceive a wondrous landscape: a world of negations, a world in which, wherever we look for presence we find absence, a world not of people but of vacant idols, a world which offers, in the places where we seek for order, friendship and moral value, only the skeleton of power. There is no creation in this world, though it is full of cleverness—a cleverness actively deployed in the cause of Nothing. It is a world of uncreation, without hope or faith or love, since no "text" could possibly mean those transcendental things. It is a world in which negation has been endowed with the supreme instruments— power and intellect—so making absence into the all-embracing presence. It is, in short, the world of the Devil.[1]

This is the conclusion of the article "Upon Nothing" in the July issue of *The Philosophical Investigations*, in which deconstruction is scrutinized and found to be the heartless lodge of the Devil. Strong words. Especially from a Professor of Philosophy at Boston University. The Devil is a term rarely used in the twentieth century. But for those raised on the pop of the 60's, the devil is little more than Janis Joplin's version of freedom, "as just another word for nothin' left to lose." However, the devil for Scruton reminds us of Dante's Satan, the king of Hell, presiding over a "city of woe" populated by forsaken people "who have lost the good of intellect," who are without remorse for their actions and are beyond asking forgiveness; so, they fester on in their rottenness. Dostoyevsky's Grand Inquisitor

1. Roger Scruton, "Upon Nothing," *Philosophical Investigations* 17/3 (1994): 481–506.

calls him "the wise and dread spirit, the spirit of self-destruction and nonexistence," which is a fitting description for a king who rules those who reject spiritual values by yielding to bestial appetites, violence or perversion of their human intellect to enact fraud and malice against their fellowman. Such people turn the world around them into the land of uncreation, a world "without hope or faith or love, ...in which negation has been endowed with the supreme instruments—power and intellect—so making absence into the all-embracing presence."

How is it that absence can be made into an all-embracing presence? Perhaps the answer to this question can be approached through the converse of the idea, of there being a presence in the all-embracing absence. The presence in an "all-embracing absence" is what cloaks a person's soul like a December hoarfrost when his parents, siblings, friends and countrymen die. When some people walk out of life, they are more alive than when they were alive. Perhaps this is because they were taken for granted and now that they have fallen into the darkness, the mystery of their ever having been present is magnified. Though they are in the ground, that they remain in a living room chair, in books, letters, and photo albums, and in the doorway through which they passed still cloaks the air. It is as though the air that became their breath, their *spiritus*, still remains behind.

To deny such a presence in the air left behind by the overwhelming absence of the dead results in a world of negation where the memories, the words and the ways of ancestors have no staying power. It is to deny the life of a creature within creation, who is aligned with creation and whose creative force passes through his life like a stream of water. Without such a force, the air is spiritless, "making absence into the all-embracing presence"—a world "not of people but of vacant idols." It is a world of people who have forsaken their souls, who are absorbed in their own stream of consciousness which is formed by immediate experiences. Such a vision is shrouded in the universe of immediacy, bobbing in the current events, of Bosnia, of Israel, of the ATT merger, of O. J. Simpson, of Dolly Parton's breasts at the super market check-out

counter, with each moment washing over the next, all equally important. Those who are lodged in the universe of immediacy are unaware
of what has come before them, the source of the breath which has
flowed through and shaped their thoughtful ancestors. The residents
of immediacy are like children whose unreflective minds are absorbed
in the needs of the moment, thinking freedom lies in the instant gratification of their desires.

To be absorbed in one's self results in self-idolatry which cuts a
person off from the source of hope, faith and love, the vessels which
nurture the soul in the relationships of a family and a community. We
are the offspring of the living stream carrying the spirit of the source.
Varsonofiev spoke of such a stream in *August 1914*:

> History is a river, it has its own laws which govern its currents, its
> twists and turns, its eddies. But wiseacres come along and say that it
> is a stagnant pond, and that it must be drained off into another and
> better channel, that it is just a matter of choosing the right place to dig
> the ditch. But you cannot interrupt a river, a stream. Disrupt its flow
> by a few centimeters—and there is no living stream. And here we are
> being asked to make a break of thousands of meters. The bonds between
> generations, institutions, traditions, customs, are what keep the stream
> flowing uninterruptedly.[2]

The spirit of "self-destruction and nonexistence" negates the spiritual side of a person's life that is the *spiritus*, "the breath of life," which
covers a person in creation like water shrouds a fish. The negators of
spirit pollute the air in Varsonofiev's river and want to free the fish by
taking him out of the water. The "wiseacre" who is abandoned in the
universe of immediacy thinks he is in a stagnant pond long polluted
by traditional ways of life no longer relevant. So now the stagnant
pond needs to be drained into a new and better channel. The question
becomes one of deciding where to dig the ditch.

2. Aleksandr Solzhenitsyn, *August 1914*, trans. Michael Glenny (New York: Farrar,
Straus and Giroux, 1972), 474.

By denying the breath of life, those who negate the spirit deflate language as the vehicle of the living word, the medium which flows through generations carrying hope and promise to those who live on in creation. For the "wiseacres" there is only the "text" in a world which humans create, where there is no transcendental creator, no meaning to life, no real reason to read as language does not flow between souls with the purpose of assisting in the development of a person's conscience. In fact, the human world is a solipsistic construct where each reading of a "text" is a new experience that is open to interpretation. It is a current view which any freshman can recite, "I am unique because no one looks like me, has had the same experiences or has the same feelings as I." This line of reasoning leads to no one being able to understand anyone else, as each person is the recipient of private sense data which has formed his private, subjective reality. In fact, if an author were to reread his own words, they would have an entirely different meaning than when he first wrote them.

The desecration of the word as the vehicle of asking, thanking, cursing, greeting, praying, discussing, promising, and making vows between souls is replaced by the nebulous intentions of the moment. In place of the spirit, the basis for order, friendship, and moral value, the wiseacre places "a cleverness actively deployed in the cause of Nothing."

Nietzsche, in the *Twilight of the Idols*, wrote of such a skeleton when he looked into the abyss of absence, of the meaningless of creation, and saw its all-embracing presence:

> Today, as we have entered into the reverse movement and we immoralists are trying with all our strength to take the concept of guilt and the concept of punishment out of the world again, and to cleanse psychology, history, nature, and social institutions and sanctions of them, there is in our eyes no more radical opposition than that of the theologians, who continue with the concept of a "moral world-order" to infect the innocence of becoming by means of "punishment" and guilt.... What alone can be our doctrine? That no one gives man his qualities—neither

God, nor society, nor his parents and ancestors, nor he himself. No one is responsible for man's being there at all.... Man is not the effect of some special purpose, of a will, and end; nor is he the object of an attempt to attain an "ideal of humanity" or an "ideal of happiness" or an "ideal of morality." It is absurd to wish to devolve one's essence on some end or other. We have invented the concept of "end": in reality there is no end.[3]

Nietzsche's "reverse movement" tears down the boundaries of civility for an unbound freedom. There is no one and no thing for a person to blame or credit, as there is no purpose to life. No one is responsible because there is nothing for which to be responsible. No one is capable of judging another man as there are no standards by which to compare people's actions. "So, which way do you want to go?" ask the immoralists, knowing all the while that there is no way to go. "Where should we dig the ditch?" is the question the wiseacre asks while looking down on the herd of humanity who they think are too timid to ask such a question as they float in the stagnant pond of tradition. But the strong, the "wiseacres" who have the "will to power" take up the shovel and begin the ditch.

The twentieth century will be remembered as one which belonged to the clever ditch diggers, the powerful who tried to channel the sacredness of the flow into their system of the Marxist, Capitalist or the Globalist. They all shared in the denial of the moral side of life for the material quality of some of the earth's people. So now is a time when health is more important than virtue, when therapists are more important than teachers, when the Sabbath is just another day of the week at the mega-mart. In this world of uncreation, people are understood as being the "products of their environment," members of a class, that is either upper, middle or lower. It is a world of the haves and the have nots. The haves live in the first world while the have-nots live in

---

3. Walter Kaufmann, ed. and trans., *The Portable Nietzsche* (New York: Viking Penguin, 1968), 500.

the third world. It is a world in which the gift of life is no longer carried into eternity. It is a world in which the "quality of life" is measured in the momentary enjoyment of a lifestyle freed from suffering. Once the quality is gone, it is time to pull the plug.

This is too philosophical?

John Lillis was right when he argued in a previous issue of *The Examined Life* that most the students who attend this university,

> are not here to imbibe the wisdom of the ages from the philosophy professor …but rather to learn a skill or acquire the credentials which will aid them in making a living in the very unsheltered world they must reenter when they leave the ivied halls of the alma mater. Very few independently wealthy people attend this or any other university, or ever have attended universities in general. The skills and credentials students acquire here are considered by them of "value" because of the way the world economy is structured.

But then again students come to a university because they are uneducated and they want to learn. It is a mistake to suppose that the primary end of education is to make a living. Especially in these times when 50% of marriages end in divorce, more children than ever are born out of wedlock, "youth development centers"—a euphemism for reform schools—are overflowing with children from broken homes, and self-abuse through drugs, food and alcohol in the young, middle aged and elderly is continuing to rise. When the health of the nation is measured by spiritual standards, we are bursting at the seams.

As a teacher I am not interested in students "making a living"; they are already able to do that. It takes but a day in America to find a job painting houses, jack hammering, washing sheets, tele-marketeering during the dinner hour, brush-hogging, building fence, waiting tables, washing dishes, driving a garbage truck, or rebuilding hydraulic pumps; unless, of course, one thinks these jobs are beneath him.

If the students of which John Lillis writes understood Latin, they would know that an *alma mater* is a "mother who fosters or nourishes," and that it was not until the 17th century that the term began to be used in English with reference to a person's former school or college, a place of intellectual and spiritual nourishment. If the veil of our university were lifted, would a place of intellectual and spiritual nourishment be found? No doubt there are teachers—and students!—who concern themselves with spiritual and intellectual nourishment, who like Socrates think teaching to be an art like midwifery, of assisting in the birth of thought in a student's soul. Such a teacher's task is not to speak his mind, not to inform students, but to have a mind. It is the sign of a liberally educated person that he is not led by fashion, fancy, or the universe of immediacy which feeds on desires.

This is not a university in the spirit of a university if its teachers are bent only on teaching "skills" which a student can market. The businesses will train our graduates for the task they wish them to perform. When John writes of universities as providing economic benefits for the faculty who have "a guaranteed job for life, at taxpayers' expense," he makes it sound as though the university was a sanatorium for wheezing intellectuals safely musing down some lazy river, (and it may be so for some!) who justify their sheltered existence by training students to be narrow-minded specialists, who will need other narrow-minded specialists to make decisions which lie outside their specialty, like being able to cope in a relationship, or some nifty techniques for handling the stress of Christmas. This university ought to be a place which houses the best minds of Nebraska and challenges her students with thoughtful discourse, which is far more valuable to the future of our state's citizenry than solely being taught the necessary skills to get gainful employment, which only addresses the lure of big bucks.

Albert Einstein once noted:

> It is not enough to teach man a specialty. Though it may become a kind of useful machine but not a harmoniously developed personality. It is essential that the students acquire an understanding of and a lively feeling for values. He must acquire a vivid sense of the beautiful and of the morally good. Otherwise he—with his specialized knowledge—more

closely resembles a well-trained dog than a harmoniously developed person.[4]

It is not enough for students, "to learn a skill or acquire the credentials which will aid them in making a living." A teacher's task is to take the student out of the shallows of self-immersion for which education is sought to make a living, so as to be some kind of "well-trained dog." Lest we forget, Man is the only creature who knows that he is going to die, so if the end, the "telos," of a university is to give a student the "means to make a living," it would be offering only half the story. A university education must discuss what is worthy of life, what ought to be loved and what ought to be done with a life while it is flowing down the stream. An alma mater ought to be remembered as the place which gave birth to a thoughtful life, as the parent who not only provided the means of living, but prepared her offspring for a meaningful life in the presence of the all-embracing presence.

(What would a university education be worth in the times of economic collapse?)

To teach is to participate in creation, to give shape to the living breath of ancestors and witness the birth of ideas in students. When John Lillis writes of the "very unsheltered world [students] must reenter when they leave the ivied halls of their alma mater," he is not using the language of creation, but of uncreation, of the fear of being left alone in creation without the "credentials for an occupation."

A teacher's task is not worth much these days, a fact I was reminded of in a recent article in the local newspaper which gave the annual state of the campus to the citizens of central Nebraska. It was a thorough report, listing the "economic input" of the university, its budget and payroll, student spending, monies spent by conference participants and other sundry events. When all was said and done the university at Kearney "pumped" over two hundred million dollars into the local

4. Einstein, 54.

economy. There were no reports on the quality of the students' writing, how many understood Shakespeare, Aristotle, Jung, Newton, the laws of inanimate nature or sung "The Messiah," or how many of our alumni celebrated wedding anniversaries, successfully raised their children, or were mourned. No, all that was presented was "the skeleton of power."

However, not everyone who works in this mental institution thinks the purpose of our lives is reflected in the monies we generate in the local economy; nor is the success of our students determined by how much money they end up making in the "real world."

When an education is judged by monetary standards we find, "a world not of people but of vacant idols, a world which offers, in the place where we seek for order, friendship and moral value only the skeleton of power." Yes, money is power King Midas. But it is a vacant idol. It is an idol because money cannot buy friendship, self-control, make a person moral or worthy of respect. Money has nothing to do with creation but everything to do with appearance. To focus upon money as a means of measuring worth implies the highest paid people are the worthiest members of the community, and we know this simply is not the case just as we know that the best parents within our community are not determined by the neighborhoods in which they live.

In all of this, I am reminded of T. S. Elliot in his *Four Quartets*:

> "Go, go, go, said the bird: humankind
> Cannot bear very much reality,
> Time past and time future
> What might have been and what has been
> Point to one end, which is always present."
> So I wonder, "What is the end which is always present?"

Henry Higgins to the Rescue!

The other day I received the newsletter of the Learning Skills Center and was privileged to some valuable information. After fifty years of research, it has been concluded by Johnson O'Connor Research Foundation Human Engineering Laboratory that "... corporate positions usually arrange themselves in a hierarchy, or rank order, of vocabulary knowledge." What is to be done? Obviously a broadened vocabulary is the key to success, if you are employed by a corporation that has positions that arrange themselves. If you are not in such a corporation then you will have to wait for someone to put you in your place.

Personally I prefer the former to the latter. Years ago, when I was a part-time graduate student, I worked for the Sperry-Vickers Corporation in Columbia, Missouri, as a warehouser (the neutered version of "warehouseman," thought to be sexist by someone in a higher circle). Of the seventy warehousepersons—how's that for a word?—twenty-five of us had college degrees, five of which were beyond the bachelor's—or should I say a single degree. Nevertheless, our vocabularies were beyond those of our supervisors and our fellow workers, and you know what, one Monday morning my time card was missing when I went to clock in. I went to my supervisor for an explanation. To my surprise the reason my time card was missing was that, while talking with a warehouseperson about physical beauty being cultural as opposed to universal, I had said, "In some societies it would be considered callipygian if it is not steatopygian." The corporate positions had

rearranged themselves in a hierarchy of vocabulary and I had unknowingly exchanged positions with my supervisor, at least until he had the
presence of mind to go to the local vocabulary-building center where
after just six weeks he added four hundred words to his vocabulary. So
the corporate positions again arranged themselves, and I found myself
clocking-in and back on the forklift. Oh well!

Back to the guys at Johnson O'Connor's, the educationalist huck-
sters who conjure up "data" for the cause of "Vocabulary Expansion"
classes taught across the land for the innocent, the eager, and the
doomed. They concluded: "The final answer seems to be that words
are the instruments by means of which men and women grasp the
thoughts of others and with which they do much of their own thinking. They are the tools of thought." Notice the Johnsons are not sure of
their conclusion: "it seems to be" is not an affirmation of a fact but a
statement of doubt. You *seem* to be my mother. You *seem* to be a man.
I *seem* to live here. But "seem" is much too common a word to be an
"instrument" in a "Vocabulary Expansion" class. Let us be philosophical and wonder for a moment. If words "seem to be the instruments by
which humans grasp the thoughts of others" then the guys and gals at
Johnson's Lab are not sure you grasp even your thoughts with words;
furthermore, they have implied that there are other ways of grasping
the thoughts of men and women, and I suppose there are, if you want
to spend your time learning body language. (Do we have a course in
that yet? Is there a "need out there"? Better check North Platte.)

Better yet, ask yourselves this: Do words "seem to be the instruments" by means of which you understand others and do your thinking? Once again the experts at the Human Engineering Laboratory are
not sure words even capture thoughts. When my wife asks me to take
out the trash am I ever sure that is what she means? Wouldn't it be
nice if we had some other means of knowing what students thought,
say looking into their eyes—I think someone at Kearney State College
is already doing that—or taking their temperature? And even if we
have to use words, why don't we just ask them if they feel good about

themselves? And if they don't, play records for them and let them sit in little circles and "share and care" about each other's experiences until they do. Or have them learn big words so they impress the interviewers from corporations? And if that doesn't work we could call in Professor Higgins to transform magically the Eliza Doolittles among us (all together now: "The R-a-i-n in S-p-a-i-n..."). Get serious! Do you think anyone is going to be charmed by an expansive vocabulary? Life should be so easy.

Why don't we at Kearney State college. concentrate our efforts on providing an academic education to the students instead of helpful hints like "dressing for success" or the promise of "safe sex" and "healthful living." We can do this by having students take courses that will discipline their thoughts, so they won't be at the mercy of their desires and end up resembling animals capable only of behaving and never of acting. It is dishonest to tell students their vocabulary is their key to success in a corporation and give them one hour of credit in Vocabulary Expansion, which may be applied to their total hours to meet graduation requirements. Give the students courses in literature and point them to the library, where I am sure there are more people willing to help them, and they will be on their way to developing a mind, and maybe even a vocabulary.

Evaluating Administrators at UNK
"There are no correct answers"

Your Dean would appreciate your candid evaluation of his/her performance. There are no "correct" answers to any of these questions. Your opinion, along with those of others, will help the Dean recognize how well he/she is meeting your expectations and his/her own professional goals. A position description for the Dean is attached.... Evaluators were selected on the basis of recommendations from a representative college committee and from the Dean. All evaluations will be anonymous and confidential.

This is the opening paragraph of an eight page—count them—questionnaire to evaluate my Dean. It is admirable that my Dean "would appreciate [my] candid evaluation of his/her professional performance." However, reason demands that I ask, why would a Dean want a "candid evaluation" of his/her performance and not want to know from whom these "candid" remarks came, as "all evaluations will be anonymous and confidential"? Furthermore, who would consent to give a "candid evaluation" of a Dean's abilities, or lack thereof, after being told "there are no 'correct' answers to any of the twenty-six questions"?

Realizing that the Dean of the College of Fine Arts and Humanities did not compose the questionnaire, as he is not a he/she or a his/her, we had our Asst. Circulation Program Director call around and he found out the questionnaire was not composed by Deans but a committee of the Faculty Senate. It appears that the members of the committee wish to remain "anonymous" as no one signed the questionnaire. And they obviously did not want to offend those who do not understand that the proper English pronoun that refers to the concept "man" is "he," so they chose to use the politically correct inclusive language.

Perhaps the liberal side of my education is too liberal when I expect that what the faculty is teaching the students in the General Studies Program should apply to the faculty themselves. You do remember the part in the university catalogue about, "the liberally educated person... [who] is able to think independently, to question, to analyze, to interpret, to judge."

So I ask, are the faculty members supposed to question, to analyze, to interpret, to judge every scrap of paper that clogs their mailboxes, or are they simply to follow directions, fill out questionnaires and become mindless team players waiting to be coached?

Imagine if the faculty of this small university were to act like liberally educated students questioning, analyzing, interpreting and judging the questionnaire regarding the Dean's performance before filling it out.

But, to shorten this assignment, we will examine the directions for the questionnaire quoted at the top of this page and only two of the twenty-six questions. We will then apply the four skills of a liberally educated person—to question, analyze, interpret and judge—to the directions and the questions.

We have been asked to give our "candid evaluation" of the Dean's performance so the Dean can "recognize how well he/she is meeting our expectations and his/her own professional goals" by answering twenty-six questions.

Question: Is there anything wrong with the directions? Our analysis: If there are "no correct answers" why would the Dean want our candid evaluation of his performance? Our interpretation: The person or committee who has made up the questionnaire thinks the Dean's position is one in which there are no correct ways in which a Dean ought to function, or, perhaps, the faculty is incapable of judgment, or the committee is trying to help a Dean realize his/her "professional goal" in a profession which has no goals. Our judgment: If there are no correct answers to the ways in which a Dean performs, then the members of the committee are posing questions to which there are no answers and wasting our time. But before passing judgment on the questionnaire, we must first look at several of the questions.

> Question twenty: Honesty: The Dean deals with faculty on many important matters and over an extended time period. Faculty should not only have faith in the Dean's good intentions, but confidence that the Dean's actions will not contradict his/her words.

The liberally educated faculty member is now asked to choose a number on a scale between one and seven. For example, number one on the scale: "The Dean is honest and sincere. One can rely on his/her word." And number seven on the scale: "The Dean is often dishonest and insincere. One cannot rely on his/her word."

The faculty member, in acting as a "liberally educated student," should now assign a number between one and seven. Simple enough. Now apply the four steps of the liberally educated person: to question, to analyze, to interpret and to judge. Question: If number one is circled we would be agreeing that "The Dean is honest and sincere," but as there are "no correct answers," then would we be wrong in thinking that the Dean is "honest and sincere" and that we should "rely on his/her word?" However, if number seven is circled we will be agreeing that the Dean is often "dishonest and insincere," but as there are "no correct answers," then we will be wrong to think that the Dean is "dishonest and insincere" every time his words fail to correspond with his/her actions. Our analysis: the logic of the directions makes the question nonsensical. Our interpretation: the people who created the questionnaire do not think honesty is a virtue—a correct way of acting, but think virtues are opinions, matters of perceptions, views, which are neither right or wrong. Our judgment: the people who created the questionnaire are relativists who think that one person cannot judge whether another person is honest, which also means they cannot judge whether they themselves are honest. Such people are not to be trusted.

Question twenty-two: Fairness: Like everyone, the Dean has social preferences. These should, however, be separated from professional feelings so that social preferences do not affect the institutional program.

Number one on the scale: "The Dean never allows social preferences to influence professional responsibilities" and number seven on the scale: "Knowingly or not, the Dean "plays favorites."

Question: What are "social preferences" and "professional feelings [which might] affect the institutional program?" Our analysis: A "social preference" is something like a "sexual preference" and the Dean, "like everyone" has certain propensities which might lead him/her to believe something like homosexuality to be a sin. But, "like everyone," this is just a "social preference," and as "there are no correct answers," ways we "ought" to live our lives, we sure do not want a Dean who cannot separate "social preferences" from "professional feelings," because the "social preferences" might "affect the institutional program." Our question: What exactly are the "professional feelings" which, "like everyone," professionals are supposed to harbor? Our analysis: It is said of prostitutes that they don't love their clients; sure, they go through the motions, their "professional feelings," and tell the he/she that he/she is wonderful. But deep down everyone is just another John/Jill, another he/she. Is a Dean supposed to have "professional feelings," which are supposed to negate his social preferences, a way of pretending to feel which is just an act, and should he/she be expected to nod his/her head in approval at every asinine quirk some faculty member wants to float by her/him? Our interpretation: a Dean is not able to think without his thought being clouded by "social preferences," which also cloud everyone else's thinking. Our judgement: A Dean is not liberally educated and is therefore unable to think independently and "to question, to analyze, to interpret and to judge." In place of thought a

Dean has "professional feelings" which override "social preferences" if, in fact, the Dean is functioning as a Dean.

Number 7 "Knowingly or not, the Dean plays favorites."

Question: Do we have Deans who are not "knowingly" aware of their actions? Our analysis: the fact that a Dean plays favorites should trouble the faculty if the "favorites" the Dean is playing lack talent and are simply agreeable sorts who are incapable of independent thought and have gravitated to committee work and "service to the university" because they cannot teach or do research. However, if the Dean is playing favorites like someone who bets at horse races, it makes good sense to bet on the favorites who are established teachers and thinkers. Our Interpretation: The people who wrote up the questionnaire do not think that a Dean is able to think, to discriminate between the faculty and judge who are the superior, marginal and inferior faculty members, and they think that equals and unequals alike ought to be treated equally. Our Judgment: A Dean ought to "play" the ablest members of his college and let the mediocre ones ride the bench. Thus, the logic of this questionnaire reflects a mind which is incapable of discriminating between who is honest and who is dishonest and which does not recognize his or her betters amongst the faculty. Such a mind, being cast in a relativistic mode, is likely to be attracted to unions which use the military model of rank and time-in-grade and years of service to determine the salaries of faculty. Being unable to make qualitative judgements—"there are no right answers!"—they proceed to quantitative judgments "how long have you been here?" as opposed to merit.

Most of the faculty who evaluate Deans and other such administrators have Doctorates of Philosophy or another terminal degree in a specific discipline, and have attended a major university for approximately seven years. Imagine for a moment if physicians, who attended four years of medical school and several years of residency, were asked in an eight-page form to evaluate the administrators of the hospital in which they practiced with the specifications that "there were no correct answers" to the questions. Do you think a physician would waste time filling out such a form? Furthermore, imagine if professors, who are required by the regents to be evaluated by every class every year of their teaching life, were to tell the students that there were no correct answers to any of the questions on the faculty evaluation form. Do you think the students would fill out the evaluation?

So why have the members of the Faculty Senate allowed for such an evaluation to be constructed, unless, of course, they wanted to see who was leading the life of a liberally educated person and who was leading a life by being led?

Discrimination

Being land-locked in Nebraska and corn-locked in Kearney cuts one off from "the world." At the University of Nebraska at Kearney we like to think of ourselves—and rightfully so!—as a university of Nebraskans, with 98.3% of our students coming from within our state.

Recently the cry has gone out that we need minorities; it is a noble cry, ranking with love of country, motherhood, and apple pie. I mean who would question the need to expose our universe, which is Nebraska (descendants of Europeans) to "minorities," especially in these times of harassment, in its countless forms?

For the sake of Reason and therefore questioning, there are several things I would like to know: How is it that a person comes to be classified as a minority? Is a person from a minority worthier by the fact of belonging to a minority? Furthermore, is a person from the majority worthier by the fact of belonging to the majority?

In answering these questions I will have to employ Reason, the ability of discrimination, of telling one thing from another, A from B, a hawk from a handsaw. If we could not reason, we would not be able to distinguish A from B, and would only see A, and A, and A, ad infinitum. But as we can reason, we can tell A from B, and are therefore capable of discriminating.

A minority stands in opposition to the majority. The majority gains its place by being more than the minority. Thus, the majority of professors, when you are discriminating, are classified as white males, and further classified as the descendants of European white parents, and yet further classified, by some, as coming equipped with a "Eurocentric perspective." Minorities are classified as anyone who does not belong to the majority. Thus, we get everyone who is not white and not male. There are other forms of discrimination. By class, you may be a Viet Nam Era Veteran, handicapped, or "over forty," and, therefore, part of a select minority which is considered a "protected class." We may further discriminate by classifying people with regard to religion, attire, length of hair, and size.

It is also possible to fall within more than one class; for example, one might be an aging, handicapped, Puerto Rican, Viet Nam Era Veteran male. All of the protected classes share the common feature of being unfortunate: it is unfortunate to serve in an unpopular war, it is unfortunate to be handicapped, and it is unfortunate that any of us should have to turn forty. But that is what you get when things are left to fortune. How unfortunate!

I do not doubt that we lack minorities among the teachers at UNK when minorities are classified by race and sex. We don't lack minorities, however, when minorities are classified by protected classes, religions, attire, length of hair and size. So there are minorities and there are minorities. Some minorities are simply more important, apparently, than other minorities.

In all of this I am reminded of a little story attributed to Aristophanes regarding the real nature of man:

> In the beginning we were nothing like we are now. For one thing, the race was divided into three; that is to say, besides the two sexes, male and female, which we have at present, there was a third which partook of the nature of both, and for which we still have a name, though the creature itself is forgotten. For though "hermaphrodite" is only used nowadays as a term of contempt, there really was a man-woman in those days, a being which was half male and half female.
>
> And secondly, gentlemen, each of these beings was globular in shape, with rounded back and sides, four arms and four legs, and two

faces, both the same, on a cylindrical neck, and one head, with one face one side and one the other, and four ears, and two lots of privates, and all the other parts to match. They walked erect, as we do our selves, backward or forward, whichever they pleased, but when they broke into a run they simply stuck their legs straight out and went whirling round and round like a clown turning cartwheels. And since they had eight legs, if you count their arms as well, you can imagine that they went bowling along at a pretty good speed.

The three sexes, I may say, arose as follows. The males were descended from the Sun, the females from the Earth, and the hermaphrodites from the Moon, which partakes of either sex, and they were round and they went round, because they took after their parents. And such, gentlemen, were their strength and energy, and such their arrogance, that they actually tried—like Ephialtes and Otus in Homer—to scale the heights of heaven and set upon the gods.

At this Zeus took counsel with the other gods as to what was to be done.... [And then Zeus decided] What I propose to do is to cut them all in half, thus killing two birds with one stone, for each one will be only half as strong, and there'll be twice as many of them, which will suit us very nicely. They can walk about, upright, on their two legs, and if, said Zeus, I have any more trouble with them, I shall split them up again, and they'll have to hop about on one.[1]

Are we the grandchildren of the hermaphrodites, who, having further angered the Gods have been split down the middle, so that now as we hop we also see halfway, as though "through a glass darkly?" We no longer see a man or a woman; we see everything as splintered. First we see a white male, or a black female. And then, as we continue to splinter, we will see a white, male, cripple.

In all of this, I think it is fair to say that there are those who think it is no longer possible to look upon another human being with both heart and mind to see a soul. We have become like the priest and the Levite who passed by the beaten man left to die alongside the road—

1. Edith Hamilton and Huntington Cairs, eds., *The Collected Dialogues of Plato*, (Princeton: Princeton University Press, 1961), 189c-190c.

he was not their neighbor! Are there no longer any Samaritans who see indiscriminately?

As we now are fractured, we have become a diversity lacking a sense of unity, so we think we need an assemblage of pieces to represent the whole person. However, this person will still be without a center and therefore incapable of rolling along.

And so we will hire by discriminating with regard to the pieces of human beings, and I fear, without being able to judge whether there is a qualified soul before us who is able to teach. We could judge as they do at the St. Louis Symphony or with Philadelphia's basketball team. In St. Louis, the musician is interviewed behind a closed curtain to insure that the judges in the audience use only their ears to make their decision. In Philadelphia, the coach of the 76'ers is interested in ability and not populating his team with a representative from each faction. (Just try arguing with any coach that there are not enough whites, Hispanics, or Orientals on the team, and that you would like to see equal representation.)

Imagine if we were to judge an incoming teacher by his ability teach rather than by one of his many minority qualities. Since the applicant professes to be a teacher, let his future colleagues take him into a classroom of undergraduates as part of his interview so that he can teach a lesson on the spot. Would not that tell his interviewers all they really need to know?

No, we will continue to discriminate using our eyes, not our minds or our hearts, and perhaps further anger the Gods, who will delight in our doing their jobs, chopping ourselves into increasingly minor pieces.

On Finding One's Self

"Who you? Why you here?" Grace Rose Martin, my three-year-old granddaughter, asked Anna Martin, her ninety-one-year-old great-grandmother at a family reunion. Lo and behold, Grace Rose is a philosopher: she has a sense of wonder and the desire to know. Philosophy begins in wonder when we affirm that the sentiment is anterior to reason. In fact, if I did not know better, I would have thought Grace knew her purpose by having read the first sentence of Aristotle's *Metaphysics*, "All men by nature desire to know."

Grace's questions are as fundamental to being human as childhood is to becoming an adult. Her questions were answered on the literal level: I am Anna Martin, and I am here for the wedding. My mother's answers satisfied Grace—for the moment—but they will not stop her from continuing to ask a plethora of questions as she seeks to weave coherence out of her surroundings.

As Grace matures, the philosophical muse of the examined life must turn inward if she is ever to fulfill herself as an adult. In other words, her questions must become "Who am I?" and "What am I doing here?"

Grace Rose is currently untroubled by self-examination as she bounces about in play. She is, as children are, in the "now," a state of innocence where each moment is sparkling new.

Philosophers have long thought the present moment—this moment—to be the least occupied of places, as most adults live in remembering or in anticipating future events.

The ancient Greeks had two different senses of time. There is *Kronos*, which is time relating before to after, time as the future passing through the present to become the past. From this Greek word, we derive such terms as "chronic" and "chronology." An illness is chronic if it lasts a long time. Chronology is the arrangement of events or dates in the order of their occurrence.

In addition to *kronos* there is *kairos*, used when speaking of appropriate time or seasonal time. This time cannot be measured. In weaving, it is the time for the weaver to draw the yarn through a gap that momentarily opens in the warp of the cloth being woven. In politics, it is the speech needed to set the eternal significance of the moment in which something needs to be said before the moment passes by and the opportunity is gone forever. Abraham Lincoln's Gettysburg Address is an example of how the word is drawn down to fix the moment that transcends the wear of time by a person who grasps the eternality of the moment in which the human spirit stands still:

> It is rather for us to be here dedicated to the great task remaining before us—that from these honored dead we take increased devotion to that cause for which they gave the last full measure of devotion—that we here highly resolve that these dead shall not have died in vain—that this nation, under God, shall have a new birth of freedom—and that government of the people, by the people, for the people, shall not perish from the earth.

Kairos is not measurable; it is an eternal quality rather than a quantity that intersects with *Kronos*.

Lincoln's words still ring true.

So, there is the time span of a person's life which can be measured chronologically from beginning to end, and there is also the span of time when the timeless intersects with the temporal, weaving context into what would otherwise be disconnected moments in a pointless life. Baptism is an example of the moment when the timeless enters time and starts a person on a spiritual journey for the sake of his soul.

Thomas Merton, in *New Seeds of Contemplation* notes:

> What is really new is what was there all the time. I say, not what has repeated itself all the time; the really "new" is that which, at every moment, springs freshly into new existence. This newness never repeats itself. Yet it is so old it goes back to the earliest beginning. It is the very beginning itself, which speaks to us.[1]

In wonder, Grace is on the edge of her unique "newness" looking out on her world for the first time. The joy of being a child is you do not know you are a child.

Grace, according to G. K. Chesterton, is in her own cosmos:

> Each one of us is living in a separate cosmos. The theory of life held by one man never corresponds exactly to that held by another. The whole of man's opinions, morals, tastes, manners, hobbies, work back eventually to some picture of existence itself which, whether it be a paradise or a battlefield, or a school or a chaos, is not precisely the same picture of existence which lies at the back of any other brain.[2]

While Ptolemy was obviously wrong to assume the earth was the center of the cosmos, Grace is the center of her universe; she is a microcosmos of the cosmos. As a part she mirrors the whole. When Grace looks out from the windows of her soul, she draws a bead which begins with her and ends on the horizon or upon whatever she is looking.

Man is the starting point of any line that can be drawn between any two points in space; it was he who drew stars into constellations. There are no points in the universe from which to measure that do not begin in a living soul.

Grace Rose is beginning to draw herself, but she is not drawing from scratch; she is endowed with an intellect and is forming a mind

1. Thomas Merton, *New Seeds of Contemplation* (New York: New Direction Books, 1972), 107.

2. *Collected Works of G. K. Chesterton* (San Francisco: Ignatius Press, 1990), vol. XVIII, 30.

each time she looks out from herself and wants to know the who, what, and why of everything in her search for order.

Grace's quest—Who you? Why you here?—shows she has a soul meant to know its end. She is being brought up in the moral virtues which are the sinews, as it were, of family life. As Aristotle says,

> Intellectual virtue or excellence owes its origin and development chiefly to teaching and for that reason requires experience and time. Moral virtue, on the other hand, is formed by habit... [and] none of the moral virtues is implanted in us by nature, for nothing which exists by nature can be changed by habit.[3]

Grace is not moral by nature, any more than she speaks by nature; however, everyone has the potential to be moral and to speak by nature. In Aristotle's terms, we are provided with the capacity first and display the activity afterwards.

Grace is everyman—and has fallen into a net, a context, where she is woven to her parents and relatives: her lifelines. It is fitting that Grace asked her questions, with which I began this reflection, of her great-grandmother: the progeny standing before the oldest living source of her life, asking for an explanation: youth in need of tradition.

Ludwig Wittgenstein noted, "Tradition is not something a man can learn; not a thread he can pick up when he feels like it; any more than a man can choose his relatives."[4]

Each person is a continuation of his thread on a continuum. A first name is uniquely individual and a last name ties a man to his people. Tradition is our skin. We do not choose our parents, nationality, or the century in which we are born—the context of our lives. We are woven bodily to the earth and spiritually to our parents in our adventure which continues their history. Our parents are lifelines, entrusted with setting the tension for the formation of the virtuous life that is essen-

3. *Nicomachean Ethics*, 15a–20.
4. L. Wittgenstein, *Culture and Value* (Chicago: University of Chicago Press, 1980), 76.

tial for our spiritual growth and achievement of our potential. Aristotle taught that the primary source of moral virtues is their presence in other beings.

Grace has fallen onto a moving platform yet is at the center of her household. In time, she will get over the shock of being in the world, as her parents bring her down to earth, schooling her in the language of household virtues through fairy tales, parables, and chores, which she currently demonstrates when she suggests, "Let's play family."

Moving from childhood to adulthood includes the awareness of the timelessness of the opportunities which are present in each moment. Each moment presents itself as a virtuous opportunity. There is a right choice in each moment that is relative to each person.

Being virtuous requires having your string pulled. Good parents start by pulling a child's string when teaching him to sit up straight, say please and thank you, be kind to others and take pride in himself.

The intellectual virtues are started at home and continued in schools. The word leisure in Greek is *skole*, and in Latin *scola*, from which comes the English word "school." Given that man is born ignorant and by nature desires to know, Aristotle in *Metaphysics* states man sets about learning only after "all the necessities of life and things that make for comfort and recreation" have been achieved.

In order to satisfy the quest to know, man needs to have the opportunity for leisure. In this respect, school is the harbor where one is outfitted for the journey of life.

The university is a playground, the leisure ground of *Kairos* for the formation of a person's self-discovery. It is at this point that a student decides to focus on a specific course of study to center his life on being a nurse, builder, banker, EMT, radiologist, exercise physiologist, farmer, teacher and the like. This is well and good. In fact, Aristotle noted in the fourth century BC that each person has a function by nature which is his calling in life. A well-governed state is one in which everyone is suited to his function, the job he is meant to do by nature, and in which work is done for the higher stakes of the greater good. This, Aristotle thought, is a good of the soul as opposed to a good of the body (an external good like a house) which though useful, is not an end in and of itself, as are the ends of life.

The individual's function should follow his formation if his life is to be virtuous. The virtues are eternal truths, the light emanating from *Kairos* that presents a mindful person with the right thing to do in this the *Kronos* of his life. There are permanent moments in every man's life. There is a right thing to do in every moment.

In effect, college is set up like a loom where the past is woven into the present. Everything we learn is behind us and a good memory is essential for a developed mind.

Within education, the purpose of being a teacher on the playground of the cosmos is to transmit the truth of disciplined thought to the next microcosm whose soul is endowed with faculty of reason. Being a teacher is like being a grandparent who is asked by his grandchild "Who am I?" and "What am I doing here? "

So, "Who you? Why you here?"

Religion at a State Institution

"Forgiveness Means Letting Go"
* To forgive another is the greatest favor you can do—for your-self....
* Be patient with yourself.... Forgiveness is a process and may take time.
* Don't expect too much. Realize that you will benefit the most from being able to let go, and that can be enough.
* Value the importance of self-forgiveness. Often times, we don't give ourselves permission to be wrong or to make mistakes. To forgive others, you need to forgive yourself.
* Forgiveness can be a wonderful way of freeing ourselves from past hurts, fears and anger. If forgiveness is an act you wish to manifest in your life, contact....

These words of self-help are from a monthly memo of a group calling itself the "Methodist Employee Assistance Program." This program is one of the many benefits available to the faculty, staff, and administration at UNK, and can be reached by dialing (800) 666–8606. No doubt the powers that be in the university system think the services M.E.A.P. offers are necessary in these times of stress, abuse and assault.

However, we at the circulation desk of *The Examined Life* were puzzled by the good-hearted people at M.E.A.P. claiming: "To forgive others, you need to forgive yourself." We thought forgiveness was an act which involves a relationship between two or more people. A person can forgive another person's loan, ask that his debts be forgiven, insult or assault other people and ask their forgiveness, or he can be insulted or assaulted and be asked to forgive his transgressors. In this respect the act of forgiveness involves the purgation of guilt: a person realizes and is bothered by his having violated another person's rights and he must ask the person's forgiveness for his transgressions. A person cannot forgive his own transgressions any more than a person can pardon his own debts.

It is hard to forgive people who have defiled us and equally difficult to humble ourselves in the dust before another person whom we have offended. Perhaps this is why forgiveness is said to be divine, as it draws a person to pardon the unpardonable.

So you can see why we were puzzled. Forgiving yourself is like borrowing money from yourself, taking yourself out to dinner, or hiding your own Easter eggs.

We wondered if the people at M.E.A.P. would think it a good idea if Lawrence Phillips of the Nebraska Cornhuskers, the preseason Heisman candidate before he punched out his ex-girlfriend, would benefit from their advice: "Lawrence you must value the importance of self-forgiveness. Often times, we don't give ourselves permission to be wrong or to make mistakes. To forgive others, you need to forgive yourself."

We could understand the former girlfriend forgiving Lawrence. She may have loved him at one time, and she may even remember Peter's question, "how oft shall my brother sin against me, and I forgive him? Seven times?" To which he was told, "Seventy times seven." And we could also understand how difficult it would be for his former girlfriend to forgive such a brutal act.

But forgiveness is divine and unless Lawrence and the rest of us are gods, we will have to continue to humble ourselves before others and ask forgiveness and maybe even serve some time with our failings until we realize our guilt.

The University as Playground

> If [the] Universities were destroyed, they would not be destroyed
> as Universities. If they are preserved, they will not be preserved
> as Universities. They will be preserved strictly and literally as
> playgrounds; places valued for their hours of leisure more than
> their hours of work. I do not say that this is unreasonable; as a
> matter of private temperament I find it attractive. It is not only
> possible to say a great deal in praise of play; it is really possible
> to say the highest things in praise of it. It might reasonably be
> maintained that the true object of all human life is play. Earth is
> a task garden; heaven is a playground.[1]

I was not surprised to hear G. K. Chesterton saying that
"Earth is a task garden and heaven is a playground," but
it was news to me that universities, if they are to be preserved, ought to
be preserved as playgrounds, especially since for the past twenty years
I have been living in, or should I say "hiding-out," in such a place as a
teacher. Then again, I should not act as though Chesterton has told me
something I did not already suspect. I have known for some time that
what I do, reading and discussing the ideas of Plato, Aristotle, Aquinas,
and Chesterton, to name a few, is looked upon as being out of fashion
and as having little to do with the real world by my colleagues in business, computer science and the various medical fields. In fact, I am surprised that those who administer the Modern University still fund our
leisure to entertain the ideas of the dead with students.

1. G. K. Chesterton, "Oxford From Without," in *All Things Considered* (originally
from *Illustrated London News*, Aug. 3, 1907).

Nevertheless, I have been caught red-handed and am obligated to offer an explanation to my students, if not their poor parents who are no doubt paying for their children to attend the Modern University where they expect them learn a skill, any skill at all, which will prove profitable in their trek through the Global economy. Convincing the sleepy-eyed students of ten o'clock classes, many of whom have been guzzling beer till three or playing computer games in their dorm till four, that they are at a playground will not take much effort. Students have always known that the university is a playground. (This is why, after students have spent several semesters at a university, you will hear them talking about being finished with their studies and getting out into the "real world" where they will, upon getting a job good enough to make big bucks, have to keep regular hours and wait many months for a holiday.)

Persuading the students' parents that their children ought to waste time in a playground before being let loose, self-sufficient in the real world will be harder. But I will give it a try.

Your children are in danger of becoming monsters. It is not your fault. You did everything that was in your power. You armed them with stories about witches and other enchanters who cast spells on innocent people. In each story, evil, which always seemed invincible, was overcome by goodness, which always appeared vincible. You took them to church where the word was revealed to them that the meek shall inherit, what you do unto the least of these you do unto me, and beware of false prophets who come to you in sheep's clothing. And now your children are about to pass through the exit of the Modern University and upon receiving a sheepskin passport into the "real" world, they will busy themselves with getting and spending and will fall into measuring themselves by the size of their house and salary.

In all of this, we have forgotten who we are. The Earth is a task garden where we ought to be busy about weeding Envy, Pride, Covetousness, Gluttony, Sloth, Lust, and Anger from our souls so that we may come to fruition.

Chesterton thought that if the universities are preserved, they ought to be preserved "as" playgrounds, and he connected these playgrounds to Heaven which is "the" playground.

It is in the University that a person is preserved, being guarded from the present by the past. In the old university, to which I belong, we open the windows and let the past walk into the now. In this timeless place we open the tombs of Plato, Augustine, Boethius, Aquinas to resurrect the living word, in order that we might know how we ought to play our lives. ("It is a place for humanizing those who might otherwise be tyrants, or even experts.") Consider:

Socrates (who asks): Why do you care so much about wealth, reputation and honor and give no care for your soul?

Aristotle: It is the nature of desire not to be satisfied, and most men live only for the gratification of it. The beginning of reform is not so much to equalize property as to train the noble sort of natures not to desire more, and to prevent the lower from getting more.

Augustine: Two cities have been formed by two loves: the earthly by the love of self, even to the contempt of God; the heavenly by the love of God, even to the contempt of self.

Francis: Where there is charity and wisdom, there is neither fear nor ignorance. Where there is patience and humility, there is neither anger nor vexation. Where there is poverty and joy, there is neither greed nor avarice. Where there is peace and meditation, there is neither anxiety nor doubt.

Aquinas: For he who seeks the favour of men must serve their will in all he says and does, and thus, while striving to please all, he becomes a slave to each one.

In short: we are busy in our recreation about our re-creation in this playground. It is our task to see that your child breathes in the words which will help to cultivate his soul so he will not fall into belonging to the world, but will plant one foot firmly in this world and the other in the next world. It is my hope that we sometimes succeed.

A Teacher's Morning

Walking out of my office into the hallway of Thomas Hall at the University of Nebraska at Kearney, I see seventeen students lining the hall before class. All but one of them is fiddling with a smartphone, maybe texting, or watching a movie piped through high-end headphones. No one notices me.

I go down the steps to meet my Philosophy 188 class, The Meaning of Life. At the bottom of the steps there is the same girl who has been seated there all semester. She is coloring in a princess costume on what looks to be a Barbie doll—Monday she was playing solitaire and last Friday she was fingering away to someone on her smartphone.

I enter my classroom to a dozen, or so, of my twenty-five students thumbing away at their phones. They speed up because class starts in two minutes, and they will be forced offline for fifty minutes.

Today we are reading Plato's "Allegory of the Cave," which depicts a form of education in 375 BC, the start of formal schooling.

Imagine people chained to a wall—they have been there since childhood ("they are like us")—looking at the opposite wall upon which shadows are cast. There is a fire behind the prisoners, and between the fire and them is a ledge upon which men walk holding cut-out figures to create the shadows on the wall at which the prisoners, who cannot turn their heads, are staring. The men behind them talk, so the shadows are connected with voices. To pass time, the prisoners see who can remember the order of the shadows and award prizes to those who are correct. Obviously, there is no one to verify the sequence of events or if the shadows have anything to do with reality, but it is the only reality the prisoners know.

One day, a prisoner's chains break, and he is free to turn around. The firelight hurts his eyes, but with time, he sees the men holding up the images and hypothesizes the cut-outs are copies of the real figures on the wall.

He eventually is pulled out of the cave into the blinding sunlight, where, after his eyes adjust, he sees reality.

The allegory is the movement of the soul upward, from the thoughtless acceptance of images projected on a blank wall by the thought-controllers, to the wisdom which comes with the direct knowledge of reality outside the cave. The students in class today see the allegory is comparable to the visual images of televised media (with advertising!), including the auditory accompaniment of politicians, teachers, ministers, priests, parents, etc., who control the sights and sounds—while fueling the fire—that reach the captive minds of those who can't unplug from whatever is titillating the eyes or stimulating the ears, thus adding up to a smoke-filled picture of a gullible mind.

Socrates uses the allegory to show the state of affairs between ignorance, opinion, and knowledge. Knowledge of reality is in the sunlight; opinion is the haze of shadows; and ignorance is the state of darkness into which all men are born.

Opinion easily holds sway over the multitude who lack the necessary self-control to disconnect from the events streaming 24/7 ad infinitum in cave land.

Class ends and the students, many of whom are back to fingering or talking to their smartphones, make their way to the door.

I walk out into the hall bustling with students—mostly quiet—reattaching to a variety of screens, eager as spelunkers gasping for fresh air.

I almost trip over a student lodged on the third step hunkered over some device as I make my way to the second floor marked by a head-phoned student seated in a chair watching a music video.

Before I enter my office, I turn to a girl who, to my surprise, says, "I love you."

She is on her iPhone, of course.

Faith and the Big Red Machine

The difference between football and public education in Nebraska was clearly illustrated in the article "Prayer Part of Husker Playbook," in the *Omaha World Herald* of October 26th. While there is a separation of church and state in the education of the children of Nebraska, there is not a separation of Christ and football at the University of Nebraska. This was made obvious in this front-page article:

> In a state where football is almost a religion and where faith in the Huskers is gospel, an increasing number of players are practicing a different kind of faith—in Jesus Christ.
>
> And that Christian atmosphere, Nebraska's coaches and players say, may be one reason for the Huskers' successes—both on and off the field.
>
> In the words of sophomore running back Dan Alexander:
>
> I think it has a lot to do with winning. Maybe everything. We have strong spiritual leaders, coaches who are really gung-ho and give 100 percent because they have the Lord backing their lives. And they try to lead by example, by a good Christian work ethic—which they take into practice and expect 100 percent out of everybody.

The article continues with examples of players who chose Nebraska because the first thing a recruiter did with potential Husker players was to help feed the homeless at a shelter. There are testimonials of players wrestling with drug abuse and returning to the straight path. The article concludes with Coach Brown starting a prayer after the victory over Missouri, and it being finished by fullback Wille Miller, "Thank you, Lord for letting us come out here today and use our God-given talents and for helping us give it our all."

Ironically, on the editorial page of the same issue there was an article about quality in education by James O'Hanlon, the Dean of UNL's teachers college. It seems there is currently a "standards movement" in education which promises to ensure our young people receive a high quality education. (May we ask, "What have our children been receiving up to the present?") O'Hanlon suggests the following standards as fundamental to reaching our educational goals:

Every child has the opportunity to attend a school that is staffed by quality teachers and is adequately financed to provide the learning materials and curriculum needed to support learning.

Every child has the support needed to benefit from the educational opportunities provided to him or her.

The community honors schools as essential to its future well-being.

O'Hanlon concludes with the end of education:

While we often think of school as existing to benefit individual students, in this country schools were established for public purposes: to prepare citizens to work together to maintain our democracy and economic system.

Now everyone connected with the schools knows schools are not overflowing with quality teachers. While the big money in state education goes to buildings, computers, athletes, and administrators, successful teachers are not rewarded like the winning coaches of Nebraska football. In fact, the schools use the military model of rank and time-in-grade to pay its teachers.

Furthermore, all children are not going to have the necessary "support needed," to accept the "educational opportunities provided to him or her." (Face it, learning is a two-way street on which the student has to want to learn like a player wants to play football for the Huskers. There simply is not enough money for tutors—the necessary "support needed"—for all the children.)

Finally, the communities do not honor schools as they honor athletics. After the win over Missouri, Nebraska's second string quarterback Monte Christo was heralded as a hero on the front page of his hometown newspaper, *The Kearney Hub*, as well as the front page of the sports section. Imagine a student who has aced a chemistry test or successfully translated a passage from Ovid waking up to find himself on the front page of his hometown newspaper?

In all of this it is quite clear that the difference between the success of Husker football and the continual search for "quality" by the administrators of public education in Nebraska is a matter of understanding a simple truth: we cannot create anything good until we have conceived it.

The coaches use their authority to address the good of life: You are all equal under God; you have different talents; you are not alone (Christ is with you); football is not the end of your life, it is a means; as a Christian you are meant for eternal life with God; and the coaching staff is 100% committed to making you all you can be as a football player, a citizen, and a Christian.

Dean James O'Hanlon, shackled by the separation of church and state ends up addressing the means of life as an end when he talks of school as a place bent on "[preparing] citizens to work together to maintain our democracy and economic system." In other words: children, the only value you have till the undertaker comes is as a citizen who can "get along" and "get and spend."

It is time for the football model of UNL which inspires players to give their all on and off the field to be applied to the public education system of Nebraska. Then we might be able to have a winning educational system instead of an educational system which is continually trying to define a quality education while offering up yet another losing season.

We can start by having all of our teachers and their students close their eyes before each class and pray, "Thank you, Lord, for letting us gather here today and use our God-given talents and for helping us give it our all."

Education in the Age of the Learning, Physically and Morally Disabled

I recently received two brochures from our University Counseling Center at the University of Nebraska at Kearney which describe the various ways faculty members might accommodate students having a variety of disabilities. The first brochure explained how the physically handicapped are guaranteed an education under the Rehabilitation Act of 1973:

> No otherwise qualified handicapped individual in the United States... shall, solely by reason of... handicap, be excluded from participation in, be denied the benefits of, or be subjected to discrimination under any program or activity receiving federal financial assistance.

Because our university receives federal financial assistance, in fact over fifty percent of our students receive government grants and loans to attend this university, it is important that we comply with the Rehabilitation Act of 1973. This explains why all of our buildings are, rightfully, accessible to the handicapped. The blind, deaf, crippled, epileptic, and, those with a chronic illness, such as cancer, aids, lupus, or arthritis, are entitled to an education. Physical disabilities were not a liability in the education of Dostoyevsky, Beethoven, Roosevelt, or Flannery O'Connor any more than they are for our disabled students who want to be educated.

However, besides the category of physical disabilities, there is an additional category, previously unknown to me, addressed in the second brochure from the Counseling Center.

"College students with Learning Disabilities" is the title of the second brochure, which comes from a Columbus, Ohio, group calling itself AHEAD (Association on Higher Education and Disability). The people at AHEAD argue that the learning disabled are entitled to the same rights of the handicapped under section 504 of the Rehabilitation Act of 1973. So, while the blind, deaf, crippled, epileptic and those with cancer, aids, lupus, and arthritis are not to be denied an education because of their handicap or disease, the learning disabled are equally protected by law to seek an education.

The brochure is designed to assist professors in recognizing students who are afflicted with "learning disabilities." As with all such matters, the brochure begins with the definition and cause of learning disabilities:

> A disorder which affects the manner in which individuals with normal or above average intelligence take in, retain, and express information. It is commonly recognized as a significant deficit in one or more of the following areas: oral expression, listening comprehension, written expression, basic reading skills, reading comprehension, mathematical calculation, or problem solving. Individuals with learning disabilities also may have difficulty with sustained attention, time management, or social skills.
> —presumably due to nervous system dysfunction.
> —cross-cultural. It occurs regardless of racial or ethnic origin.

Put the two brochures together and here is what follows: universities and colleges receiving federal financial assistance must not, by law, discriminate in the recruitment, admission, or treatment of students who are physically or mentally handicapped. Furthermore, under Section 504 universities and colleges *may not*:

> —limit the number of students with disabilities admitted or make

preadmission inquiries as to whether or not an applicant is disabled,

—limit eligibility to a student with a disability from any course of study,

—counsel a student with a disability toward a more restrictive career,

—establish rules and policies that may adversely affect students with disabilities.

Our university has an admissions requirement: In order for a student to be admitted in *Good Standing* as an entering freshman, an applicant who is under 21 years of age, must be a graduate of an accredited high school, and meet one of three criteria: have completed a specific number of courses in language arts, mathematics, science and social sciences, or rank in the upper one-half of his high school class, or present a composite ACT score of 20 or a combined score of 850 on the SAT.

However, these admissions standards clearly discriminate against those suffering from a *learning disability*. What follows are some of the symptoms from the brochure of those suffering from learning disabilities:

—Slow reading rate and/or retention of material.

—Difficulty identifying points and themes.

—Difficulty reading for long periods of time.

—Difficulty with sentence structure, e.g. incomplete sentences, run-ons, and poor use of grammar.

—Frequent spelling errors.

—Difficulty following oral or written directions.

—Incomplete mastery of basic facts (e.g., mathematical tables.)

—Difficulty comprehending word problems.

—Difficulty with organization skills.

—Time management difficulties.

—Difficulty preparing for and taking tests.

—Fluctuating attention span during lectures.

Admission counselors cannot expect students to meet the current admission standards and professors must be able to recognize the symptoms of those who have learning disabilities which are attributed to a "presumed central nervous system dysfunction."

(I must admit that while reading over the symptoms of the learning disabled, I realized my own occasional "central nervous system dysfunction." I am guilty of a "slow reading rate" when working through Aristotle, Hume, Bacon, and Dante; and, when reading the newspaper, I skip over words and entire lines of print. I also admit to have difficulty proofreading which forces me to rely on others. I am, however, relieved to find my faults are due to a "central nervous system dysfunction.")

Thanks to our counselors, and the people at AHEAD, professors will now realize that the students who miss fifteen classes a semester suffer "time management difficulties"; those who do not read assigned material are ailing from a "slow reading rate"; and those who cannot write a logically structured paper, spell, proofread, or complete a sentence have tested positive to this *nervous system dysfunction.*

All ideas of a university being a place to develop the intellect of students through a series of academic intensive courses in the arts and sciences must be dismissed as elitist. If this institution is to continue to receive federal funds in the form of grants and student loans, it must comply with Section 504. What would happen to the enrollment of universities if the students with learning disabilities were excluded from a course of study?

A general studies curriculum must be developed which is accessible to those who are suffering from learning disabilities. If we are going to abide by the law, we must follow the directions from the people from AHEAD and not:

—limit the number of students with disabilities admitted;

—make preadmission inquiries as to whether or not an applicant is disabled;

—limit eligibility of a student with a disability from any course of study.

The disabled, besides having the right to attend class, also have the right to participate in all the activities on the campus.

What next? I predict the people at AHEAD will soon be sending a brochure to the administration and faculty concerning the rights of those suffering from *Coordination System Dysfunction* (CSD). These students not only have the right to an education, but also the right to participate in all activities at the local and intercollegiate level.

Some characteristics of college students with Coordination System Dysfunction (which may be coupled with learning disabilities) include:

—Difficulty stretching, lifting weights, and doing calisthenics.
—Difficulty running for long periods of time.
—Difficulty understanding a play.
—Difficulty attending practice (time management dysfunction).
—Difficulty following oral or written directions.
—Difficulty reviewing films.
—Difficulty eating a balanced diet.
—Difficulty identifying numbers and colors.
   —presumably due to nervous system dysfunction;
   —cross cultural: it occurs regardless of racial or ethnic origin.

There will be those who will argue the "separate but equal" position: that we need two athletic complexes to accommodate the needs of the athletically able and the athletically disabled. If this argument proves persuasive, the precedent will be established which will be used by those on the academic side of campus, for the duplication of facilities; more labs, a separate library, theater, music hall and classrooms. This would create two campuses within one which would necessitate a separate administration to coordinate the studies of the Able and the Disabled. Degrees would be granted for the "Able Bachelor of Science," or the "Disabled Bachelor of Science," with an emphasis in Disabled Chemistry, with a coaching endorsement in Secondary Coordination Disabled Volleyball and Track.

Furthermore, I predict the people at AHEAD will soon notice another disability, even more wide spread than the two previously mentioned disabilities, which is right before their eyes: the Morally Disabled. The definition:

> A disorder which affects the way in which individuals with normal and above average intelligence act when relating to others. It is commonly recognized as a significant deficit in one or more of the following areas: oral expression, control over the members of the body, basic social skills, interpreting body language, or understanding personal space. Individuals with moral disabilities also may have difficulty with self-examination, attention, and time management.

—presumably due to nervous system dysfunction.

—cross-cultural. It occurs regardless of racial or ethnic origin.

Some Characteristics of those with morality disabilities:

—Difficulty telling the truth.

—Tendency to walk with the certainty of a somnambulist.

—Tendency to express sadness in the face of spiritual good.

—Tendency to think a position is to be revered above a person's character.

—Tendency to identify genitals as the seat of reason.

—Difficulty recognizing people who are morally superior.

—Tendency to think morals a matter of opinion.

—Tendency to think might makes right.

Remember, the common thread linking the Learning, the Coordination, and the Morally Disabled is their presumed *nervous system dysfunction*. These disabilities are recognized by Affirmative Action and Equal Opportunity as being cross-cultural and occurring regardless of class, race, religion, or ethnic origin.

Remember, if you want to get AHEAD, you must recognize we are now on our way to creating, "a pleasant constitution, which lacks rulers but not variety and which distributes a sort of equality to both equals and unequals alike."

And so it goes.

The Demise of Writing (Thinking) Intensive Courses at UNK

S tudents who are reluctant to write will be relieved by the recent decision of an ad-hoc committee of the faculty senate to reduce the requirements of "writing intensive" courses from twelve to six hours. Such students will be further comforted to know that of the two required writing intensive courses, only one must be from outside their major course of study.

I must confess the decision of the ad-hoc committee surprised me as the vast majority of students I teach in general studies courses (a UNK misnomer for the liberal arts) are not good writers. This means many of my students have trouble understanding and thinking about Marx, Plato, Aristotle, Dostoyevsky, Rousseau, Locke or whomever it is we are reading. This is to be expected of students who are beginning to think and who have had the misfortunate of graduating from high schools in which they were not asked to reflect in writing on the primary sources they read in literature or history. Too many students graduated from high schools where writing for literature or history, for example, could be avoided by using Cliff Notes or an internet search engine to explicate in writing some concept, idea or historical event by cutting and pasting information or by paraphrasing someone else's words for a report of some sort or another. Worse yet, many teachers have turned from having students write to having them sharpen their computer skills by giving poster presentations instead. Oh, joy.

So why did an ad-hoc committee of the faculty senate suggest a reduction of writing intensive courses, and why did the faculty senate and the academic vice chancellor approved its recommendation?

In search of an answer, I asked the past president of the faculty senate, Martha Cruz. She told me that a survey was sent to the faculty, and the majority of the faculty respondents (how many did reply?) thought that enough writing was being done in classes which were not designated as writing intensive.

The wonderful thing about doing a survey is that the results are anonymous. Who exactly are the teachers who think our students are writing enough and what is their definition of having a student write? How many classes are there in which the vast amount of "student writing" is the short paragraph (a sentence or two) at the end of a multiple-choice exam? How many classes are there where writing amounts to accessing a search engine on the internet to cut and paste information on the problem of obesity in American children, the rights of illegal immigrants, the amount of calories burned in various types of aerobic exercise or other such information gathering?

Ironically, at the same time some of the faculty surveyed were circling whichever letter indicated our students are writing enough, the National Center for Education Statistics reported that "only 31 percent of college graduates can read a complex book and extrapolate from it."

I must be one of the only teachers on this campus whose students are not from places like Lake Wobegon where "the women are strong, all the men are good-looking, and all the children are above-average."

Regardless of the results of this faculty survey, I know the majority of students at our university are not above the national average that can read and "extrapolate" from *The Brothers Karamazov*, *Social Contract*, or *Nicomachean Ethics*.

There is more to a student being able to write than turning out papers in the form of a social scientist, a biologist, a construction management expert, economist, or artist. A student must learn to write for himself, as he must learn to read and think for himself.

Writing is essential in developing a well-ordered mind. Good writing comes from attentive thoughtfulness in the service of truth. This form of writing transcends a student's being able to "write across the curriculum" as it involves his self-examination throughout life. Henry David Thoreau in his journal on July 6, 1840, writes:

> Have no mean hours, but be grateful for every hour, and accept what it brings. The reality will make any sincere record respectable. No day will have been wholly misspent, if one sincere, thoughtful page has been written. Let the daily tide leave some deposit on these pages, as it leaves sand and shells on the shore. So much increase of terra firma. This may be a calendar of the ebbs and flows of the soul; and on these sheets as on a beach, the waves may cast up pearls and seaweed.

This is worth repeating, "No day will have been wholly misspent, if one sincere, thoughtful page has been written."

This is not to say that thoughtful writing, even if sincere, is good writing, as the ideas may not be true. For example, what does a student think of this bit of thoughtful, and perhaps even sincere, writing?

> There were few Jews in Linz. In the course of the centuries, their outward appearance had become Europeanized and had taken on a human look; in fact, I even took them for Germans.[1]

These sentences are grammatically correct and certainly one man's honest reflection, but are they true? If they are not true, what is it that makes them false? Thoughtfulness in the service of the truth creates a tension in the mind of the reader, especially when he must put his thoughts on paper. (The words, as you may have surmised, are from *Mein Kampf* and belong to Hitler.)

Good writing is to thinking what good weeding is to gardening. If the University of Nebraska at Kearney were a college of horticulture, there would be courses required of students which were weed-

---

1. Adolf Hitler, *Mein Kampf*, trans. Ralph Manheim (Boston: Houghton Mifflin, 1971), 52.

ing intensive. While it is possible to plant a garden without weeding, there is no surer way to reduce the yield of lettuce, cabbage, cucumbers, broccoli, spinach, tomatoes, chickpeas, or whatever else is fighting to see the light of day, than by not weeding out the morning glories, cockleburs, and other noxious weeds.

It is important to remember that a mind is not a bodily organ like the brain. Human beings do not have minds by nature. In fact, we are born ignorant and do not speak, read, write or think by nature. However, we have the potential to develop a mind and need to be taught to speak, read, write, and think thoughtfully in the service of truth. The traditional way to develop a mind is by studying those who have good minds. In this respect, writing is connected to reading good thinkers in the service of truth.

Learning to write for yourself in the service of truth is the beginning of being thoughtful. A student learns the logic of thinking clearly by weeding out hasty generalizations, false assumptions, misleading analogies and ad hominines, and by avoiding slippery slopes, contradictions, vacuous jargon and redundancy in his writing. Therefore, as a gardener is known by the fruits of his garden, a thinker is known by the truth of his compositions.

John Henry Newman in the section "Elementary Studies" of his book *The Idea of a University* addresses the task of developing a mind,

> I say, that the one main portion of intellectual education, of the labours of both school and university, is to remove the original dimness of the mind's eye; to strengthen and perfect its vision; to enable it to look out into the world right forward, steadily and truly; to give the mind clearness, accuracy, precision; to enable it to use words aright, to understand what it says, to conceive justly what it thinks about, to abstract, compare, analyze, divide, define, and reason correctly.[2]

The purpose of the mind is to "reason correctly." The mind by nature is meant to come to a point. As we come to conclusions in our

2. Newman, 248.

writing, we are dogmatic, like Hitler, and have doctrines, which are held as truths upon which our lives are based. Imagine, if the British and American leaders had taken what is implicit in Hitler's words seriously before World War II, what could have been, instead of what was the case for millions of Jews.

I am here reminded of G. K. Chesterton's definition of man:

> [Man is] an animal that makes dogma. As he piles doctrine on doctrine and conclusion on conclusion in the formation of some tremendous scheme of philosophy and religion, he is, in the only legitimate sense of which the expression is capable, becoming more and more human. When he drops one doctrine after another in a refined skepticism, when he declines to tie himself to a system, when he says that he has outgrown definitions, when he says that he disbelieves in God, holding no form of creed but contemplating all, then he is by that very process sinking slowly backwards into the vagueness of the vagrant animals and unconsciousness of the grass. Trees have no dogmas. Turnips are singularly broad-minded.[3]

It is the purpose of an "intellectual education" to teach students to "reason correctly" in the service of truth unless, of course, one is a skeptic who aligns himself with the animals as a thoughtless creature who, even though able to use the faculty of reason to write reports, spout statistical data from surveys, master accounting, play chess, write a grocery list, design a can opener, or attempt to square the circle.

Newman continues,

> It is the haziness of intellectual vision which is the malady of all classes of men by nature, of those who read and write and compose, quite as well as of those who cannot,—of all who have not had a really good education.[4]

Newman knows that graduating from a university does not ensure a student's ability to reason correctly as he may graduate from a voca-

---

3. *Collected Works of G. K. Chesterton* (San Francisco: Ignatius Press, 1990), vol. I, 196.
4. Newman, 249.

tional university which does not offer a liberal education. Thinking, like weeding, is not easy; it requires the daily discipline of thoughtfully paying attention to ideas so as not to be in the intellectual haze of a false dogma like Marxism that creates man as a "social construct," a soulless animal whose education is only necessary to prepare him to work for the good of the state.

Let us practice weeding: look at this passage from the beginning of Rousseau's *Social Contract* and examine what is implicit in its dogma:

> The earliest of all societies, and the only natural one, is the family; yet children remain attached to their father only so long as they have need of him for their own preservation. As soon as this need ceases, that natural bond is dissolved. The children being freed from the obedience which they owed to their father, and the father from the cares which he owed to this children, become equally independent. If they remain united, it is no longer naturally but voluntarily; and the family itself is kept together by convention.[5]

How does Rousseau know that the family is the only natural society? Does he mention a child's attachment and obligation to his mother? What must he think his obligation to his mother to be once she finished nursing him? Are the obligations to our fathers and their obligations to us a matter of convention or is there some universal moral standard which holds us responsible to our fathers and mothers throughout the days of their lives? Finally, did what Rousseau think make it easier for him to turn over his own five children to foundling homes?

Keep in mind that what we write, what we think—and they are one and the same—*may be a calendar of the ebbs and flows of the soul; and on these sheets as on a beach, the waves may cast up pearls and seaweed.*

Does Rousseau give us pearls of wisdom or only seaweed drying on the beach for our soul's sake?

---

5. Jean-Jacques Rousseau, *The Social Contract*, trans. G. D. H. Cole, (Buffalo: Prometheus Books, 1988), 14.

A Man for All Seasons... A Teacher

Rich: Well, there! A friend of Sir Thomas and still no office? There must be something wrong with him.

More: I thought we said friendship.... The Dean of St. Paul's offers you a post; with a house, a servant and fifty pounds a year.

Rich: What? What post?

More: At the new school.

Rich: (Bitterly disappointed) A teacher!

More: A man should go where he won't be tempted... in office they offer you all sorts of things. I was once offered a whole village, with a mill, and a manor house, and heaven knows what else—a coat of arms, I shouldn't be surprised. Why not be a teacher? You'd be a fine teacher. Perhaps even a great one.

Rich: And if I was, who would know it?

More: You, your pupils, your friends, God. Not a bad public, that.... Oh, and a quiet life.

Rich: (Laughing) You say that!

More: Richard, I was commanded into office; it was inflicted on me.... Can't you believe that?

Rich: It's hard.

More: (Grimly) Be a teacher[1].

$\mathbf{T}$his conversation takes place between Sir Thomas More and Richard Rich in the play *A Man For All Seasons*. Richard Rich has recently graduated from Cambridge and is in search of a position. He is in his late twenties and eager to make his way in the world. He is picky. He does not want to land just "any" posi-

1. Robert Bolt, *A Man for All Seasons* (New York: Vintage Books, 1990), 7–9.

tion. He is attracted to titles and is trying to find friends amongst the nobles of 16th Century England so as to gain a political post. During the last six months of networking, a Duke mistakenly waved at him, and he once got past the "outer doorman" of a Cardinal, only to be ushered out by the Cardinal's chamberlain. Thomas More is the most important government official he knows. (He envies the bribes that are sent to More (and returned by him) meant to sway his judgment.)

Thomas More understands how easily Rich is taken in by titles. In the above passage, More, knowing Rich's weaknesses and his talents, tells Richard to be a teacher; in fact, he thinks Richard might have the makings of a "great one." However, Richard is after worldly recognition and does not see the merit of being a great teacher, "Who would know it?" More's response "You, your pupils, your friends, God" goes right over his head. The recognition of pupils, friends and God, coupled with the "quiet life" and the possibility of being a "fine teacher," is not the notoriety Richard Rich has in mind.

Richard Rich eventually bears false witness against More, sacrificing More's *head* that he might get ahead in the world. Eventually this lands him the position of Attorney-General for Wales. He lives a long and prosperous life and dies in his sleep.

In all of this we see that nothing has changed: there is little money in teaching, few students notice you; friends—never more than a few—understand your talents, and God only knows if you make a difference in the lives of those you teach.

Nevertheless, More's response "You, your pupils, your friends, and God" to Richard Rich's "Who would know?" captures the extent of a teacher's public.

From what we see of Rich's character, there is nothing to suggest he has the makings of a teacher: he is too captivated by the world of appearance to serve the truth. In fact, he is a bottom-feeder, a real muck-sucker who will do anything to advance his own position. He is a character all too common in political and educational institutions, worlds which have long been populated with untalented people enamored by titles and the power to laud over those they perceive to be their underlings while padding their pockets as wards of the state.

Nevertheless, Thomas More thought Rich had the makings of a teacher—"perhaps even a great one"—so he must have been able to see something in his character that is hidden from the reader. Then again, if More can see this in Richard, he can see it in every man.

Thomas More addresses the vocation of a teacher when he calls it a "a quiet life." The life of a teacher may be a quiet life, but it is not a calm life. Anyone who teaches for life is immersed for hours in the solitude of correcting student papers, reading (rereading!) and reflecting upon the ancestors of a discipline. The time when a teacher is not in quiet is spent with family and a few friends. Yet, this is not true of all teachers any more than it is true that all Catholics would join Thomas More in upholding marriage as a sacrament in the face of Henry VIII, who had More beheaded for refusing to go against the Church and join the King's new church.

When More advises Richard to become a teacher he knows Richard is lured by bribes and can be turned to the fancy of whomever tempts him. More is trying to save Richard from himself when he offers him the position of a teacher. Perhaps in the confines of the quiet life of teaching Richard would learn to pay attention to the truths of the subjects he is teaching.

More could have been direct with Rich, "Hell Rich, titles are meaningless, especially in England where Kings are the pick of the litter, and Henry's divorce is being argued on the grounds that his Queen is "barren as a brick," when in fact it is his own licentiousness that is eating at him. He cannot justify his adultery nor forgive his own sins so he is starting his own church where infidelity is to be made a sacrament. But he chose an indirect answer to Rich's question, "Who would know it?"

Notice who is at the beginning and the end of More's response to Richard: "you" and "God." What is between the teacher and God is his pupils and his friends. Now a teacher is given pupils the way we are given our neighbors—at random (Thank God we can choose our friends!), and he is given those students for a set period of time: for the day as an elementary teacher or hours as a college teacher. Few parents can demand such control over a child's time.

Furthermore, rarely will anyone not enrolled ever join a class to see what a teacher is doing with his students. A teacher is in the unique position of being free to have his students read and to focus upon whatever he wishes. A "good" teacher will have students focus upon the truth, be it objective as in mathematics, chemistry, carpentry or subjective as in literature and philosophy, where the task is to elucidate the moral acts of virtuous characters before students.

If Rich had accepted More's offer, he would have read, in sixteenth century England, Boethius' *The Consolation of Philosophy* with his students, using Boethius' questions on himself and his students. Here is how it might have gone. Rich assigns the first book of Boethius' work in which lady philosophy has come to console him. In this book she asks the author, "Do you believe that this life consists of haphazard and chance events, or do you think it is governed by some rational principle?" Now Rich must put to his students the question which has been put to Boethius. Given they are students, more than likely they have read the assignment, but they are not yet able to grasp the intent. They are like beginning music students who can play all the notes, but what they play is far from being musical. Such a question is meant to initiate a dialogue on the nature of man, on whether his actions are chaotic reactions to pain and pleasure or a response to a purpose beyond this world. Anyway, the question confronts the teacher as he prepares to test the students with the question. As such a question is meant to initiate a conversation between teacher and student, it has the power to initiate an internal dialogue between Boethius, in this case, and Rich. The question, demanding an answer, gnaws on the teacher as he prepares to face his students.

Clearly Rich as a teacher would have been privileged to read with his students Socrates' apology before the Athenian Senate and to reflect upon his question:

> Good Sir, you are an Athenian, a citizen of the greatest city with the greatest reputation for both wisdom and power; are you not ashamed of your eagerness to possess as much wealth, reputation and honours as possible, while you do not care for nor give thought to wisdom, truth, or the best possible state of your soul?[2]

The dialogue begins in quiet preparation for class when Rich is alone with Socrates. "Rich do you care about wealth, reputation and honour more than the state of your soul?" We know, by looking as it is played out before us, what his honest answer would be, but if he would have accepted Thomas More's offer to be a teacher, his life may have been very different.

After wrestling with Socrates' question he would have turned to his students. The indirect question is the best when planting the inquisitive seed in a student's mind. "What do you intend on doing with your education?" Young students, thinking that the profession makes the man instead of the converse, will respond with what they know to be lucrative, respectable professions: " I am going to be a chemical engineer; ...a doctor; ...a lawyer, ...a CEO." By asking this question, Rich, in effect would be asking Socrates question, "Why do you care so much about wealth and reputation?" There is nothing wrong with any of these positions. What *is* wrong may be the reason for wanting them. If you want to be a doctor so as to make lots of money, then you are going into medicine for the wrong reason. You are not concerned with the "best possible state of your soul." Being a doctor is a respectable profession, but it does not necessarily follow that if you are a doctor you are worthy of respect. The same holds true for engineers, lawyers, CEO's, garbage men, and Presidents. There are riches in every profession.

2. Plato, *Five Dialogues*, trans. G. M. A. Grube (Indianapolis: Hackett Publishing, 1992), Apology, 29d.

274 | *Death of the Soul*

A Man for All Seasons is as much about Richard Rich as it is about Thomas More. Richard Rich depicts how the common man judges his position in the world and Thomas More depicts how the uncommon man judges the world by the position he takes.

We have already seen what Rich ended up doing in order to get a "worthy" position. Now we will turn to a brief scene at the end of the play in which Thomas More's daughter Margaret is allowed to visit her father in prison under the condition that she would persuade him to swear to the Act of Succession from the Catholic Church and so that Henry VIII could spare his life.

> More: You want me to swear to the Act of Succession?
> Margaret: God more regards the thoughts of the heart than the words of the mouth. Or so you've always told me.
> More: Yes.
> Margaret: Then say the words of the oath and in your heart think otherwise.
> More: What is an oath but the words we say to God?
> Margaret: That's very neat.
> More: Do you mean it isn't true?
> Margaret: No, it's true.
> More: Then it's a poor argument to call it "neat," Meg. When a man takes an oath, Meg, he's holding his own self in his own hands. Like water. (He cups his hands) And if he opens his fingers *then*—he needn't hope to find himself again. Some men aren't capable of this, but I'd be loathe to think you father one of them.
> Margaret: In any State that was half good, you would be raised up high, not here, for what you've done already. It's not your fault the State's three-quarters bad. Then if you elect to suffer for it, you elect yourself a hero.
> More: That's very neat. But look now.... If we lived in a State where virtue was profitable, common sense would make us good, and greed would make us saintly. And we'd live like animals or angels in the happy land that *needs* no heroes. But since in fact we see that avarice, anger, envy, pride, sloth, lust and stupidity commonly profit far beyond humility, chastity, fortitude, justice and thought, and have to choose to

be human at all... why then perhaps we *must* stand fast a little—even at the risk of being heroes.[3]

It goes without saying, in the end, More is the teacher, the really "great one."

3. Ibid., 138–40.

74510066R00174

Made in the USA
Columbia, SC
31 July 2017